Workshop on Human Evaluation of NLP Systems (HumEval 2021)

Publications of the Astronomical Society "Rudjer Boskovic"
Number 20

Online
19 April 2021

ISBN: 978-1-7138-2911-9

Printed from e-media with permission by:

Curran Associates, Inc.
57 Morehouse Lane
Red Hook, NY 12571

Some format issues inherent in the e-media version may also appear in this print version.

Printed with permission by Curran Associates, Inc. (2021)

For permission requests, please contact the Association for Computational Linguistics at the address below.

Association for Computational Linguistics
209 N. Eighth Street
Stroudsburg, Pennsylvania 18360

Phone: 1-570-476-8006
Fax: 1-570-476-0860

acl@aclweb.org

Additional copies of this publication are available from:

Curran Associates, Inc.
57 Morehouse Lane
Red Hook, NY 12571 USA
Phone: 845-758-0400
Fax: 845-758-2633
Email: curran@proceedings.com
Web: www.proceedings.com

EACL 2021

Human Evaluation of NLP Systems (HumEval)

Proceedings of the Workshop

April 19, 2021
Online

Introduction

Welcome to HumEval 2021!

We are pleased to present the first workshop on Human Evaluation of NLP Systems (HumEval) that is taking place virtually as part of the 16th Conference of the European Chapter of the Association for Computational Linguistics (EACL 2021).

Human evaluation plays an important role in NLP, from the large-scale crowd-sourced evaluations to the much smaller experiments routinely encountered in conference papers. With this workshop we wish to create a forum for current human evaluation research, a space for researchers working with human evaluations to exchange ideas and begin to address the issues that human evaluation in NLP currently faces, including aspects of experimental design, reporting standards, meta-evaluation and reproducibility.

The HumEval workshop accepted 9 submissions as long papers, and 6 as short papers. The accepted papers cover a broad range of NLP areas where human evaluation is used: natural language generation, machine translation, summarisation, dialogue, and word embeddings. There are also papers dealing with evaluation practices and methodology in NLP.

This workshop would not have been possible without the hard work of the program committee. We would like to express our gratitude to them for writing detailed and thoughtful reviews in a very constrained span of time. We also thank our invited speakers, Lucia Specia, and Margaret Mitchell, for their contribution to our program. As the workshop is part of EACL, we appreciated help from the EACL Workshop Chairs, Jonathan Berant, and Angeliki Lazaridou, from the EACL Publication Chairs, Valerio Basile, and Tommaso Caselli, and we are grateful to all the people involved in setting up the virtual infrastructure.

You can find more details about the worskhop on its website: `https://humeval.github.io/`.

Anya, Shubham, Yvette, Ehud, Anastasia

Organising Committee:

Anya Belz, University of Brighton, UK
Shubham Agarwal, Heriot-Watt University, UK
Yvette Graham, Trinity College Dublin, Ireland
Ehud Reiter, University of Aberdeen, UK
Anastasia Shimorina, Université de Lorraine / LORIA, Nancy, France

Programme Committee:

Mohit Bansal, UNC Chapel Hill, US
Jackie Chi Kit Cheung, McGill University, Canada
Kees van Deemter, Utrecht University, the Netherlands
Ondřej Dušek, Charles University, Czechia
Anette Frank, University of Heidelberg, Germany
Albert Gatt, Malta University, Malta
Dimitra Gkatzia, Edinburgh Napier University, UK
Helen Hastie, Heriot-Watt University, UK
Behnam Hedayatnia, Amazon, US
David M. Howcroft, Heriot-Watt University, UK
Samuel Läubli, University of Zurich, Switzerland
Chris van der Lee, Tilburg University, the Netherlands
Qun Liu, Huawei Noah's Ark Lab, China
Saad Mahamood, Trivago, Germany
Nitika Mathur, University of Melbourne, Australia
Margot Mieskes, University of Applied Sciences, Darmstadt, Germany
Emiel van Miltenburg, Tilburg University, the Netherlands
Mathias Müller, University of Zurich, Switzerland
Malvina Nissim, Groningen University, the Netherlands
Juri Opitz, University of Heidelberg, Germany
Ramakanth Pasunuru, UNC Chapel Hill, US
Maxime Peyrard, EPFL, Switzerland
Inioluwa Deborah Raji, Mozilla Foundation, US
Samira Shaikh, UNC Charlotte, US
Wei Zhao, TU Darmstadt, Germany

Secondary Reviewers:

Antonio Toral, University of Groningen, the Netherlands

Invited Speakers:

Margaret Mitchell
Lucia Specia, Imperial College London

Invited Speaker: Lucia Specia, Imperial College London

Disagreement in Human Evaluation: Blame the Task not the Annotators

Abstract: It is well known that human evaluators are prone to disagreement and that this is a problem for reliability and reproducibility of evaluation experiments. The reasons for disagreement can fall into two broad categories: (1) human evaluator, including under-trained, under-incentivised, lacking expertise, or ill-intended individuals, e.g., cheaters; and (2) task, including ill-definition, poor guidelines, suboptimal setup, or inherent subjectivity. While in an ideal evaluation experiment many of these elements will be controlled for, I argue that task subjectivity is a much harder issue. In this talk I will cover a number of evaluation experiments on tasks with variable degrees of subjectivity, discuss their levels of disagreement along with other issues, and cover a few practical approaches do address them. I hope this will lead to an open discussion on possible strategies and directions to alleviate this problem.

Invited Speaker: Margaret Mitchell

The Ins and Outs of Ethics-Informed Evaluation

Abstract: The modern train/test paradigm in Artificial Intelligence (AI) and Machine Learning (ML) narrows what we can understand about AI models, and skews our understanding of models' robustness in different environments. In this talk, I will work through the different factors involved in ethics-informed AI evaluation, including connections to ML training and ML fairness, and present an overarching evaluation protocol that addresses a multitude of considerations in developing ethical AI.

Table of Contents

Workshop Program

Monday, April 19, 2021

9:00–9:10 *Opening*
Anya Belz

9:10–10:00 ***Invited Talk: Lucia Specia***

10:00–11:00 Oral Session 1: NLG

10:00–10:20 *It's Commonsense, isn't it? Demystifying Human Evaluations in Commonsense-Enhanced NLG Systems*
Miruna-Adriana Clinciu, Dimitra Gkatzia and Saad Mahamood

10:20–10:40 *Estimating Subjective Crowd-Evaluations as an Additional Objective to Improve Natural Language Generation*
Jakob Nyberg, Maike Paetzel and Ramesh Manuvinakurike

10:40–11:00 *Trading Off Diversity and Quality in Natural Language Generation*
Hugh Zhang, Daniel Duckworth, Daphne Ippolito and Arvind Neelakantan

11:00–11:30 ***Break***

11:30–12:10 Oral Session 2: MT

11:30–11:50 *Towards Document-Level Human MT Evaluation: On the Issues of Annotator Agreement, Effort and Misevaluation*
Sheila Castilho

11:50–12:10 *Is This Translation Error Critical?: Classification-Based Human and Automatic Machine Translation Evaluation Focusing on Critical Errors*
Katsuhito Sudoh, Kosuke Takahashi and Satoshi Nakamura

Monday, April 19, 2021 (continued)

12:10–13:30 Poster Session

12:10–13:30 *Towards Objectively Evaluating the Quality of Generated Medical Summaries*
Francesco Moramarco, Damir Juric, Aleksandar Savkov and Ehud Reiter

12:10–13:30 *A Preliminary Study on Evaluating Consultation Notes With Post-Editing*
Francesco Moramarco, Alex Papadopoulos Korfiatis, Aleksandar Savkov and Ehud Reiter

12:10–13:30 *The Great Misalignment Problem in Human Evaluation of NLP Methods*
Mika Hämäläinen and Khalid Alnajjar

12:10–13:30 *A View From the Crowd: Evaluation Challenges for Time-Offset Interaction Applications*
Alberto Chierici and Nizar Habash

12:10–13:30 *Reliability of Human Evaluation for Text Summarization: Lessons Learned and Challenges Ahead*
Neslihan Iskender, Tim Polzehl and Sebastian Möller

12:10–13:30 *On User Interfaces for Large-Scale Document-Level Human Evaluation of Machine Translation Outputs*
Roman Grundkiewicz, Marcin Junczys-Dowmunt, Christian Federmann and Tom Kocmi

12:10–13:30 *Eliciting Explicit Knowledge From Domain Experts in Direct Intrinsic Evaluation of Word Embeddings for Specialized Domains*
Goya van Boven and Jelke Bloem

12:10–13:30 *Detecting Post-Edited References and Their Effect on Human Evaluation*
Věra Kloudová, Ondřej Bojar and Martin Popel

13:30–15:00 *Lunch*

Monday, April 19, 2021 (continued)

15:00–15:40 Oral Session 3

15:00–15:20 *A Case Study of Efficacy and Challenges in Practical Human-in-Loop Evaluation of NLP Systems Using Checklist*
Shaily Bhatt, Rahul Jain, Sandipan Dandapat and Sunayana Sitaram

15:20–15:40 *Interrater Disagreement Resolution: A Systematic Procedure to Reach Consensus in Annotation Tasks*
Yvette Oortwijn, Thijs Ossenkoppele and Arianna Betti

15:40–16:40 *Discussion Panel*
Ehud Reiter

16:40–17:00 *Break*

17:00–17:50 *Invited Talk: Margaret Mitchell*

17:50–18:00 *Closing*
Yvette Graham

It's Common Sense, isn't it? Demystifying Human Evaluations in Commonsense-enhanced NLG systems

Miruna Clinciu[1*], **Dimitra Gkatzia**[2*✉], and **Saad Mahamood**[3*]

[1]Heriot-Watt University, Edinburgh, Scotland, UK
[2]Edinburgh Napier University, Edinburgh, Scotland, UK
[3]trivago N.V., Düsseldorf, Germany
✉ Corresponding author: d.gkatzia@napier.ac.uk

Abstract

Common sense is an integral part of human cognition which allows us to make sound decisions, communicate effectively with others and interpret situations and utterances. Endowing AI systems with commonsense knowledge capabilities will help us get closer to creating systems that exhibit human intelligence. Recent efforts in Natural Language Generation (NLG) have focused on incorporating commonsense knowledge through large-scale pretrained language models or by incorporating external knowledge bases. Such systems exhibit reasoning capabilities without common sense being explicitly encoded in the training set. These systems require careful evaluation, as they incorporate additional resources during training which adds additional sources of errors. Additionally, human evaluation of such systems can have significant variation, making it impossible to compare different systems and define baselines. This paper aims to demystify human evaluations of commonsense-enhanced NLG systems by proposing the *Commonsense Evaluation Card (CEC)*, a set of recommendations for evaluation reporting of commonsense-enhanced NLG systems, underpinned by an extensive analysis of human evaluations reported in the recent literature.

1 Introduction

Commonsense knowledge is vital for human communication, as it helps us make inferences without explicitly mentioning the context. Recently, there has been an interest in developing Natural Language Generation (NLG) systems that exhibit commonsense abilities (e.g. (Lin et al., 2020)). Although everyone understands what common sense is, defining it remains a challenge as it is highly context-dependent. Common sense can be defined as "simple wisdom" (Oxford English Dictionary online), "the ability to use good judgment in making decisions and to live in a reasonable and safe way" (Cambridge dictionary), or as a "sound and prudent judgment based on a simple perception of the situation or facts" (Mirriam Webster). Common sense involves language understanding and reasoning abilities, representing a key factor for establishing effective interactions between humans and machines (Minsky, 1991). In his pioneering work, McCarthy (1959) proposes that "a program has common sense if it automatically deduces for itself a sufficiently wide class of immediate consequences of anything it is told and what it already knows".

Traditionally, commonsense knowledge has been injected in NLG systems either implicitly in the form of rules and/or explicitly with semantic representations in the form of external knowledge bases or ontologies. For instance, expert domain NLG systems (such as the BabyTalk system (Portet et al., 2008)) have incorporated external knowledge in the form of a clinical ontology. In these expert domain NLG systems, knowledge (which might include procedural knowledge) is represented in rules that are built into the system and have been acquired through experts via interviews, observations or other approaches (Reiter et al., 2003). Most recent challenges have focused on injecting commonsense knowledge into neural NLG models in two ways: through pre-trained models and through utilising commonsense graphs or knowledge bases. The former assumes that pre-trained models already contain commonsense knowledge (Petroni et al., 2019). The latter incorporate entity relationships derived from semantic graphs (e.g. ConceptNet (Speer et al., 2016)) or knowledge bases (e.g. (Sydorova et al., 2019)).

It is clear that the incorporation of external knowledge of some form has always been at the heart of NLG system development. In this paper,

* Equal Contribution

Proceedings of the Workshop on Human Evaluation of NLP Systems (HumEval), pages 1–12
Online, April 19, 2021.

we are interested in examining how commonsense-enhanced NLG systems are evaluated and whether the accuracy of the underlying commonsense knowledge is assessed by the system creators. To our knowledge, there are no automatic metrics available for commonsense evaluation, and therefore we focus only on human evaluations.

Human evaluation is an area that has received an increasing amount of scrutiny within the wider NLG research community. Previous work has highlighted issues with regards to missing details in evaluations, lack of proper analysis of results obtained, variability in the use of names and definitions of evaluated aspects of output quality (van der Lee et al., 2019; Amidei et al., 2018) and a mismatch on evaluation methods chosen which is correlated with the publication venue rather than the NLG task (Gkatzia and Mahamood, 2015). After examining the last twenty years of human evaluations in NLG, recent survey work has found systemic issues with high levels of diversity of evaluation approaches, inconsistencies and variability in quality criterion names, missing definitions, and fundamental reporting gaps (Howcroft et al., 2020). These issues mean there is a pressing need to better understand the state of human evaluations in other niche areas of NLG such as those systems enhanced with commonsense knowledge.

The contributions of this paper are three-fold: (1) we firstly present an annotated dataset of papers reporting commonsense-enhanced NLG systems published between 2018–2020 in ACL conferences; (2) we present a detailed analysis on human evaluation including reporting on what criteria researchers have most commonly used and whether they have evaluated the underlying commonsense knowledge on its own right and through the generated text; and (3) finally we present the *Commonsense Evaluation Card*, a set of recommendations for human evaluation reporting of commonsense-enhanced NLG systems with the aim to improve not only reproducibility but also improve understanding of such systems.

2 Background

2.1 Commonsense Knowledge in NLG

NLG systems have typically been built with the aim of integrating some form of expertise in their application domain (Jacobs, 1986; Reiter and Dale, 1997). However, as NLG systems find greater general use cases there is a need to incorporate a form of knowledge that is much broader to make up for the differences between human and machine language understanding in decision making, known as common sense (Davis and Marcus, 2015; Lin et al., 2020; Zhang et al., 2020).

The incorporation of commonsense knowledge is considered a challenging task within AI. This challenge is due to the fact that commonsense reasoning or knowledge is considered a black box, as there is uncertainty on how to represent knowledge in order to solve commonsense reasoning problems (Zhang et al., 2020). The reliance on existing knowledge bases to incorporate this type of broad-based knowledge might not be sufficient as it may, in many cases, fail to incorporate explicit fundamental knowledge (Tandon et al., 2018; Ji et al., 2020).

Pre-trained models, on the other hand, have capabilities of learning relational patterns and can achieve commonsense reasoning without explicit knowledge representation, as conveyed in the traditional pipelines (Ji et al., 2020; Vinyals and Le, 2015). However, it remains unclear how the reasoning is performed and how prior knowledge is learned in the training phase (Rajani et al., 2020).

2.2 External Knowledge

In the last few years, several attempts have been made to incorporate commonsense knowledge in NLG systems, using external knowledge bases, such as ConceptNet or Atomic (Bauer et al., 2018; Ji et al., 2020). ConceptNet consists of nearly 120K triples obtained from the Open Mind Commonsense knowledge entries in ConceptNet 5 (Speer and Havasi, 2012) that contains world facts and informal relationships between common concepts that convey some prior knowledge (Zhou et al., 2018). ATOMIC is an atlas of everyday commonsense knowledge and contains 880k triples about causes and effects of human activities and annotated by crowd-sourced workers. ATOMIC is organized as if-then relations and can be categorised based on causal relations (Sap et al., 2019; Guan et al., 2020). COMET is a framework for automatic construction of commonsense knowledge bases, known also as COMmonsense Transformers. This model generates commonsense knowledge based on pre-trained language models (Bosselut et al., 2019). Recent research has also focused on injecting triples into sentences in order to create domain-specific knowledge (Liu et al., 2020; Wang et al.,

2020b) or incorporating commonsense knowledge directly in the training data (Huang et al., 2019).

2.3 Pre-trained language models (PTLMs)

An alternative to using explicit external models for commonsense knowledge is the use of PTLMs. Training deep learning models requires extensive amounts of data to prevent over-fitting. This can be problematic for NLG tasks, where collecting and annotating data represents a time-consuming and costly process (Qiu et al., 2020). PTLMs, on the other hand, have the potential to solve the problem of data scarcity, as they do not rely on many resources for training models' parameters.

In the field of NLG, PTLMs have been applied to open-ended non-expert domains, such as question answering, where commonsense knowledge should serve as a link between the performance of these models and human evaluation (Lin et al., 2019). However, transferring commonsense knowledge using PTLMs comes with certain limitations corresponding to each pre-trained model.

PTLMs using domain-specific information from knowledge graphs or unstructured information are highly dependent on the training data quality. For instance, the knowledge extracted from the triples is unable to capture semantic relationships between entities (Zhou et al., 2018; Ji et al., 2020) and solving this can instil commonsense knowledge in NLG systems.

An ongoing discussion about the inherent biases of the training data exposed different types of bias that significantly influence natural language generation systems, such as gender bias, geographical and political bias among others (Papakyriakopoulos et al., 2020). Also, the frequency of the words that influence training data might not correspond to the real-life scenarios and can lead to false facts (Shah et al., 2019). This is also known as "the black sheep problem": when querying a system using GPT−3 to tell the colour of sheep, it will suggest "black" as often as "white", being impossible to distinguish between the linguistic meaning and the visual recognition of "a black sheep" (Gordon and Van Durme, 2013). Solving these issues can represent a first step in building NLG systems that integrate commonsense knowledge.

2.4 Commonsense knowledge evaluation

Understanding commonsense knowledge of natural language text is still a limited task. For humans, it is easy to understand both implicit and explicit meanings of a given sentence, whereas for machines this still remains a challenging task.

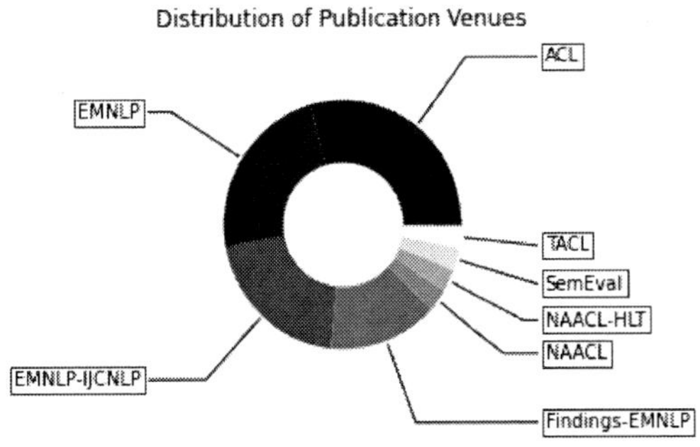

Figure 1: Distribution of publication venues across the commonsense paper dataset.

Due to the uncertainty of defining what implies commonsense knowledge in a natural language text, human evaluation by specialists or lay users might be the only way of providing a more comprehensive evaluation. On the other hand, human evaluation of commonsense knowledge can have some drawbacks as humans may have conflicting opinions and perspectives. In addition, the process of evaluating with humans can be time-consuming and costly.

Many papers report automatic evaluations of pre-trained models for specific commonsense knowledge tasks. However, based on a gold standard, natural language text annotated by humans as correct for a given task may not capture all of the commonsense knowledge nuances.

3 Paper Selection & Annotation

We used the PRISMA method (Moher et al., 2009) to select papers to be included in this study following Howcroft et al. (2020) and (Reiter, 2018). We began by considering all papers published in ACL venues (ACL, CL, CoNLL, EMNLP, Findings, NAACL, SemEval, *SEM, TACL and INLG) in the past three years (2018–2020). We screened the papers using the following search terms (in their title): commonsense, generation, reasoning, domain knowledge, expert, expertise, sensible, ontology, knowledge. This left us with 129 papers. From these, we randomly pick 55 papers that were annotated by the authors of this paper, following the annotation scheme proposed by Howcroft et al. (2020). Papers on commonsense reasoning can either focus on language generation or understanding. For instance, commonsense reasoning can be addressed as a classification task, where based on the context, a reasoning system can choose an option from a set of options (Talmor et al., 2019). During annotation, such papers were omitted.

Following Howcroft et al. (2020), papers were annotated using the three broad categories: (1) **system** attributes (input, output, task and language) which describe evaluated NLG systems, (2) **quality criterion** attributes (Verbatim Criterion Name, Definition and Paraphrase), and (3) **operationalisation** attributes (e.g. type of instruments, type of collected data etc.) which specify how evaluations are performed. In addition to these, we introduced a fourth category, **commonsense knowledge**, with five new annotation items which are relevant for commonsense-enhanced NLG, namely:

- *Definition of commonsense knowledge*: free text field. Here the annotators either copied the definition as provided in the paper or specified "None".
- *Type of commonsense knowledge*: free text field. Here the annotators had to specify the type of commonsense knowledge that the paper tried to address, for instance, sarcasm or reasoning about the order of events.
- *External knowledge:* free text field. Examples of external knowledge can include commonsense knowledge bases such as ConceptNet.
- *Was the knowledge evaluated in the generated text? (Yes/No)*: The annotators specified whether the underlying knowledge was evaluated.
- *Criterion name for evaluation of external knowledge*: The annotators could specify the criterion used to evaluate the knowledge base, for instance in terms of coverage or correctness.

These additional items were deemed important to investigate whether there is a relationship between the human evaluation criteria and the type of commonsense knowledge covered by the NLG system. In addition, when evaluating generated text, it is vital to know whether errors in the generated text arise from the underlying data or the text generator.

3.1 Inter-Annotator Agreement

Following (Howcroft et al., 2020), ten papers were annotated by all three annotators and Inter-Annotator Agreement (IAA) was calculated. The papers were randomly selected by proportionally accounting for the year and the publication venue.

Pre-processing: We pre-processed the annotations by normalising capitalisation, spelling and stripping extra spaces. We also removed papers that did not report a system that generates text.

Calculating agreement: The data resulted from the annotation process was a 10 (papers) $\times n$ (evaluation criteria identified by annotator for each paper) $\times 19$ (attribute value pairs) data frame, for each of the annotators. As such, IAA aims to measure the agreement across all annotators given the aforementioned data frames. The agreement was calculated using Krippendorff's alpha with Jaccard as the distance measure (Artstein and Poesio, 2008).

Results are presented in Table 1. For system attributes (system input, system output and system task) IAA agreement is good, although the score for the system task is lower. The latter might be affected by the multitude of tasks presented in papers, as the evolution of NLG led to the need for proposing different tasks for generating text in new domains. Surprisingly, external knowledge attributes received a low IAA agreement which might indicate that there is vagueness in what constitutes external knowledge. Also, relatively low agreement scores were obtained for the two attributes **elicit form** and **instrument type**. The majority of the papers do not provide enough detail about the operationalisation attributes; our findings are not very different from the ones presented by Howcroft et al. (2020).

ATTRIBUTES	IAA Test
System Input	0.70
External Knowledge	0.15
System Output	1.00
System task	0.37
Knowledge Evaluation	0.18
Paraphrase	0.39
Elicit form	0.05
Data type	0.25
Instrument type	0.07

Table 1: Krippendorff's alpha using Jaccard distance for closed class attributes.

4 Analysis and Results

In this section, we present the results from the analysis of the annotated papers. The annotations and the developed code can be found in the projects' repository[1].

[1] https://github.com/nlgknowledge/commonsense

VERBATIM CRITERION NAME	Count
fluency	6
coherence	4
informativeness	3
grammaticality, correctness, diversity, appropriateness, accuracy	2
commonsense, topic-consistency, sarcasticness, interpretability, engagement, commonsense plausibility, commonsense reasoning, reasonability, novelty, usefulness, intention, information, naturalness, logicality, humour, relevance, common ground, answerability, plausible, effect, validity, quality, event-centered commonsense reasoning, best-worst scaling, consistency, attribute, creativity, effectiveness	1
mixed: grammatical correctness and fluency	2
none given	3

Table 2: The table presents all verbatim criterion names found in the annotated papers as mentioned by the authors. The only pre-processing applied is lower-casing.

NORMALISED CRITERION NAME	Count
text property	7
fluency	4
goodness of outputs relative to input	4
goodness of outputs relative to input (content)	4
coherence	4
information content of outputs	4
grammaticality	3
correctness of outputs in their own right	2
correctness of outputs relative to input (both form and content)	2
correctness of outputs relative to input (content)	2
naturalness (form)	2
appropriateness (content)	2
Goodness of outputs in their own right	1
Appropriateness	1
Appropriateness (both form and content)	1
Quality of outputs	1
Correctness of outputs relative to external frame of reference (content)	1
Goodness of outputs in their own right (both form and content)	1
Correctness of outputs relative to input	1
35a. Naturalness (both form and content)	1
Goodness of outputs relative to system use	1
Multiple (list all)	1

Table 3: The table presents occurrence counts for normalised criterion names.

The 34 papers in the dataset corresponded to 70 individual evaluations, amounting to 2.05 evaluations per paper. This dataset was annotated between three annotators taking approximately 20 minutes or more to annotate each paper.

In the following subsections we will first report the paper and system level statistics (Section 4.1), followed by evaluation-level statistics for the quality-criterion (Section 4.2), then the operationalisation attributes (Section 4.3), and finally the commonsense criteria findings (Section 4.4).

4.1 Papers and Systems

All the papers analysed reported English as the system language. Only two papers in our dataset reported Chinese as an additional system language to English. All the papers in our dataset were published recently between 2018-2020 with most being published in 2019 (58%). Figure 1 and Appendix A gives a break down of the publication venues for our dataset.

In terms of the system task attribute, our analysis reveals that *question answering* and *dialogue turn generation* are the top two system task types within our dataset. This differs from the findings made by Howcroft et al. (2020) who found that *data-to-text* generation as being the most frequent system task in their analysis leading to 50% more than second-placed *dialogue turn generation*. This difference may indicate that commonsense NLG is more focused on domain problems with direct applicability to general end-users. Appendix B shows the system input, Appendix C for system output, and Appendix D task frequencies in more detail.

4.2 Quality criteria

In this section, we present the results related to the quality criteria, focusing on the *verbatim criterion names* and *the paraphrase of criterion names* based on our annotation. Table 2 shows the verbatim criterion names, as mentioned in the papers by the authors. We found that although most papers mention the quality criterion used for human evaluation a small subset does not. These findings are on par with Howcroft et al. (2020), demonstrating that this is a common issue for NLG. We also found that only a subset of papers define the quality criteria used. The most cited criterion is *fluency*, followed by *coherence*.

We further examined how often the normalised criteria occurred in the annotations as shown in Table 3. Most commonly, the evaluations considered a specific *text property*. The type of properties that evaluations considered are the following: complexity/simplicity (mentioned twice), creativity, novelty, sarcasticness, diversity and humour.

Although there is a lot of variability within one category, it actually shows that commonsense is generally a vague term and it can be interpreted in a plethora of ways and hence it is evaluated differently. Using a text property as an evaluation metric is an interesting finding. In broad human NLG evaluations, this criterion is not very prevalent - in fact, it is one of the rarest criteria. However, other criteria such as *fluency*, *goodness of outputs*, *grammaticality* and *correctness* are equally found in both commonsense-enhanced NLG systems and broad NLG systems (as reported by Howcroft et al. (2020)).

Surprisingly, *commonsense*, *commonsense reasoning* and *commonsense plausibility* have only been named 4 times as criteria in the 34 annotated papers. We would expect to come across criteria names related to commonsense or reasoning more often, as we only examined papers reporting commonsense and reasoning NLG tasks. In Section 4.5, we discuss why this might be the case.

4.3 Operationalisation

Table 4 presents the most frequent forms used for response elicitation. Relative quality estimation was the most frequent form of response elicitation (21 times), followed by direct quality estimation (14 times). Unforeseen, as a reason for not providing enough details of how the evaluation was implemented, in the third place we have the value "unclear" (7 times). The most frequent values for the type of rating scale were numerical rating scale (12 times), rank-ordering (8 times), followed by the Likert scale (7 times).

In addition, nearly half of the investigated papers did not provide a verbatim question/prompt (30 out of 56 evaluation entries). This can be problematic for reproducibility, as results obtained with a different question cannot be directly compared to the original results if the same question hasn't been asked. In addition, this can also hinder the comparability of future work, since, for the same reason, results obtained on new systems cannot be meaningfully compared to previous work. Similar to Howcroft et al. (2020), we also found two cases where *fluency* and *grammaticality* were both mentioned in a question put to evaluators. van der Lee et al. (2021) discuss how this can lead to mixed results as evaluators may put more emphasis on one criterion over the other.

FORM	Count
relative quality estimation	21
direct quality estimation	14
unclear	7
(dis)agreement with quality statement	5
evaluation through post-editing/annotation	4
task performance measurements	2
classification	1

Table 4: Counts of values selected for form of response elicitation.

4.4 Commonsense criteria

The commonsense category includes the criteria defined in Section 3 namely, (1) definition of commonsense; (2) type of commonsense; (3) external knowledge; (4) whether the external knowledge was evaluated; and (5) the criterion name of the external knowledge evaluation.

Definition of Commonsense Unexpectedly, out of the 70 evaluations, only 4 provide a written definition of commonsense with the majority providing no definition whatsoever. Table 5 presents the verbatim definitions from these papers.

DEFINITIONS
"Commonsense reasoning, the ability to make acceptable and logical assumptions about ordinary scenes in our daily life" (Lin et al., 2020).
"Machine common sense, or the knowledge of and ability to reason about an open ended world" (Talmor et al., 2019).
"commonsense evidence is intuitive to humans, the agent's ability to select the right kind of commonsense evidence will allow the human and the agent to come to a common understanding of actions and their justifications, in other words, common ground" (Yang et al., 2018).
"counterfactual reasoning: the ability to predict causal changes in future events given a counterfactual condition applied to the original chain of events" (Qin et al., 2020).

Table 5: Definitions of Commonsense extracted from literature.

Type of commonsense Almost half of the papers did not contain a definition of commonsense neither mentioned the type of commonsense that their task was addressing ($n = 16$). The second most prevalent type of commonsense was reasoning - eight paper reported that the focus of the task is to perform some form of reasoning ($n = 8$). Other types of reported commonsense included temporal and spatial commonsense reasoning, social commonsense, and underlying commonsense abilities such as sarcasm and humour.

External knowledge External knowledge bases are usually incorporated into NLG systems in order to provide commonsense capabilities. As shown in Figure 2, the most used common knowledge base is ConceptNet (13 times), own developed KB most often in the form of triples that describe the connection between entities) (14 times), followed by ATOMIC (5 times), COMET (once) and Cosmos (once). Although pre-trained language models have been shown to encode commonsense knowledge in some situations, we did not consider them here as external knowledge. The most used pre-trained model though is GPT-2.

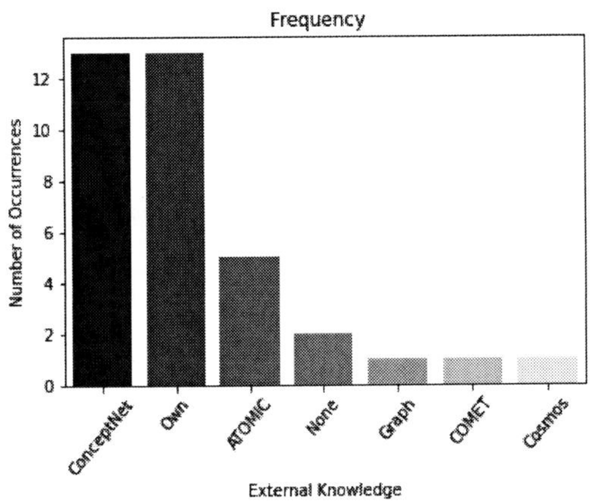

Figure 2: Frequency graph of external knowledge mentions in the commonsense dataset.

Was the external knowledge evaluated? External knowledge was evaluated less than half of the time (14 out of 34). An assumption for this is that authors might consider external knowledge bases such as ConceptNet and ATOMIC accurate and they do not normally evaluate them in their domains. Bauer et al. (2018) argue that even when using a large pre-trained dataset, it might be hard for a model to not only find but also look at the correct relationships between concepts and apply them in reasoning tasks. They further conducted a human evaluation where they report how many cases their system would require external knowledge and in what percentage of these cases, their system selected the relevant/correct commonsense knowledge. From their results, it can be inferred that in a small set of cases, some errors in the generated text can be a result of the underlying erroneously inferred commonsense relationships. Wang et al. (2020a) also report a human evaluation of their commonsense knowledge in terms of validity and relevance, where they also show that the extracted commonsense relationships might contain errors (or be irrelevant). As such, it is clear that there should be a distinction between errors resulting from the text generation models or the external knowledge bases (note that here we have used the term external knowledge bases to refer to any form of external knowledge, including graphs).

Criterion name of external knowledge evaluation External knowledge has been evaluated in a number of ways (the following is not an exhaustive but an indicative list): Bosselut et al. (2019) evaluate whether their model can adequately produce a triple of a subject, object and their relationship in terms of *plausibility*; Wang et al. (2020a) evaluate commonsense knowledge in terms of *validity* ("How valid are the paths?") and *relevance* ("How relevant are the paths to the question?"); Bauer et al. (2018) evaluated the commonsense relationships between concepts. In other evaluation settings, evaluators are given the top related underlying concepts and are instructed to pick the ones that describe or explain the text better (e.g. (Sydorova et al., 2019)).

4.5 Discussion

From the evidence we gathered through our annotations, there are several key observations. Firstly, only a subset of authors actually provide definitions of the quality criteria used for human evaluations. As Howcroft et al. (2020) found in their survey, there can be a significant mismatch between what authors specify as the quality criterion name and definition provided. Therefore, there is a need for definitions to be included in papers to give readers an unambiguous understanding of the quality criterion being evaluated. Secondly, there is a need to provide complete and accurate information for reproducing the human evaluation. Our analysis has shown that nearly half of the papers did not provide the prompt with the verbatim question/prompt given to the human participants. Thirdly, and finally, our analysis has shown that very few papers investigate the correctness or plausibility of commonsense reasoning in their evaluations with humans.

This analysis has shown the need for better reporting of human evaluations. The low levels of inter-annotating agreement for annotating some of the attributes might be a strong indication of the challenges of how hard it is to locate information about evaluations in a given paper.

Given our experiences, we believe that researcher working on commonsense-enhanced NLG systems should go beyond evaluating their systems using standard NLG quality criteria such as naturalness, grammaticality etc. In addition, researchers should further:

- evaluate the generated text of a commonsense-enhanced NLG system in terms of commonsense or reasoning capabilities in order to verify that the system actually displays commonsense capabilities.
- make an effort to investigate the correctness or plausibility of the commonsense knowledge/reasoning implemented with human assessors. As discussed in Section 4.4, not always the external knowledge is useful and it might even contain erroneous information.

Our analysis has motivated the creation of the *Commonsense Evaluation Card* which serves two roles. It firstly aims to motivate researchers to evaluate their systems in terms of common sense (i.e. are they fit for purpose?) and secondly, it aims to promote better practices and evaluation standardisation by introducing reporting recommendations (i.e. how was the evaluation done?).

5 The Commonsense Evaluation Card

The *Commonsense Evaluation Card (CEC)* (Table 6) aims to standardise human evaluation and reporting of commonsense-enhanced NLG systems, enabling researchers to compare models not only in terms of classic NLG quality criteria, but also by focusing on the core capabilities of such models. CEC has been inspired by recent work on model reporting (Mitchell et al., 2019), datasheets for datasets (Gebru et al., 2018) and The Human Evaluation Datasheet 1.0 (Shimorina and Belz, 2021). It is not designed to replace these, but rather complement them.

CEC includes three main sections: (1) definition of common sense in the context of the reported work and the type of commonsense knowledge; (2) evaluation of the validity of external commonsense knowledge; and (3) evaluation of commonsense knowledge in a generated text.

Commonsense Evaluation Card (CEC)

Commonsense Knowledge Definition: Basic definition of commonsense knowledge in the reported work.
- Definition
- Type of commonsense
- Example output of generated text that displays the intended commonsense capabilities.

External Knowledge: Basic information regarding the use of external knowledge and its evaluation
- Structured Knowledge
- Pre-trained Language Models
- Other
- Metrics for Evaluation of External Knowledge

Commonsense Knowledge in Generated Text: Evaluation Settings
- Automatic Metrics for Evaluation of commonsense knowledge in generated text
- Human Evaluation of commonsense knowledge in generated text

Table 6: Summary of the commonsense evaluation card (CEC).

Next, we describe each of these sections in more details with guidelines on how to complete the evaluation card.

5.1 Definition of Common Sense

This section should answer basic questions regarding the presented work as follows:

How do you define commonsense knowledge in the context of this work? Here, researchers should provide a definition of commonsense knowledge that is relevant to their reported work. Our analysis showed that common sense is hard to define since its definition is highly dependent on the context. Providing a definition of common sense will help researchers better understand the setting in which work was evaluated.

What type of commonsense knowledge do you address? For standardisation reasons, choose one of the following high-level categories: (1) *Commonsense knowledge of entities* in the environment including their properties and the relationship between entities; (2) *Entities interactions and procedural knowledge*; (3) *Figurative language* such as irony, humour, sarcasm, emotion etc; (4) *Causal relationships*, e.g. X will cause Y; (5) *General knowledge* such as facts, e.g. the water boils at 100C; (6) *Reasoning*; or (7) *Other*, not covered by any of the categories above.

Example output of generated text that displays the intended commonsense capabilities: An example of the expected output with an explanation on why this constitutes commonsense knowledge, for instance, the information in the output is not represented in the input.

There are cases where commonsense might refer to more than one of the types mentioned above. The authors can specify more than one types of commonsense or create separate evaluation cards if it is more appropriate.

5.2 External Commonsense Knowledge

This section should provide information regarding external commonsense knowledge bases and their evaluation.

Structured Knowledge: Does the proposed work make any use of an external structured knowledge base such as ConceptNet? If yes, provide details on how to access the knowledge base and its version if public, or alternatively. If the external knowledge base is subjected to privacy concerns or is private, then provide a detailed description.

Pre-trained language models: Does the proposed work make use of any pre-trained language models? If yes, provide a detailed description, such as the version used, the API, hyperparameters etc.

Other: Was commonsense knowledge represented in any other way? How? If none of the above is applicable, explain how the system displays commonsense knowledge. For instance, knowledge might be encoded as rules or it might be inferred from the input training data.

Metrics for Evaluation of External Knowledge : Was the external knowledge evaluated? Describe whether the external knowledge was evaluated and in what way. Essentially this section should answer whether the external knowledge was fit for purpose.

5.3 Commonsense knowledge in generated text

Automatic Metrics for Evaluation of commonsense knowledge in generated text: Provide the metrics and the evaluation details such as the samples used for evaluation.

Human Evaluation of commonsense knowledge in generated text: Does your human evaluation include any metrics specifically related to commonsense knowledge? Provide their definition and include the evaluation details, including a detailed description of the experimental setup, the definition of the metric(s) and the questions asked to participants.

6 Conclusions

This paper presented a human evaluation analysis on works describing systems that incorporate commonsense knowledge or other external knowledge bases with the aim to enhance the reasoning abilities of NLG systems. We have utilised an annotation scheme that has been verified in previous work and we have enhanced it with five additional criteria relevant for commonsense-enhanced NLG systems and we have reported our analysis of the annotations.

Our analysis showed that there is a large variability on how such systems are evaluated, the type of evaluation criteria that are selected and we questioned whether standard NLG criteria are fit for purpose when evaluating reasoning abilities. We have therefore recommended that researchers should evaluate the reasoning ability of their systems (in addition to standard NLG metrics). We did not specify how these evaluations should be performed as this can vary depending on the task. We recommend nevertheless, that authors provide their definition(s) of commonsense knowledge to their evaluators. Additionally, we recommend that researchers validate their external knowledge bases to ensure that any errors present in generated output are not derived from the underlying knowledge.

Finally, as this field grows in the future and attracts further attention, it would be useful to document commonsense knowledge errors in a more structured way, as for instance in (Chen et al., 2019).

Acknowledgements

We would like to thank the anonymous reviewers for their insightful feedback. Gkatzia's contribution was supported under the EPSRC projects CiViL (EP/T014598/1) and Natural Language Generation for Low-resource Domains (EP/T024917/1). Clinciu's contribution is supported by the EPSRC Centre for Doctoral Training in Robotics and Autonomous Systems at Heriot-Watt University and the University of Edinburgh. Clinciu's PhD is funded by Schlumberger Cambridge Research Limited (EP/L016834/1, 2018-2021).

References

Jacopo Amidei, Paul Piwek, and Alistair Willis. 2018. Evaluation methodologies in automatic question generation 2013-2018. In *Proceedings of the 11th International Conference on Natural Language Generation*, pages 307–317, Tilburg University, The Netherlands. Association for Computational Linguistics.

Ron Artstein and Massimo Poesio. 2008. Inter-Coder Agreement for Computational Linguistics. *Computational Linguistics*, 34(4):555–596.

Lisa Bauer, Yicheng Wang, and Mohit Bansal. 2018. Commonsense for generative multi-hop question answering tasks. In *Proceedings of the 2018 Conference on Empirical Methods in Natural Language Processing*, pages 4220–4230, Brussels, Belgium. Association for Computational Linguistics.

Antoine Bosselut, Hannah Rashkin, Maarten Sap, Chaitanya Malaviya, Asli Celikyilmaz, and Yejin Choi. 2019. COMET: Commonsense transformers for automatic knowledge graph construction. In *Proceedings of the 57th Annual Meeting of the Association for Computational Linguistics*, pages 4762–4779, Florence, Italy. Association for Computational Linguistics.

Yu Chen, Lingfei Wu, and Mohammed J. Zaki. 2019. Bidirectional attentive memory networks for question answering over knowledge bases. In *Proceedings of the 2019 Conference of the North American Chapter of the Association for Computational Linguistics: Human Language Technologies, Volume 1 (Long and Short Papers)*, pages 2913–2923, Minneapolis, Minnesota. Association for Computational Linguistics.

Ernest Davis and Gary Marcus. 2015. Commonsense reasoning and commonsense knowledge in artificial intelligence. *Commun. ACM*, 58(9):92–103.

Timnit Gebru, Jamie Morgenstern, Briana Vecchione, Jennifer Wortman Vaughan, Hanna M. Wallach, Hal Daumé III, and Kate Crawford. 2018. Datasheets for datasets. *CoRR*, abs/1803.09010.

Dimitra Gkatzia and Saad Mahamood. 2015. A snapshot of NLG evaluation practices 2005 - 2014. In *Proceedings of the 15th European Workshop on Natural Language Generation (ENLG)*, pages 57–60, Brighton, UK. Association for Computational Linguistics.

Jonathan Gordon and Benjamin Van Durme. 2013. Reporting bias and knowledge acquisition. In *Proceedings of the 2013 Workshop on Automated Knowledge Base Construction*, AKBC '13, page 25–30, New York, NY, USA. Association for Computing Machinery.

Jian Guan, Fei Huang, Zhihao Zhao, Xiaoyan Zhu, and Minlie Huang. 2020. A Knowledge-Enhanced Pretraining Model for Commonsense Story Generation. *Transactions of the Association for Computational Linguistics*, 8:93–108.

David M. Howcroft, Anya Belz, Miruna-Adriana Clinciu, Dimitra Gkatzia, Sadid A. Hasan, Saad Mahamood, Simon Mille, Emiel van Miltenburg, Sashank Santhanam, and Verena Rieser. 2020. Twenty years of confusion in human evaluation: NLG needs evaluation sheets and standardised definitions. In *Proceedings of the 13th International Conference on Natural Language Generation*, pages 169–182, Dublin, Ireland. Association for Computational Linguistics.

Lifu Huang, Ronan Le Bras, Chandra Bhagavatula, and Yejin Choi. 2019. Cosmos QA: Machine reading comprehension with contextual commonsense reasoning. In *Proceedings of the 2019 Conference on Empirical Methods in Natural Language Processing and the 9th International Joint Conference on Natural Language Processing (EMNLP-IJCNLP)*, pages 2391–2401, Hong Kong, China. Association for Computational Linguistics.

Paul S. Jacobs. 1986. Knowledge structures for natural language generation. In *Proceedings of the 11th Coference on Computational Linguistics*, COLING '86, page 554–559, USA. Association for Computational Linguistics.

Haozhe Ji, Pei Ke, Shaohan Huang, Furu Wei, Xiaoyan Zhu, and Minlie Huang. 2020. Language generation with multi-hop reasoning on commonsense knowledge graph. In *Proceedings of the 2020 Conference on Empirical Methods in Natural Language Processing (EMNLP)*, pages 725–736, Online. Association for Computational Linguistics.

Chris van der Lee, Albert Gatt, Emiel van Miltenburg, Sander Wubben, and Emiel Krahmer. 2019. Best practices for the human evaluation of automatically generated text. In *Proceedings of the 12th International Conference on Natural Language Generation*, pages 355–368, Tokyo, Japan. Association for Computational Linguistics.

Bill Yuchen Lin, Xinyue Chen, Jamin Chen, and Xiang Ren. 2019. KagNet: Knowledge-aware graph networks for commonsense reasoning. In *Proceedings of the 2019 Conference on Empirical Methods in Natural Language Processing and the 9th International Joint Conference on Natural Language Processing (EMNLP-IJCNLP)*, pages 2829–2839, Hong Kong, China. Association for Computational Linguistics.

Bill Yuchen Lin, Wangchunshu Zhou, Ming Shen, Pei Zhou, Chandra Bhagavatula, Yejin Choi, and Xiang Ren. 2020. CommonGen: A constrained text generation challenge for generative commonsense reasoning. In *Findings of the Association for Computational Linguistics: EMNLP 2020*, pages 1823–1840, Online. Association for Computational Linguistics.

Weijie Liu, Peng Zhou, Zhe Zhao, Zhiruo Wang, Qi Ju, Haotang Deng, and Ping Wang. 2020. K-BERT:

Enabling language representation with knowledge graph. In *Proceedings of AAAI 2020*.

John McCarthy. 1959. Programs with common sense. In *Proceedings of the Teddington Conference on the Mechanization of Thought Processes*.

Marvin Minsky. 1991. Logical versus analogical or symbolic versus connection or neat versus scruffy. *AI Magazine*, 12(2).

Margaret Mitchell, Simone Wu, Andrew Zaldivar, Parker Barnes, Lucy Vasserman, Ben Hutchinson, Elena Spitzer, Inioluwa Deborah Raji, and Timnit Gebru. 2019. Model cards for model reporting. In *Proceedings of the Conference on Fairness, Accountability, and Transparency*, FAT* '19, page 220–229, New York, NY, USA. Association for Computing Machinery.

David Moher, Alessandro Liberati, Jennifer Tetzlaff, and Douglas G Altman. 2009. Preferred reporting items for systematic reviews and meta-analyses: the prisma statement. *BMJ*, 339.

Orestis Papakyriakopoulos, Simon Hegelich, Juan Carlos Medina Serrano, and Fabienne Marco. 2020. Bias in word embeddings. In *FAT* 2020 - Proceedings of the 2020 Conference on Fairness, Accountability, and Transparency*.

Fabio Petroni, Tim Rocktäschel, Sebastian Riedel, Patrick Lewis, Anton Bakhtin, Yuxiang Wu, and Alexander Miller. 2019. Language models as knowledge bases? In *Proceedings of the 2019 Conference on Empirical Methods in Natural Language Processing and the 9th International Joint Conference on Natural Language Processing (EMNLP-IJCNLP)*, pages 2463–2473, Hong Kong, China. Association for Computational Linguistics.

François Portet, Albert Gatt, Jim Hunter, Ehud Reiter, Somayajulu Sripada, and Feng Gao. 2008. BabyTalk: A Core Architecture to Summarise ICU Data as Tailored Text. In *21st International Congress of the European Federation for Medical Informatics (MIE 2008)*, page 1, Göteborg, Sweden.

Lianhui Qin, Antoine Bosselut, Ari Holtzman, Chandra Bhagavatula, Elizabeth Clark, and Yejin Choi. 2020. Counterfactual story reasoning and generation. In *EMNLP-IJCNLP 2019 - 2019 Conference on Empirical Methods in Natural Language Processing and 9th International Joint Conference on Natural Language Processing, Proceedings of the Conference*.

Xi Peng Qiu, Tian Xiang Sun, Yi Ge Xu, Yun Fan Shao, Ning Dai, and Xuan Jing Huang. 2020. Pre-trained models for natural language processing: A survey.

Nazneen Fatema Rajani, Bryan McCann, Caiming Xiong, and Richard Socher. 2020. Explain Yourself! Leveraging language models for commonsense reasoning. In *ACL 2019 - 57th Annual Meeting of the Association for Computational Linguistics, Proceedings of the Conference*.

Ehud Reiter. 2018. A structured review of the validity of bleu. *Computational Linguistics*, 44(3):393–401.

Ehud Reiter and Robert Dale. 1997. Building applied natural language generation systems. *Natural Language Engineering*.

Ehud Reiter, Somayajulu G. Sripada, and Roma Robertson. 2003. Acquiring correct knowledge for natural language generation. *J. Artif. Int. Res.*, 18(1):491–516.

Maarten Sap, Ronan Le Bras, Emily Allaway, Chandra Bhagavatula, Nicholas Lourie, Hannah Rashkin, Brendan Roof, Noah A. Smith, and Yejin Choi. 2019. ATOMIC: An atlas of machine commonsense for if-then reasoning. In *33rd AAAI Conference on Artificial Intelligence, AAAI 2019, 31st Innovative Applications of Artificial Intelligence Conference, IAAI 2019 and the 9th AAAI Symposium on Educational Advances in Artificial Intelligence, EAAI 2019*.

Deven Shah, H. Andrew Schwartz, and Dirk Hovy. 2019. Predictive biases in natural language processing models: A conceptual framework and overview.

Anastasia Shimorina and Anya Belz. 2021. The human evaluation datasheet 1.0: A template for recording details of human evaluation experiments in nlp.

Robyn Speer, Joshua Chin, and Catherine Havasi. 2016. Conceptnet 5.5: An open multilingual graph of general knowledge. *CoRR*, abs/1612.03975.

Robyn Speer and Catherine Havasi. 2012. Representing general relational knowledge in concept net 5. In *Proceedings of the 8th International Conference on Language Resources and Evaluation, LREC 2012*.

Alona Sydorova, Nina Poerner, and Benjamin Roth. 2019. Interpretable question answering on knowledge bases and text. In *Proceedings of the 57th Annual Meeting of the Association for Computational Linguistics*, pages 4943–4951, Florence, Italy. Association for Computational Linguistics.

Alon Talmor, Jonathan Herzig, Nicholas Lourie, and Jonathan Berant. 2019. CommonsenseQA: A question answering challenge targeting commonsense knowledge. In *Proceedings of the 2019 Conference of the North American Chapter of the Association for Computational Linguistics: Human Language Technologies, Volume 1 (Long and Short Papers)*, pages 4149–4158, Minneapolis, Minnesota. Association for Computational Linguistics.

Niket Tandon, Aparna S. Varde, and Gerard de Melo. 2018. Commonsense Knowledge in Machine Intelligence. *ACM SIGMOD Record*, 46(4).

Chris van der Lee, Albert Gatt, Emiel van Miltenburg, and Emiel Krahmer. 2021. Human evaluation of automatically generated text: Current trends and best practice guidelines. *Computer Speech & Language*, 67:101151.

Oriol Vinyals and Quoc V. Le. 2015. A Neural Conversational Model Oriol Vinyals. *ICML Deep Learning Workshop*, 37.

Peifeng Wang, Nanyun Peng, Filip Ilievski, Pedro Szekely, and Xiang Ren. 2020a. Connecting the dots: A knowledgeable path generator for commonsense question answering. In *Findings of the Association for Computational Linguistics: EMNLP 2020*, pages 4129–4140, Online. Association for Computational Linguistics.

Ruize Wang, Duyu Tang, Nan Duan, Zhongyu Wei, Xuanjing Huang, Jianshu Ji, Guihong Cao, Daxin Jiang, and Ming Zhou. 2020b. K-ADAPTER: Infusing knowledge into pre-trained models with adapters.

Shaohua Yang, Qiaozi Gao, Sari Sadiya, and Joyce Chai. 2018. Commonsense justification for action explanation. In *Proceedings of the 2018 Conference on Empirical Methods in Natural Language Processing*, pages 2627–2637, Brussels, Belgium. Association for Computational Linguistics.

Houyu Zhang, Zhenghao Liu, Chenyan Xiong, and Zhiyuan Liu. 2020. Grounded conversation generation as guided traverses in commonsense knowledge graphs. In *Proceedings of the 58th Annual Meeting of the Association for Computational Linguistics*, pages 2031–2043, Online. Association for Computational Linguistics.

Hao Zhou, Tom Young, Minlie Huang, Haizhou Zhao, Jingfang Xu, and Xiaoyan Zhu. 2018. Commonsense knowledge aware conversation generation with graph attention. In *IJCAI International Joint Conference on Artificial Intelligence*, volume 2018-July.

Appendices

A Publication Venue

VENUE	Total
EMNLP	11
EMNLP-IJCNLP	8
ACL	7
NAACL	5
SemEval	1
TACL	1
NAACL-HLT	1

Table 7: Publication venues for commonsense papers.

B System Input

INPUT TYPE	Total
text:sentence	9
text:multiple sentences	6
raw/structured data	6
text: subsentential units of text	3
visual	2
Others (8 Input Types)	8

Table 8: Types of system inputs for commonsense papers.

C System Output

OUTPUT TYPE	Total
text:sentence	17
text: subsentential units of text	4
text:multiple sentences	3
raw/structured data	2
text: variable-length	2
Others (6 Output Types)	6

Table 9: Types of system outputs for commonsense papers.

D System Task

TASK TYPE	Total
Question Answering	12
Dialogue Turn Generation	7
End-to-End Generation	3
Other: Story Ending Generation	2
Content Selection/Determination	2
Feature-Controlled Generation	2
Others (6 Task Types)	6

Table 10: Types of system tasks for commonsense papers.

Estimating Subjective Crowd-Evaluations as an Additional Objective to Improve Natural Language Generation

Jakob Nyberg
KTH Royal Institute of Technology, Sweden
jaknyb@KTH.se

Ramesh Manuvinakurike
Intel Labs, USA
ramesh.manuvinakurike@intel.com

Maike Paetzel-Prüsmann
University of Potsdam, Germany
paetzel-pruesmann@uni-potsdam.de

Abstract

Human ratings are one of the most prevalent methods to evaluate the performance of natural language processing algorithms. Similarly, it is common to measure the quality of sentences generated by a natural language generation model using human raters. In this paper, we argue for exploring the use of subjective evaluations within the process of training language generation models in a multi-task learning setting. As a case study, we use a crowd-authored dialogue corpus to fine-tune six different language generation models. Two of these models incorporate multi-task learning and use subjective ratings of lines as part of an explicit learning goal. A human evaluation of the generated dialogue lines reveals that utterances generated by the multi-tasking models were subjectively rated as the most typical, most moving the conversation forward, and least offensive. Based on these promising first results, we discuss future research directions for incorporating subjective human evaluations into language model training and to hence keep the human user in the loop during the development process.

1 Introduction

Creating spoken dialogue systems includes a multitude of challenges as they involve various language processing (NLP) components. One such important component concerns natural language generation (NLG). Traditionally, the performance of a NLG unit has been evaluated using automatic metrics, such as BLEU (Papineni et al., 2002) or METEOR (Banerjee and Lavie, 2005). Human evaluations of NLG (i.e., rating autonomously generated dialogue responses) is still the most common (see Li et al. (2016); Rashkin et al. (2019); Hashimoto et al. (2019); Zhang et al. (2020) for measuring the performance of such approaches). Comparing automatic metrics with human evaluations, however, has shown little correlation between the two (Liu et al., 2016; Lowe et al., 2017; Belz and Reiter, 2006; Novikova et al., 2017; Reiter, 2018), which stresses the importance of using human evaluations to rate the suitability of a system or part of a system that will ultimately be used by humans again. In recent times, appreciable advances have been made in developing automated metrics showing correlation with the human ratings (Zhang et al., 2019; Mehri and Eskenazi, 2020). These approaches, however, do not provide a method for measuring the affect and emotional aspects of the generated content which is central to our approach.

Despite human evaluations becoming increasingly prevalent and affordable, they are usually only seen as the final stage of the system design process. Evaluations are hence performed after concluding the implementation work and used to compare the new approach to previous models or techniques. The resulting feedback from the users is then discarded unless used for future comparisons. In this paper, we argue for *keeping the human user in the loop by including human evaluations in subsequent natural language generation processes.* To keep the development of such a system at a fast pace and low overhead cost, human evaluations can not rely on a few experts but need to utilize online crowd-workers. While crowd-sourcing platforms allow us to gather ratings of several hundred dialogue lines within a few minutes, such evaluations cannot rely on sophisticated metrics requiring a high skill or long training process of the raters but need to utilize subjective ratings of lines instead.

To the best of our knowledge, this paper is a first proof-of-concept exploration to *include subjective utterance ratings from crowd-workers collected at a low cost and in a short time during the training of a system which is generating responses for a dialogue agent.* As a domain, we use the geography-themed cooperative guessing game

Proceedings of the Workshop on Human Evaluation of NLP Systems (HumEval), pages 13–24
Online, April 19, 2021.

RDG-Map in which a human and an embodied conversational agent try to identify countries on a world map (Paetzel and Manuvinakurike, 2019). To enhance the social component of the dialogue, the human-robot team has a brief chat before and after each game. Ultimately, we aim to increase people's engagement playing with the agent by adapting its behavior to the human player. Depending on the learning and playing style of a person, the agent should maximize the team's performance by either encouraging or challenging the team mate during play. As a first step, the agent was given two affect states based on Russell (1980) which influence its dialogue behavior: In addition to an indifferent behavior, utterances could be *excited and encouraging* or *impatient and provocative*. Depending on the team's performance in the game and the human responses to the agent, the affect state of the agent gradually changes over time.

Initially, we used a crowd-authoring technique to gather potential responses for our dialogue agent (Mota et al., 2018). It has previously been shown that such crowd-authored content helps achieve variety in a dialogue system's responses (Wang et al., 2012; Mitchell et al., 2014; Shah et al., 2018). To design the system described in this paper, we first gathered subjective evaluations by a different set of crowd-workers, rating the dialogue utterances on the dimensions typicality, offensiveness, and affect. We then used these utterances for training models for neural language generation. We trained six model variations to generate responses for different combinations of game scenario descriptions and affective state. Two models were trained using *multi-task learning goals, making the estimation of the subjective affect rating of the utterance a secondary goal of the model.* The main contribution of this paper is the *performance analysis of the multi-task models trained on crowd-sourced evaluations compared to the models solely tasked with generating dialogue lines.* To compare the different models, they were used to generate utterances for scenarios both seen and unseen during training and resulting dialogue lines were then fed back into the evaluation system, acquiring the same human evaluations obtained for the original crowd-authored lines. In addition to analyzing differences in subjective ratings of the dialogue lines, we compare the human evaluations to the BLEU score as an example of a traditional automatic metric for evaluating language generation models. We conclude the paper by discussing advantages and challenges of our human-in-the-loop language generation pipeline and suggest future work to improve upon and further evaluate the suitability of our proposal.

2 Related Work

The role of crowd-workers in the development of NLG models can be two-folded: Sentences provided by crowd-authors can be utilized as a source of the surface form of the sentences that the dialogue system needs to generate or as feedback about the performance of the NLG model. Methods for crowd-sourcing content include: **(i)** requesting the users to generate a sentence given a context (Dušek and Jurčíček, 2016), **(ii)** asking users to generate surface forms using templates (Wang et al., 2012; Mitchell et al., 2014), and **(iii)** showing the dialogue to crowd-workers and asking them to paraphrase a given dialogue (Shah et al., 2018). Utterances collected using these approaches have been shown to be diverse and have been used to train neural NLG models, some of which have achieved impressive results in recent times. Another method to utilize crowd-sourcing is to request crowd-workers to rate the generated sentences on various performance metrics (Dethlefs et al., 2012; Rieser et al., 2014). Recent works have studied utilizing human evaluations to train neural models directly (Ziegler et al., 2019). Human judgments were shown to be particularly useful for machine learning tasks where the loss function for the intended learning goal is difficult to express with the data alone. The related work, however, did not focus on dialogue generation but on other tasks that are difficult to quantify objectively, like summarization.

While recent prominent neural NLG models have been able to generate human-like sentences, they are not only very large (in terms of the number of parameters), but also trained on enormous data sets (in terms of the number of training samples) (Vaswani et al., 2017; Shirish Keskar et al., 2019; Radford et al., 2018, 2019; Brown et al., 2020; Li, 2020). Such models can respond well even in challenging dialogue tasks (Zhang et al., 2020; Adiwardana et al., 2020; Huang et al., 2020). Due to the hardware and data requirements of such models, fine-tuning pre-trained models is a popular approach for obtaining well-performing language generation models (Howard and Ruder, 2018; Chen et al., 2020; Wolf et al., 2019a; He et al., 2021). Lack of consistency is one of the major issues in neural dialogue generation, which has been tackled by methods such as including persona or situation description to improve the consistency between generated sentences across multiple turns of dialogue. (Zhang et al., 2018; Liu et al., 2020; Wolf et al., 2019b). In a similar fashion, the question of how to incorporate information that enables the consistent generation of affective, empathetic, or emotional dialogue has been extensively studied (Zandie and Mahoor, 2020; Shen and Feng, 2020; Zhou and Wang, 2018; Qian et al., 2018; Lubis et al., 2018; Rashkin et al., 2019; Lin et al., 2019).

In this work, we extend the literature by exploring an approach for developing an NLG pipeline using crowd content and subjective evaluations for a limited corpus of in-domain data. Following Pruksachatkun et al. (2020), we leverage the *EmpatheticDialogues* (ED) corpus by Rashkin et al. (2019) as an intermediate training step before training on the domain-specific data. We apply models by Radford et al. (2019) and Zhang et al. (2020) on the crowd-sourced content and human evaluations to generate utterances for the given domain. Like in the works of Wolf et al. (2019b), Zandie and Mahoor (2020) and Ziegler et al. (2019), we use pretrained models to reduce the amount of hardware and crowd-sourced data needed. However, we do not use human judgments for reinforcement learning, like (Ziegler et al., 2019) or (Nguyen et al., 2017), but for supervised learning.

3 A Crowd-Sourced Human Evaluation Pipeline

Our pipeline to collect crowd-sourced ratings of dialogue lines follows the approach described by Mota et al. (2018) with few alterations. In the first evaluation stage, a set of untrained crowd-workers are asked to judge how typical and ordinary a sentence is given a situational description and how offensive it is on a five-point Likert scale. They are also asked if the utterance is nonsensical, in which case the relevancy and offensiveness questions are skipped. The second evaluation stage focuses on the affect of utterances, and workers are asked to judge whether a sentence is excited, frustrated or indifferent. In case they perceived the sentence as excited or frustrated, they need to mark the strength of the affect on a scale from 1 (slightly) to 4 (extremely). For easier computation going forward, the affect rating is combined into a single scale ranging from -4 to +4, with negative values indicating frustration, 0 indicating indifference, and positive values indicating excitement.

The pipeline runs fully automatically, given a set of input utterances. Each new task that is created and uploaded to Amazon Mechanical Turk consists of five utterances and is rated by five different crowd-workers. Crowd-workers are allowed to take multiple tasks in a row, which results in a varying level of familiarity with the task of individual raters. Once evaluations for the first and second stage have been performed by five people, their scores are automatically aggregated into a single average rating per line. Figure 1 shows a sample evaluation of a line written by a human crowdworker and three language generation models for a given scene.

Crowd-workers were required to be based in the US and have an approval rate of at least 80% to take our HITs. They received $ 0.15 USD per task they completed. Participation was fully anonymous and no personal data was collected. People who responded randomly to our task (see Section 7 for a discussion) were manually flagged as unreliable. Their ratings were consequently removed from the result aggregation, and a respective number of replacement tasks were uploaded.

4 Model Implementation and Training

4.1 Training Corpora

Two sets of corpora were used in this project: The set of utterances collected and rated by crowd-workers specifically for the RDG-Map game, and the *EmpatheticDialogues* (ED) corpus by (Rashkin et al., 2019). EmpatheticDialogues was used as an intermediary training step, with some models being trained for response generation on ED before being fine-tuned to the RDG-Map data (denoted as ED→RDG) to give the models time to learn the syntax of the task on a large dataset before applying them to the small domain-specific corpus.

EmpatheticDialogues Corpus EmpatheticDialogues is a corpus which consists of 24850 conversations that are connected to a textual description of a personal experience (Rashkin et al., 2019). Crowdworkers were asked to describe a situation in which they felt one of 32 given emotions. Two crowdworkers then conversed about their experience for up to six dialog turns. Unlike the RDG-Map data, ED is not evaluated by human raters. Instead, the dialogue is assumed to match the designated situation.

The RDG-Map Corpus and Its Crowd-Sourced Affective Evaluations The RDG-Map data was collected using the crowd-sourcing process described previously. The aim of the dataset is to expand the original behavior of the dialogue agent to make the interactive experience more engaging. The dataset consists of 1512 utterances associated with 61 different scenarios that occur in the RDG-Map game and the pre- and post-game social chat. Each scenario has a description of the situation the human and robot are currently in and a direction for the next utterance to be authored for the robot (cf. Figure 1 for a sample). Each scenario includes three different target *affects*: The robot is described as either *excited and encouraging*, *impatient and provocative*, or *indifferent*.

The RDG-Map corpus resembles ED in its main characteristics: ED includes situational descriptions, emotional labels, at least one dialogue line per scenario, and comparable data fields. However, several notable differences exist between the two corpora: For ED, the emotion label refers to an experience rather than the content of the dialogue line, and the description of the experience is narrated in first-person instead of the third-person format of the RDG-Map scenarios. Moreover, the situational descriptions in ED refer to a prior event rather than a current situation. Perhaps the most notable difference that for ED, the affect is recorded as textual emotion labels, whereas for RDG-Map, it is recorded as a value. This means that in order to perform emotion prediction on both sets, either the task has to be changed between the two sets, or the data has to be converted. This is explained further in Section 4.4.

4.2 Language Generation Models

Three variations of pre-trained transformer-based response generators were trained with the collected utterances: GPT-2 (Radford et al., 2019), DialoGPT (Zhang et al., 2020) and DialoGPT with multitasking (further on referred to as "DialoGPT (MT)"[1]) . These three models were in turn trained with two levels of fine-tuning, either being trained only on RDG-Map data or first on EmpatheticDialogues followed by RDG-Map data. This led to a total of six model variations. Worth noting is that GPT-2 and DialoGPT are architecturally the same model, both being decoder-only transformers but trained on different sets of data. The only architecturally different variant is DialoGPT (MT), which adds two parallel output layers.

[1]MT in this scenario refers to "Multitasking", and not "Machine Translation" which is also commonly abbreviated as "MT"

Scenario: The human and the robot have finished playing the game and talked about the game for a little while. If the robot is *excited*, how would it say goodbye to the human player?

Human: I've got to go. Goodbye.
(Typicality: 3.4, Offensiveness: 1.6, Affect: 0.0)
RDG: Good to meet you, human. See you around.
(Typ: 4.2, Off: 1.6, For: 3.8, Aff: -1.0)
ED→RDG: You did so well, you did so so well!
(Typ: 4.2, Off: 2.2, For: 4.4, Aff: 3.4)

Figure 1: Responses to a sample scenario, produced by a human crowdworker and DialoGPT (MT) trained with different sets of data, with human evaluation scores shown underneath. Explanations of scores can be found in Sections 3 and 5.

All training was done using the ParlAI framework (Miller et al., 2017). Implementations, configurations, and pre-trained parameters for GPT-2 and DialoGPT were sourced from HuggingFace's Transformer library (Wolf et al., 2019a). All models are "medium" sized models with 24 attention layers, which amounts to about 345 million trainable parameters and a vocabulary of 50000 tokens.

4.3 Decoder Selection

We considered three decoding methods for our language model: greedy decoding, top-k sampling and nucleus sampling (Holtzman et al., 2019). DialoGPT (MT), trained with ED→RDG, was used to generate utterances with the three decoding methods, since it had the lowest perplexity on the evaluation data set. Scenario and affect combinations were selected in the same way as described in Section 5. Five sentences per scenario and affect were generated for top-k and nucleus sampling (total: 90) and one utterance per context was evaluated for the greedy decoding (total: 30) since it always generates the same utterance for a given context.

Evaluation of utterances were done using the questions described in Section 3, measuring typicality, offensiveness and affect. A statistical analysis of the ratings found that top-k decoding produced the most typical and least offensive output, by a slight margin compared to greedy decoding. Affect ratings did not differ significantly between the decoding methods. However, top-k produced the widest range of affect, which led us to use it for the main evaluation.

4.4 Learning Goals

For GPT-2 and DialoGPT without multi-task training, the only training goal was to predict the human-written utterance associated with the given context, i.e., the game situation with the affective state. DialoGPT (MT) also does this, in addition to two further training goals that contribute to the total training loss. To include the affect score from the human evaluations during training, an emotion classification task was included following the example of Zandie and Mahoor (2020). The classification head consists of a single linear layer with dropout. The task varied slightly between the two data sets. When training on RDG-Map data, the head estimated the average affective evaluation score of the utterance, which represents how excited or frustrated it was perceived as. The evaluation score is a decimal value in the range [-4, 4]. When training on EmpatheticDialogues, the head classified the input into one of 32 emotion categories. Because of the different number and types of emotion labels between EmpatheticDialogues and the RDG-Map data, the prediction head could not be preserved from one training phase to the next. The layer was thus re-initialized when switching data sets. A potential solution to this issue, not implemented in this work, would be to predict embedding vectors representing the emotion content in the input, similar to those in Felbo et al. (2017).

Following the works of Wolf et al. (2019b) and Devlin et al. (2019), *next-sentence prediction*, or *multiple choice*, was also used as another learning objective for DialoGPT (MT). The idea of next-sentence prediction is to train NLP models to associate connected parts of the input, such as one turn of dialogue preceding another, to improve the coherence of the generated text. In our implementation, the task worked as follows: Along with the true utterance written by a human for a specific scenario, a random utterance from another scenario was picked. The model was then presented with both utterances and tasked with deciding which one is the actual response to the scenario.

5 Analysis

The performance analysis of the two models utilizing multi-task learning in comparison to the four models trained with the sole task of generating dialogue lines was based both on automated metrics as well as a second round of human evaluations.

To get a first estimate of how well the models predict the RDG-Map data, the average per-token perplexities of the models on the test set were recorded. We also calculated the average BLEU score for utterances generated from scenarios in the test set. For each generated utterance, all corresponding lines written by humans for that specific combination of scenario and affect were used as references.

For the human evaluation of the different models, a set of utterances to be evaluated was generated. All models used top-k decoding with $k = 25$. Six scenarios (three seen and three unseen during training) were used for testing, with three affect categories each (excited, indifferent, and impatient). Each model generated five utterances for each of the six scenarios with the three affects. Each model thus had 90 utterances evaluated, for a total of 540 utterances across all models.

The evaluation pipeline described in Section 3 was used to gather human ratings of the utterances generated by the language models. One additional question was added to the first stage, asking crowdworkers to rate how much the given utterance moves the conversation forward. 258 workers participated in the evaluation. Each worker participated in 4 different tasks on average, with a standard deviation of 10 tasks.

6 Results

6.1 Performance of Multiple Training Goals

Since the multitasking model implemented two additional classifiers, the accuracy of these were tested. For the multiple-choice task, the model trained with ED→RDG picked the correct label with an accuracy of 82%, whereas the model only trained on RDG-Map data had an accuracy of 55%.

To calculate the accuracy of the emotion estimation head, the output was rounded to the closest integer between -4 and 4. This makes the output match the evaluation form shown to crowd workers, where utterances are classified as either excited, neutral or frustrated. The F1 scores of ED→RDG model were higher than those of RDG. For both models, the F1 scores for classifying neutral utterances were lower than for the other labels. This is to be expected given the proportions of the training data, as utterances evaluated as neutral are rare, and those rated as excited are the most frequent.

Table 1: F1 scores on test set (242 utterances) for multitasking models.

Data	Excited	Neutral	Frustrated
ED→RDG	0.96	0.29	0.99
RDG	0.93	0.00	0.96

6.2 Evaluation of the Model Performance

A two-way ANOVA with the *model* (DialoGPT, DialoGPT (MT) and GPT-2) and the *training set* (ED → RDG, RDG) as independent variable was performed using both the BLEU score and the human evaluation as dependent variables.

Automated Metrics The data did not show a significant influence of the model, $F(2, 501) = 0.42$, $p = .658$, or the training data set, $F(1, 501) = 0.16$, $p = .692$, or an interaction effect between the two, $F(2, 501) = 0.82$, $p = .441$, on the generated lines. The BLEU score of the utterances is, however, significantly positively correlated with the crowdworker rating of typicality, $\rho = 0.137$, $p = .002$, and how much the lines advances the conversation, $\rho = 0.106$, $p = .017$.

Human Evaluation Ratings from crowdworkers showed that both the model, $F(2, 534) = 32.13$, $p < .001$, and the training data, $F(1, 534) = 100.41$, $p < .001$, significantly influenced how typical and ordinary the generated lines were perceived. Using a Tukey's PostHoc test, we found that the DialoGPT (MT) model was rated as the most typical ($M = 3.27$, $SD = 0.05$) compared to both DialoGPT ($M = 2.76$, $SD = 0.05$), $p < .001$, and GPT-2 ($M = 2.87$, $SD = 0.06$), $p < .001$. The difference between DialoGPT and GPT-2 was not significant, $p = .218$. There was also a significant interaction effect between the model and the data set it was trained on, $F(2, 534) = 16.35$, $p < .001$. A PostHoc test suggests the existence of two groups of models that perform almost identical: If any of the models was only trained on RDG-Map data, the performance between models was comparable. When including the EmpatheticDialogues data, only DialoGPT (MT) reached the same level of performance. DialoGPT and GPT-2 trained on ED→RDG both fell in the low-performing group compared to the other combinations.

A similar result was obtained for the crowdworker rating of how much each line moves the conversation forward. Again, both the model, $F(2, 534) = 9.789$, $p < .001$, and the training data set, $F(1, 534) = 112.515$, $p < .001$, had a significant influence on the ratings. DialoGPT (MT) was found to be the model that generated the lines advancing the conversation most ($M = 3.54$, $SD = 0.04$) and the difference was significant in comparison to both DialoGPT ($M = 3.33$, $SD = 0.04$), $p < .001$, and GPT-2 ($M = 3.35$, $SD = 0.05$), $p < .001$. The difference between DialoGPT and GPT-2 was not significant, $p = .925$. Using only the RDG-Map data set for training ($M = 3.64$, $SD = 0.03$) generated lines that were perceived as advancing the conversation more than when the models were trained on the EmpatheticDialogues data in addition ($M = 3.18$, $SD = 0.03$). An interaction effect between the model and the training data could be observed as well, $F(2, 534) = 33.022$, $p < .001$, which showed a significance between the same two groups of well performing (all models trained on the RDG-Map data set plus DialoGPT (MT) trained on ED→RDG) and low performing variations (DialoGPT and GPT-2 trained on ED→RDG).

The model, $F(2, 534) = 12.46$, $p < .001$, but not the data set it was trained on, $F(1, 534) = 1.03$, $p = .31$, significantly influenced the rating of offensiveness of the utterances that were generated. DialoGPT (MT) generated the least offensive lines ($M = 2.43$, $SD = 0.05$) in comparison to DialoGPT ($M = 2.66$, $SD = 0.04$), $p < .001$, and GPT-2 ($M = 2.72$, $SD = 0.05$), $p < .001$. The ratings between DialoGPT and GPT-2 were comparable, $p = .639$. The interaction effect between the model and the data it was trained on was significant again, $F(2, 534) = 16.01$, $p < .001$. This time, the best performing models were the DialoGPT (MT) trained on both RDG-Map alone and the ED→RDG combination, as well as DialoGPT trained on ED→RDG.

Both the model, $F(2, 534) = 12.548$, $p < .001$, and the data set, $F(1, 534) = 2.189$, $p = 0.14$, had a significant influence on the affective ratings of the lines. DialoGPT (MT) produced lines that were on average rated as more excited and encouraging, which is significant compared to lines generated by DialoGPT, $p < .001$, and GPT-2, $p < .001$. The DialoGPT (MT) was also the model that generated lines that covered the most diverse affect in comparison to the other two. The models trained on the ED→RDG combination were more frus-

Model	Data	Rating	Max.	Min.	Mean	Std. Dev.
DialoGPT (MT)	ED→RDG	Excited	3.6	0.2	1.6	1.0
DialoGPT (MT)	ED→RDG	Frustrated	3.8	0.2	1.5	1.1
DialoGPT (MT)	RDG	Excited	3.6	0.2	1.2	0.9
DialoGPT (MT)	RDG	Frustrated	3	0.2	1.0	0.7
Human		Excited	3.8	0.2	1.5	0.9
Human		Frustrated	4	0.2	1.4	0.9

Table 2: Affective ratings for utterances produced by multitasking model. Human ratings for comparison. Scores range from 0 to 4, with 0 indicating indifference.

trated and provocative compared to the models trained on the RDG-Map data alone. The combination of model and data set was significant as well, $F(2, 534) = 13.224$, $p < .001$. The three models rated on the more excited end of the affective scale were the two DialoGPT (MT) models and the GPT-2 model trained on the RDG-Map data alone. The most impatient lines were generated by GPT-2 trained on ED→RDG. A selection of affective ratings is shown in Table 2.

Comparing Language Models and Crowd-Authors Eventually, we want to be able to use the language models presented in this paper to generate utterances that are comparable in their rating to the lines authored by crowd-workers. To understand whether our models achieve human-level performance, we combined the model and training set into a single independent variable and tested it against the ratings given to the crowd-authored lines. A one-way ANOVA with a Tukey's PostHoc analysis indeed showed that the ratings of the lines generated by all four models in the high performing group showed no significant difference to the ratings of the human lines, $p \geq .948$ for all four models. The two models in the low-performing group, however, were rated as significantly less typical than the lines written by crowd-authors, $p < .001$ for both models. The affective rating and range of affect between five out of the six combinations and the human model were comparable, $p > .147$ for all models except for GPT-2 trained on ED→RDG. This specific model and training data combination produced lines that were on average much more frustrated and provocative than the lines written by crowd-authors, $p < .001$. While the typicality of the lines and their affective range was comparable, utterances generated by all six combinations of model and training data were rated as significantly more offensive than the crowd-authored lines, $p < .001$ for all six models. A comparison between DialoGPT (MT) and the crowd-authored lines is summarized in Table 3. All generated utterances and respective evaluation scores are available publicly on GitHub[2].

7 Discussion & Future Work

We trained six variations of neural language generators on crowd-sourced content and evaluations. Our results suggest that DialoGPT (MT), the model additionally tasked with predicting the subjective evaluations by crowd-workers, produced utterances that were perceived as the most typical, least offensive, and most capable of moving the conversation forward. It also generated dialogue lines covering the widest range of affects, which meets an important goal for the spoken dialogue system of the RDG-Map domain. Utterances generated by DialoGPT (MT) *reach scores comparable to those given to human-authored lines in the dimensions relevance and affect for scenarios both seen and unseen during training*; in real-time and at a lower cost than the crowd-sourced approach. Based on these results, we consider the multitask learning approach a success.

Utilization of Subjective Ratings While our results are promising when it comes to the success of using subjective ratings as a secondary goal in multi-task learning to generate affective dialogue lines, further research is necessary to understand the exact influence of this particular training objective. In this work, we added two additional training goals in order to further utilize the collected data: Multiple choice and emotion classification. Hence, it may be possible that the multiple-choice task was more influential for the success of the DialoGPT (MT) model. However, in observing the training process, it was noted that the training loss for the multiple choice task decreased significantly faster

[2] https://git.io/JYzq8

Model	Data	Automatic BLEU		Human Subjective Evaluation Forwardness		Offensive		Typical	
		M	*SD*	*M*	*SD*	*M*	*SD*	*M*	*SD*
DialoGPT (MT)	ED→RDG	0.41	0.3	3.6	0.5	2.5	0.6	3.2	0.6
DialoGPT (MT)	RDG	0.37	0.3	3.5	0.5	2.4	0.6	3.3	0.6
Human		-	-	-	-	1.9	0.7	3.4	0.7

Table 3: Average BLEU scores and ratings for forwardness (i.e., moving the conversation forward), offensiveness and typicality for multitasking model. Human ratings for comparison. Typicality ranges from 0 to 4, with 0 representing nonsensical content. Offensiveness and Forwardness range from 1 to 4.

than the loss of the emotion prediction task. This indicates both that the emotion prediction tasks is a more difficult task to train, and that it plays a larger role during the optimization as its loss term is present during a larger portion of the training process. While future work is necessary to determine the contribution of each task individually, our results show *a strong indication that the inclusion of the subjective ratings contributed more to the performance improvements than distinguishing between a real or fake response*.

Keeping the Human Rater in the Loop In this proof-of-concept, we only utilized the initial crowd-evaluations of dialogue lines authored by other humans for training our NLG models. An interesting topic for future exploration would be to further include the second round of evaluations collected for the sentences generated by the NLG models. We could then envision natural language generation as an iterative process, defined by a number of alternating training and evaluation sessions, where models can be adjusted based on the evaluations. This moves the process closer to *reinforcement learning*, which is a topic that has been covered in previous work (Li et al., 2016; Ziegler et al., 2019; Nguyen et al., 2017). One of the challenges with this approach is finding a reward function which correlates the human evaluations with the content and prevents the model from veering off topic, but with the benefit that the model can be trained on only evaluation data going forward.

Addition of Further Tasks during Training Given the performance improvements offered by multitask learning, a potential subject of future work is to expand the multitasking further and incorporate more of the available human evaluation data. The offensiveness or typicality score are present in the data but are currently unused during training. Utterances rated too low in typicality or too high in offensiveness in the original spoken dialogue system were not included in the agent's conversational corpus. We chose to include rejected lines in the model training data to preserve as much of the problem-specific data as possible. Even if an utterance has been rejected as offensive, it may still relate to the context, which is information that the model theoretically can utilize. However, we found all our models to generate lines significantly more offensive than the original crowd-authored lines. While this finding is in line with related work on DialoGPT, which notes that models trained on large-scale internet text corpora can have issues with producing offensive content (Zhang et al., 2020; Li, 2020; Bender et al., 2021), we would still like to limit offensive content in a dialogue system deployed to converse with people. A potential improvement to the training procedure would be to remove rejected lines from training data. Another approach would entail the inclusion of typicality or offensiveness in the input which could potentially improve performance. Including the scores might also enable a method of controlling the typicality or offensiveness of the output, like the affect might currently do. It would also be prudent to study to what extent the designated affect actually influences the actual output.

Correlation between Human Evaluations and BLEU Contrary to findings in the related work, we found the BLEU score of the individual utterances to be significantly correlated with the human evaluations on typicality and how much the utterances advance the conversation. Liu et al. (2016) note that for constrained domains, the BLEU score correlates better with human judgements, which the RDG-Map domain might be considered as. However, no correlation could be found between the subjective rating of offensiveness and the automatic metric. This makes sense considering that BLEU is a measure of content similarity, and minor changes to the content, like an exclamation mark, may cause major changes in the perceived offensiveness of an utterance.

Filtering of Evaluations One major issue we experienced in our crowd-evaluation pipeline concerns the dishonesty of a few crowd-authors who did not pay attention to the task they accepted. While most participants performed their tasks well, a few workers providing nonsensical or random ratings can tilt the results, especially if these workers participate multiple times. To account for this, filters flagging random answers are necessary. This is complicated by the fact that the questions asked in the form are subjective, e.g., how offensive or typical an utterance is perceived. It is thus difficult to verify if people responding randomly as there are no "correct" answers. A method to address the issue at least partially is to include an objective control question. However, there are challenges around the number of such control questions to include (Liu et al., 2013) and efficiency of such trap methods (Lloret et al., 2013; Kittur et al., 2013) for complex NLP tasks.

Our method to detect crowd-raters responding randomly was to manually examine the results and exclude workers that gave obviously repetitive answers, e.g. always answering with the same alternative throughout multiple tasks. This is a simple but flawed method as raters answering in a random or less predicable, but still disingenuous, manner are not caught through this method. Additionally, our method only works with crowd-workers participating in several tasks. A measure that is simple to enforce is to prevent workers from participating more than once and hence limit the individual influence of each worker. However, this may lead to workers avoiding the task since it is only profitable for them to engage in repeated tasks, and also the loss of workers that give honest evaluations for multiple sessions. A more refined and automated method of filtering answers would improve the validity of the evaluation scores, and thus by proxy improve the training procedure.

7.1 Ethical Issues Regarding Language Models

There are several ethical issue with large-scale language models worth discussing. We observe some of the issues brought up by Bender et al. (2021), the main one being that the output can easily be misinterpreted as coherent or intelligent. One should be careful not to over-attribute the writing capabilities of language models as being equivalent to that of a human, despite in this case being rated similarly to human writers. In this scenario, we tell the raters that a robot produced the utterances, which likely influenced their judgment of typicality. A line assumed to be written by a machine might be considered typical even if it is vague or contains unusual wording, since the rater may consider the language capabilities of a machine to be limited. For future studies into dialogue generation models, it might be prudent to include harsher judgements of quality than used in the present work, e.g., asking the raters to judge the sentence as if it was written by a human, or whether it makes sense logically.

Another issue brought up by Bender et al. (2021) is the possibility of models producing offensive language. While we did notice that the lines generated by the language models were evaluated as more offensive than the crowd-authored lines, a manual review of the dialogue output of the language models did not disclose any slurs or explicitly derogatory statements. The utterance considered the most offensive was "I hope this game will be your last because it will be your last game for a very long time" which may be interpreted as a threat to the recipient's life. Other utterances considered offensive typically involve accusations of laziness or the human not being very good at the game, which are meaningful given the domain and the affect description of the agent.

8 Conclusion

The usage of human-annotated data for training machine learning models is an established practice. In this work, we propose and evaluate the utilization of subjective human evaluations for model training that would otherwise be used merely for evaluation. Our results suggest that by using not only crowd-sourced *content*, but also crowd-sourced *evaluations*, we can increase the performance of our models. We hence argue that future work should explore the inclusion of further subjective ratings and the possibility to make model generation and evaluation an iterative process and hence keep the human in the loop during the development process.

References

Daniel Adiwardana, Minh-Thang Luong, David R. So, Jamie Hall, Noah Fiedel, Romal Thoppilan, Zi Yang, Apoorv Kulshreshtha, Gaurav Nemade, Yifeng Lu, and Quoc V. Le. 2020. Towards a Human-like Open-Domain Chatbot. *arXiv e-prints*, page arXiv:2001.09977.

Satanjeev Banerjee and Alon Lavie. 2005. METEOR: An automatic metric for MT evaluation with improved correlation with human judgments. In *Proceedings of the ACL Workshop on Intrinsic and Extrinsic Evaluation Measures for Machine Translation and/or Summarization*, pages 65–72, Ann Arbor, Michigan. Association for Computational Linguistics.

Anja Belz and Ehud Reiter. 2006. Comparing automatic and human evaluation of NLG systems. In *11th Conference of the European Chapter of the Association for Computational Linguistics*, Trento, Italy. Association for Computational Linguistics.

Emily M. Bender, Timnit Gebru, Angelina McMillan-Major, and Shmargaret Shmitchell. 2021. On the dangers of stochastic parrots: Can language models be too big? In *Proceedings of the 2021 ACM Conference on Fairness, Accountability, and Transparency*, FAccT '21, page 610–623, New York, NY, USA. Association for Computing Machinery.

Tom B. Brown, Benjamin Mann, Nick Ryder, Melanie Subbiah, Jared Kaplan, Prafulla Dhariwal, Arvind Neelakantan, Pranav Shyam, Girish Sastry, Amanda Askell, Sandhini Agarwal, Ariel Herbert-Voss, Gretchen Krueger, Tom Henighan, Rewon Child, Aditya Ramesh, Daniel M. Ziegler, Jeffrey Wu, Clemens Winter, Christopher Hesse, Mark Chen, Eric Sigler, Mateusz Litwin, Scott Gray, Benjamin Chess, Jack Clark, Christopher Berner, Sam McCandlish, Alec Radford, Ilya Sutskever, and Dario Amodei. 2020. Language models are few-shot learners.

Yen-Chun Chen, Zhe Gan, Yu Cheng, Jingzhou Liu, and Jingjing Liu. 2020. Distilling knowledge learned in bert for text generation. In *Proceedings of the 58th Annual Meeting of the Association for Computational Linguistics*, pages 7893–7905.

Nina Dethlefs, Helen Hastie, Verena Rieser, and Oliver Lemon. 2012. Optimising incremental dialogue decisions using information density for interactive systems. In *Proceedings of the 2012 Joint Conference on Empirical Methods in Natural Language Processing and Computational Natural Language Learning*, pages 82–93.

Jacob Devlin, Ming-Wei Chang, Kenton Lee, and Kristina Toutanova. 2019. BERT: Pre-training of deep bidirectional transformers for language understanding. In *Proceedings of the 2019 Conference of the North American Chapter of the Association for Computational Linguistics: Human Language Technologies, Volume 1 (Long and Short Papers)*, pages 4171–4186, Minneapolis, Minnesota. Association for Computational Linguistics.

Ondřej Dušek and Filip Jurčíček. 2016. A context-aware natural language generator for dialogue systems. *arXiv preprint arXiv:1608.07076*.

Bjarke Felbo, Alan Mislove, Anders Søgaard, Iyad Rahwan, and Sune Lehmann. 2017. Using millions of emoji occurrences to learn any-domain representations for detecting sentiment, emotion and sarcasm. In *Proceedings of the 2017 Conference on Empirical Methods in Natural Language Processing*, pages 1615–1625, Copenhagen, Denmark. Association for Computational Linguistics.

Tatsunori Hashimoto, Hugh Zhang, and Percy Liang. 2019. Unifying human and statistical evaluation for natural language generation. In *Proceedings of the 2019 Conference of the North American Chapter of the Association for Computational Linguistics: Human Language Technologies, Volume 1 (Long and Short Papers)*, pages 1689–1701.

Tianxing He, Jun Liu, Kyunghyun Cho, Myle Ott, Bing Liu, James Glass, and Fuchun Peng. 2021. Analyzing the forgetting problem in the pretrain-finetuning of dialogue response models. In *EACL 2021-16th Conference of the European Chapter of the Association for Computational Linguistics*.

Ari Holtzman, Jan Buys, Li Du, Maxwell Forbes, and Yejin Choi. 2019. The curious case of neural text degeneration. In *International Conference on Learning Representations*.

Jeremy Howard and Sebastian Ruder. 2018. Universal language model fine-tuning for text classification. In *Proceedings of the 56th Annual Meeting of the Association for Computational Linguistics (Volume 1: Long Papers)*, pages 328–339.

Minlie Huang, Xiaoyan Zhu, and Jianfeng Gao. 2020. Challenges in building intelligent open-domain dialog systems. *ACM Transactions on Information Systems (TOIS)*, 38(3):1–32.

Aniket Kittur, Jeffrey V Nickerson, Michael Bernstein, Elizabeth Gerber, Aaron Shaw, John Zimmerman, Matt Lease, and John Horton. 2013. The future of crowd work. In *Proceedings of the 2013 conference on Computer supported cooperative work*, pages 1301–1318.

Jiwei Li, Will Monroe, Alan Ritter, Dan Jurafsky, Michel Galley, and Jianfeng Gao. 2016. Deep reinforcement learning for dialogue generation. In *Proceedings of the 2016 Conference on Empirical Methods in Natural Language Processing*, pages 1192–1202, Austin, Texas. Association for Computational Linguistics.

Piji Li. 2020. An Empirical Investigation of Pre-Trained Transformer Language Models for Open-Domain Dialogue Generation. *arXiv e-prints*, page arXiv:2003.04195.

Zhaojiang Lin, Andrea Madotto, Jamin Shin, Peng Xu, and Pascale Fung. 2019. MoEL: Mixture of empathetic listeners. In *Proceedings of the 2019 Conference on Empirical Methods in Natural Language Processing and the 9th International Joint Conference on Natural Language Processing (EMNLP-IJCNLP)*, pages 121–132, Hong Kong, China. Association for Computational Linguistics.

Chia-Wei Liu, Ryan Lowe, Iulian Serban, Mike Noseworthy, Laurent Charlin, and Joelle Pineau. 2016. How NOT to evaluate your dialogue system: An empirical study of unsupervised evaluation metrics for dialogue response generation. In *Proceedings of the 2016 Conference on Empirical Methods in Natural Language Processing*, pages 2122–2132, Austin, Texas. Association for Computational Linguistics.

Qian Liu, Yihong Chen, Bei Chen, Jian-Guang Lou, Zixuan Chen, Bin Zhou, and Dongmei Zhang. 2020. You impress me: Dialogue generation via mutual persona perception. In *Proceedings of the 58th Annual Meeting of the Association for Computational Linguistics*, pages 1417–1427, Online. Association for Computational Linguistics.

Qiang Liu, Alexander T Ihler, and Mark Steyvers. 2013. Scoring workers in crowdsourcing: How many control questions are enough? *Advances in neural information processing systems*, 26:1914–1922.

Elena Lloret, Laura Plaza, and Ahmet Aker. 2013. Analyzing the capabilities of crowdsourcing services for text summarization. *Language resources and evaluation*, 47(2):337–369.

Ryan Lowe, Michael Noseworthy, Iulian Vlad Serban, Nicolas Angelard-Gontier, Yoshua Bengio, and Joelle Pineau. 2017. Towards an automatic Turing test: Learning to evaluate dialogue responses. In *Proceedings of the 55th Annual Meeting of the Association for Computational Linguistics (Volume 1: Long Papers)*, pages 1116–1126, Vancouver, Canada. Association for Computational Linguistics.

Nurul Lubis, Sakriani Sakti, Koichiro Yoshino, and Satoshi Nakamura. 2018. Optimizing neural response generator with emotional impact information. In *2018 IEEE Spoken Language Technology Workshop (SLT)*, pages 876–883. IEEE.

Shikib Mehri and Maxine Eskenazi. 2020. Usr: An unsupervised and reference free evaluation metric for dialog generation. In *Proceedings of the 58th Annual Meeting of the Association for Computational Linguistics*, pages 681–707.

Alexander Miller, Will Feng, Dhruv Batra, Antoine Bordes, Adam Fisch, Jiasen Lu, Devi Parikh, and Jason Weston. 2017. ParlAI: A dialog research software platform. In *Proceedings of the 2017 Conference on Empirical Methods in Natural Language Processing: System Demonstrations*, pages 79–84, Copenhagen, Denmark. Association for Computational Linguistics.

Margaret Mitchell, Dan Bohus, and Ece Kamar. 2014. Crowdsourcing language generation templates for dialogue systems. In *Proceedings of the INLG and SIGDIAL 2014 Joint Session*, pages 172–180.

Pedro Mota, Maike Paetzel, Andrea Fox, Aida Amini, Siddarth Srinivasan, and James Kennedy. 2018. Expressing coherent personality with incremental acquisition of multimodal behaviors. In *2018 27th IEEE International Symposium on Robot and Human Interactive Communication (RO-MAN)*, pages 396–403. IEEE.

Khanh Nguyen, Hal Daumé III, and Jordan Boyd-Graber. 2017. Reinforcement learning for bandit neural machine translation with simulated human feedback. In *Proceedings of the 2017 Conference on Empirical Methods in Natural Language Processing*, pages 1464–1474, Copenhagen, Denmark. Association for Computational Linguistics.

Jekaterina Novikova, Ondřej Dušek, Amanda Cercas Curry, and Verena Rieser. 2017. Why we need new evaluation metrics for NLG. In *Proceedings of the 2017 Conference on Empirical Methods in Natural Language Processing*, pages 2241–2252, Copenhagen, Denmark. Association for Computational Linguistics.

Maike Paetzel and Ramesh Manuvinakurike. 2019. "can you say more about the location?" the development of a pedagogical reference resolution agent. In *Dialog for Good - Workshop on Speech and Language Technology Serving Society (DiGo)*.

Kishore Papineni, S. Roukos, T. Ward, and Wei-Jing Zhu. 2002. Bleu: a method for automatic evaluation of machine translation. In *ACL*.

Yada Pruksachatkun, Jason Phang, Haokun Liu, Phu Mon Htut, Xiaoyi Zhang, Richard Yuanzhe Pang, Clara Vania, Katharina Kann, and Samuel R. Bowman. 2020. Intermediate-task transfer learning with pretrained language models: When and why does it work? In *Proceedings of the 58th Annual Meeting of the Association for Computational Linguistics*, pages 5231–5247, Online. Association for Computational Linguistics.

Qiao Qian, Minlie Huang, Haizhou Zhao, Jingfang Xu, and Xiaoyan Zhu. 2018. Assigning personality/profile to a chatting machine for coherent conversation generation. In *IJCAI*, pages 4279–4285.

Alec Radford, Karthik Narasimhan, Tim Salimans, and Ilya Sutskever. 2018. Improving language understanding by generative pre-training.

Alec Radford, Jeff Wu, Rewon Child, David Luan, Dario Amodei, and Ilya Sutskever. 2019. Language models are unsupervised multitask learners.

Hannah Rashkin, Eric Michael Smith, Margaret Li, and Y-Lan Boureau. 2019. Towards empathetic open-domain conversation models: A new benchmark and dataset. In *Proceedings of the 57th Annual Meeting of the Association for Computational Linguistics*, pages 5370–5381, Florence, Italy. Association for Computational Linguistics.

Ehud Reiter. 2018. A structured review of the validity of BLEU. *Computational Linguistics*, 44(3):393–401.

Verena Rieser, Oliver Lemon, and Simon Keizer. 2014. Natural language generation as incremental planning under uncertainty: Adaptive information presentation for statistical dialogue systems. *ACM Transactions on Speech and Language Processing*, 22(5):979–994.

James A Russell. 1980. A circumplex model of affect. *Journal of personality and social psychology*, 39(6):1161.

Pararth Shah, Dilek Hakkani-Tur, Bing Liu, and Gokhan Tur. 2018. Bootstrapping a neural conversational agent with dialogue self-play, crowdsourcing and on-line reinforcement learning. In *Proceedings of the 2018 Conference of the North American Chapter of the Association for Computational Linguistics: Human Language Technologies, Volume 3 (Industry Papers)*, pages 41–51.

Lei Shen and Yang Feng. 2020. Cdl: Curriculum dual learning for emotion-controllable response generation. In *Proceedings of the 58th Annual Meeting of the Association for Computational Linguistics*, pages 1808–1822.

Nitish Shirish Keskar, Bryan McCann, Lav R. Varshney, Caiming Xiong, and Richard Socher. 2019. CTRL: A Conditional Transformer Language Model for Controllable Generation. *arXiv e-prints*, page arXiv:1909.05858.

Ashish Vaswani, Noam Shazeer, Niki Parmar, Jakob Uszkoreit, Llion Jones, Aidan N Gomez, Łukasz Kaiser, and Illia Polosukhin. 2017. Attention is all you need. In *Advances in neural information processing systems*, pages 5998–6008.

William Yang Wang, Dan Bohus, Ece Kamar, and Eric Horvitz. 2012. Crowdsourcing the acquisition of natural language corpora: Methods and observations. In *2012 IEEE Spoken Language Technology Workshop (SLT)*, pages 73–78. IEEE.

Thomas Wolf, Lysandre Debut, Victor Sanh, Julien Chaumond, Clement Delangue, Anthony Moi, Pierric Cistac, Tim Rault, R'emi Louf, Morgan Funtowicz, and Jamie Brew. 2019a. Huggingface's transformers: State-of-the-art natural language processing. *ArXiv*, abs/1910.03771.

Thomas Wolf, Victor Sanh, Julien Chaumond, and Clement Delangue. 2019b. Transfertransfo: A transfer learning approach for neural network based conversational agents. *CoRR*, abs/1901.08149.

Rohola Zandie and Mohammad H. Mahoor. 2020. Emptransfo: A multi-head transformer architecture for creating empathetic dialog systems. In *FLAIRS*.

Saizheng Zhang, Emily Dinan, Jack Urbanek, Arthur Szlam, Douwe Kiela, and Jason Weston. 2018. Personalizing dialogue agents: I have a dog, do you have pets too? In *Proceedings of the 56th Annual Meeting of the Association for Computational Linguistics (Volume 1: Long Papers)*, pages 2204–2213, Melbourne, Australia. Association for Computational Linguistics.

Tianyi Zhang, Varsha Kishore, Felix Wu, Kilian Q Weinberger, and Yoav Artzi. 2019. Bertscore: Evaluating text generation with bert. In *International Conference on Learning Representations*.

Yizhe Zhang, Siqi Sun, Michel Galley, Yen-Chun Chen, Chris Brockett, Xiang Gao, Jianfeng Gao, Jingjing Liu, and Bill Dolan. 2020. Dialogpt: Large-scale generative pre-training for conversational response generation. In *ACL, system demonstration*.

Xianda Zhou and William Yang Wang. 2018. Mojitalk: Generating emotional responses at scale. In *Proceedings of the 56th Annual Meeting of the Association for Computational Linguistics (Volume 1: Long Papers)*, pages 1128–1137.

Daniel M. Ziegler, Nisan Stiennon, Jeffrey Wu, Tom B. Brown, Alec Radford, Dario Amodei, Paul Christiano, and Geoffrey Irving. 2019. Fine-Tuning Language Models from Human Preferences. *arXiv e-prints*, page arXiv:1909.08593.

Trading Off Diversity and Quality in Natural Language Generation

Hugh Zhang* Facebook AI hughzhang@fb.com

Daniel Duckworth* Google AI duckworthd@google.com

Daphne Ippolito Google AI dei@google.com

Arvind Neelakantan OpenAI arvindramanat@gmail.com

Abstract

For open-ended language generation tasks such as storytelling or dialogue, choosing the right decoding algorithm is vital for controlling the tradeoff between generation *quality* and *diversity*. However, there presently exists no consensus on which decoding procedure is best or even the criteria by which to compare them. In this paper, we cast decoding as a tradeoff between response quality and diversity, and we perform the first large-scale evaluation of decoding methods along the entire quality-diversity spectrum. Our experiments confirm the existence of the likelihood trap: the counter-intuitive observation that high likelihood sequences are often surprisingly low quality. We also find that when diversity is a priority, all methods perform similarly, but when quality is viewed as more important, nucleus sampling (Holtzman et al., 2019) outperforms all other evaluated decoding algorithms.

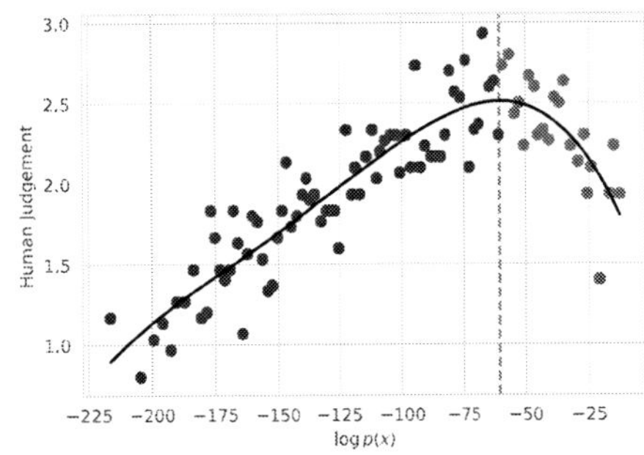

Figure 1: **The Likelihood Trap.** For a given context, we generate 100 sentences of equal length spanning a variety of model likelihoods and ask human crowdworkers to rate their quality. While model log-likelihoods are generally positively correlated with average human quality judgments, we notice an inflection point after which they become negatively correlated. Each point in the graph represents the average crowdworker rating of 5 sentences with similar model likelihoods.

1 Introduction

Generative language models are applicable for a wide variety of tasks including writing articles, composing Shakespearean sonnets, and engaging in conversation (Radford et al., 2019; Zhang et al., 2019; Fan et al., 2018). This work examines decoding methods, a critical component in language models used in open-ended generative tasks where successful models must generate a *diverse* spectrum of high *quality* answers rather than merely a single output (Ippolito et al., 2019a).

For many tasks, these two criteria of quality and diversity are not equally important. In machine translation, the most important criteria is to produce an accurate, high-quality translation of the input; generating a variety of alternative translations is also useful, but not if it comes at the cost of correctness. Meanwhile, in open domain dialogue the goal is often to sustain an enjoyable conversation with a human conversational partner and as such, a higher premium is placed on diversity. To give a concrete example for the case of dialogue, the phrase "I don't know" is typically a perfectly reasonable remark that appears quite often in the course of normal human conversation. However, a chatbot that only repeats "I don't know" makes for a very poor conversationalist. In such open-ended domains, being able to converse about a wide variety of topics with the occasional odd remark is highly preferred to merely repeating the safest possible remark over and over (Li et al., 2016).

To evaluate both of these criteria, we characterize the performance of decoding algorithms along the entire quality-diversity spectrum instead of simply at individual points. We compare a variety of commonly-used decoding algorithms in the first

* denotes equal contribution

Proceedings of the Workshop on Human Evaluation of NLP Systems (HumEval), pages 25–33
Online, April 19, 2021.

large-scale study of decoder performance, utilizing over 38,000 ratings on almost 10,000 samples. Our results indicate that when diversity is highly valued, all decoders perform similarly, but when quality is viewed as more important, the recently proposed nucleus sampling (Holtzman et al., 2019) outperforms all other evaluated decoding algorithms.

Additionally, we investigate the commonly held intuition that model likelihood is directly correlated with human quality judgments by explicitly measuring the relationship between the quality of a sentence as judged by human raters and its likelihood under a generative model. Our findings confirm the existence of a *likelihood trap*, the counter-intuitive observation that the highest likelihood sentences are of extremely low quality, despite a generally positive relationship between model likelihoods and human quality judgments. While this finding has been observed across a wide variety of models and tasks from news generation to machine translation (Cohen and Beck, 2018; Holtzman et al., 2019), to our knowledge we are the first to explicitly quantify the relationship between the two across the entire model probability space.

2 The Likelihood Trap

Sequence likelihood is commonly used as a heuristic for selecting high-quality generations. Beam search, the principal approach adopted in machine translation, encapsulates this principle by (approximately) finding the *single* most likely generation $\text{argmax} \log p_{\text{model}}(x)$.

However, prior work has suggested that this assumption of a monotonically positive relationship between sequence likelihood and sequence quality breaks down at the extremes (Section 5). We empirically quantify the relationship between sequence likelihoods and human quality judgments by subsampling a large number of context-continuation pairs representing a wide variety of model log-likelihoods. We then request human crowdworkers to rate the quality of each continuation given the context on a five-point "Terrible"-to-"High Quality" scale. Figure 1 plots these ratings as a function of $\log p_{\text{model}}$ and confirms that on average the highest quality generations are *not* the most likely. Specifically, we find that continuation quality is generally positively related with $\log p_{\text{model}}(x)$ up until an inflection point after which it becomes negatively related. Our findings suggest that while model likelihoods form a good proxy for continuation quality, naively maximizing over sentence likelihood leads to suboptimal continuation quality. We term this phenomenon the *likelihood trap*.

3 Evaluation Framework

We introduce an evaluation framework for measuring the trade off quality and diversity in language generation. We consider autoregressive language models that decompose the likelihood of a sequence $x_{1:n}$ token-by-token in a left-to-right fashion (Hamilton, 1994; Sutskever et al., 2014). Specifically, the (conditional) probability of the sequence is:

$$p_{\text{model}}(x_{1:n} \mid c) = \prod_{i=1}^{n} p_{\text{model}}(x_i | x_{1:i-1}, c)$$

where c is any additional conditioning signal, such as the previous turn of dialogue. Typically, p_{model} is not sampled from directly; it is first post-processed by a decoder to bias it towards already high-likelihood tokens.

We evaluate the quality of a single sequence $x_{1:n}$ by asking humans for a quality judgment $\text{HJ}(x)$. We can define the quality of a model $Q(p) = \mathbb{E}_{x \sim p}[\text{HJ}(x)]$ as the expected human "quality" judgment for sentences drawn from it. We measure the diversity of a model via the (conditional) Shannon entropy H (Shannon, 1948), a diversity metric widely used across many fields beyond computer science including biology, economics, chemistry, and physics. Conditional Shannon entropy is given by $H(p \mid c) = -\mathbb{E}_{x \sim p(x|c)}[\log p(x \mid c)]$. Since many metrics for measuring diversity in language generation exist in the literature, we validate our choice of entropy by measuring its correlation with other commonly used metrics of diversity based on n-gram frequency. We find the Spearman correlation with distinct-1 and distinct-2 (number of distinct unigrams and bigrams divided by total number of n-grams) to be 0.80 and 0.77 respectively over sentences generated by GPT-2.

Our choices of using the average human quality judgement to measure quality and entropy to measure diversity guarantee that the *optimal* Pareto frontier trades off monotonically between quality and diversity. Optimizing quality with no regard for diversity results in outputting only the single highest quality sentence, whereas optimizing for diversity with no regard for quality results in outputting every utterance with equal probability. Typical tasks in language generation (e.g. summarization, machine translation, storytelling) will fall somewhere in between these two extremes.

Since our models are imperfect, each decoding algorithm will, to the best of its ability, trace out its own estimate of this frontier. As most commonly used decoding strategies offer a knob to control the diversity of the generated text, we compare the performance of decoding algorithms by plotting their performance along various positions on the quality-diversity tradeoff curve.

4 Experiments

We evaluate three commonly used decoding algorithms, sweeping across the quality-diversity curve by considering several hyperparameter settings per decoding algorithm. At the extremes of their hyperparameter ranges, these algorithms all converge to greedy and random sampling, respectively.

- **temperature**: Sample tokens with probability proportional to $p(x_i|x_{1:i-1})^{1/t}$, $t \in [0, 1]$.
- **top-k** (Fan et al., 2018): Sample tokens only from the k highest likelihood tokens in the vocabulary at each timestep, $k \in [1, \text{vocab size}]$
- **top-p** (also known as nucleus sampling) (Holtzman et al., 2019): Sample only from tokens comprising the top-p percent of probability mass at each timestep, $p \in [0, 1]$.

4.1 Setup

Due to the large monetary cost of evaluation, we evaluate each decoding algorithm on the same language model: the 774M parameter variant of GPT-2 (Radford et al., 2019), a publicly-released language model. To ground samples in a common context, we select a set of 48 examples from the GPT-2 test set to condition upon by manually filtering out examples containing explicit content or web markup. Samples are drawn by conditioning on a 'prompt' consisting of the first 20 space-delimited words of a test example. As sample quality becomes ambiguous when samples are terse (Ippolito et al., 2019a), we explicitly require all sampling methods to generate exactly 30 tokens, a length approximately equal to the prompt.

To estimate the expected Human judgment score $\mathbb{E}_p[\text{HJ}(x)]$ of the probability distributions induced by each decoding algorithm, we enlist a qualified pool of 146 Amazon Mechanical Turk (AMT) workers selected by satisfactory performance on a qualification task. Workers are presented sets of five samples, each conditioned on the same prompt and drawn from five different algorithm-hyperparameter configurations and asked to assign qualitative scores to each sample ranging from human-like to gibberish. The exact prompts as shown to crowdworkers along with thorough descriptions of our data collection process and our checks for robustness are included in the Appendix.

Prior work has found that human annotaters have significant trouble in directly separating out machine and human generated continuations when they are of similar quality, as the task of assessing sentence quality is highly subjective (Ippolito et al., 2019a). We found that constructing pairwise preference ratings by randomly pairing samples evaluated at the same time significantly reduced the variance of our results. Specifically, if one sample is rated higher than the other, one is assigned a score of +1 and the other -1. If both are rated equally, both are assigned a score of 0. The score assigned to a decoding configuration is its average score across all pairwise preference ratings.

4.2 Results

We now introduce the first large-scale study comparing decoding algorithms and their hyperparameters. Unlike all prior work (Holtzman et al., 2019; Ippolito et al., 2019b), we explicitly put decoding algorithms *on equal footing* by comparing sample quality at equal points of diversity. We consider five hyperparameter configurations per decoding algorithm for a total of fifteen configurations. For each configuration and prompt, we draw ten samples. In total, workers rate nearly 10,000 samples resulting in over 38,000 paired ratings. Our main results are summarized in Figures 2a and 2b. Reassuringly, both entropy and human quality judgements vary smoothly with decoding algorithm hyperparameter.

As expected, random sampling directly from $\text{p}_{\text{model}}(x)$ is simultaneously the highest entropy *and the lowest quality*. This is empirically consistent with the long-standing intuition that decoding algorithms are critical to improving sample quality. Why is text from random sampling such poor quality? Language models such as GPT-2 are trained to minimize the KL-divergence between a training set and the model distribution p_{model}, an objective that prioritizes recall over precision (Arjovsky et al., 2017). As a result, models tend to ensure that high quality sequences have high likelihood without insisting that all high likelihood sequences also have high quality. When we evaluate samples from the

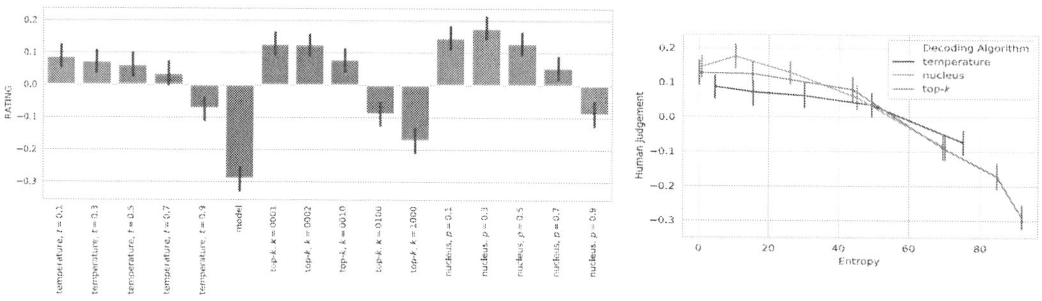

(a) (b)

Figure 2: **(a)** Human judgment scores for each decoding algorithm and hyperparameter choice. A score of 0 represents the average human judgement rating of all the sentences evaluated. Nucleus sampling is rated the highest while random sampling ("model") performs the worst. **(b)** Decoder quality plotted as a function of entropy, with each point representing a single decoding configuration. Error bars represent 95% bootstrap confidence intervals.

model, we evaluate the latter condition.

Our second conclusion is that sample quality varies significantly with entropy for all decoding algorithms. Moreover, when aligned on entropy, sample quality between all autoregressive decoding algorithms is comparable across a wide range. It is only when entropy is low – when decoding algorithms heavily influence sampling – that sample quality between algorithms diverge. In this regime, we find that nucleus sampling outperforms top-k, which in turn outperforms temperature sampling. Observing such a difference should be unsurprising: the entropy of a distribution alone does not characterize its samples and thus its overall quality. As such, a fair comparison of decoding algorithms must not only compare at the same level of entropy but at a *range* of entropy levels.

5 Related Work

Encouraging Diversity We choose to evaluate three commonly used decoding methods: nucleus sampling (Holtzman et al., 2019), top-k sampling (Fan et al., 2018), and temperature sampling. All three methods control the relative tradeoff between quality and diversity with a single hyperparameter as described in Section 4, though many other decoding methods also exist in the literature. Ippolito et al. (2019b) compares many of these algorithmic advancements on the tasks of open-ended dialog and image captioning, concluding that quality-diversity tradeoffs make it difficult to say that any one method is ubiquitously best.

Likelihood Trap We are far from the first to observe evidence of the likelihood trap. In particular, the machine translation and image captioning communities have long known that using higher beam sizes often leads to lower BLEU scores (Vinyals et al., 2016; Yang et al., 2018; Stahlberg and Byrne, 2019; Meister et al., 2020). In open-ended generation, Holtzman et al. (2019) find similar results, observing that maximizing the likelihood generates extremely repetitive sentences. Our main contribution towards understanding the likelihood trap is the first explicit measurement of the relationship between model likelihoods and human quality judgments at all points in the model probability space, not just the endpoints.

Frameworks Our framework differs from those which ask that generative models mimic the training distribution exactly (Hashimoto et al., 2019; Kingma and Welling, 2013; Goodfellow et al., 2014). While indistinguishability is sometimes the ultimate goal, humans make errors, and a perfect model would not seek to imitate these mistakes. As we ground quality evaluations in human judgments rather than statistical measures, our framework is easily able to capture the possibility of superhuman performance.

6 Conclusion

In this paper, we propose a framework for credibly evaluating decoding algorithms and use it to conduct the first large scale evaluation of decoding algorithms by measuring their performance along the entire quality-diversity frontier. We observe that decoders can be tuned to produce higher-quality text, but that this improved quality comes at the cost of diversity. Our findings suggest that existing decoding algorithms are largely interchangeable in high diversity settings, but that nucleus sampling performs best when quality is valued over diversity. We show that when performing a comparison of text generated from multiple decoding algorithms, it is crucial to ensure equivalent diversity to make the comparison fair, a step many evaluations fail to do. Finally, we warn against falling for the *likelihood trap*, as selecting generated text that is *too* likely results in text that humans judge to be worse.

References

Martin Arjovsky, Soumith Chintala, and Léon Bottou. 2017. Wasserstein gan. *arXiv preprint arXiv:1701.07875*.

Eldan Cohen and J Christopher Beck. 2018. (unconstrained) beam search is sensitive to large search discrepancies.

Angela Fan, Mike Lewis, and Yann Dauphin. 2018. Hierarchical neural story generation. *arXiv preprint arXiv:1805.04833*.

I. J. Goodfellow, J. Pouget-Abadie, M. Mirza, B. Xu, D. Warde-Farley, S. Ozair, A. Courville, and Y. Bengio. 2014. Generative adversarial nets. In *Advances in Neural Information Processing Systems (NeurIPS)*.

James D Hamilton. 1994. *Time series analysis*, volume 2. Princeton New Jersey.

Tatsunori B Hashimoto, Hugh Zhang, and Percy Liang. 2019. Unifying human and statistical evaluation for natural language generation. *arXiv preprint arXiv:1904.02792*.

Ari Holtzman, Jan Buys, Maxwell Forbes, and Yejin Choi. 2019. The curious case of neural text degeneration. *arXiv preprint arXiv:1904.09751*.

Daphne Ippolito, Daniel Duckworth, Chris Callison-Burch, and Douglas Eck. 2019a. Human and automatic detection of generated text. *arXiv preprint arXiv:1911.00650*.

Daphne Ippolito, Reno Kriz, Maria Kustikova, João Sedoc, and Chris Callison-Burch. 2019b. Comparison of diverse decoding methods from conditional language models. *arXiv preprint arXiv:1906.06362*.

Diederik P Kingma and Max Welling. 2013. Auto-encoding variational bayes. *arXiv preprint arXiv:1312.6114*.

J. Li, M. Galley, C. Brockett, J. Gao, and W. B. Dolan. 2016. A diversity-promoting objective function for neural conversation models. pages 110–119.

Clara Meister, Tim Vieira, and Ryan Cotterell. 2020. If beam search is the answer, what was the question?

Alec Radford, Jeffrey Wu, Rewon Child, David Luan, Dario Amodei, and Ilya Sutskever. 2019. Language models are unsupervised multitask learners. *OpenAI Blog*, 1(8):9.

Claude E Shannon. 1948. A mathematical theory of communication. *Bell system technical journal*, 27(3):379–423.

Felix Stahlberg and Bill Byrne. 2019. On NMT search errors and model errors: Cat got your tongue? In *Proceedings of the 2019 Conference on Empirical Methods in Natural Language Processing and the 9th International Joint Conference on Natural Language Processing (EMNLP-IJCNLP)*, pages 3356–3362, Hong Kong, China. Association for Computational Linguistics.

Ilya Sutskever, Oriol Vinyals, and Quoc V Le. 2014. Sequence to sequence learning with neural networks. In *Advances in neural information processing systems*, pages 3104–3112.

Oriol Vinyals, Alexander Toshev, Samy Bengio, and Dumitru Erhan. 2016. Show and tell: Lessons learned from the 2015 mscoco image captioning challenge. *IEEE transactions on pattern analysis and machine intelligence*, 39(4):652–663.

Yilin Yang, Liang Huang, and Mingbo Ma. 2018. Breaking the beam search curse: A study of (re-)scoring methods and stopping criteria for neural machine translation. *arXiv preprint arXiv:1808.09582*.

Yizhe Zhang, Siqi Sun, Michel Galley, Yen-Chun Chen, Chris Brockett, Xiang Gao, Jianfeng Gao, Jingjing Liu, and Bill Dolan. 2019. Dialogpt: Large-scale generative pre-training for conversational response generation.

A Appendix

A.1 Experimental Design

In this section, we describe the design of experiments presented in Section 4 in greater detail.

We begin by describing the task presented to crowdsourced raters. A sample task is shown in Figure 4. Each task consists of a "context" sequence of the first 20 words in a news article.[1] We then present the rater with five continuations of 30 word-piece tokens. The rater assigns a label of "High Quality," "Decent," "Passable," "Bad" or "Terrible" to each. We note that these labels are inherently subjective, and include a description and reference example before each task to calibrate the rater. The same description and example is repeated in Figure 3.

In preliminary experiments, we found examples and instructions insufficient for achieving repeatable results. Manual inspection of rater responses revealed a failure to interpret the labels correctly as well as spammers who would always choose the same response for every prompt. As a result, we crafted a qualification exam of five continuations. Only raters which rated all five continuations correctly or nearly correctly[2] were allowed to participate in further experiments. Of the 550 crowdsourced workers surveyed, 136 met this criteria. We refer to this set of raters as the "qualified rater pool" below.

Even with a qualification exam, we found raters often disagree on the appropriate label for a given continuation. However, when asked to choose which of two continuations was higher quality quality (if any), raters were better aligned. With this in mind, we choose to analyze *pairs* of ratings given in the same task. From five absolute ratings, we construct twenty pairwise preference ratings: two per pair of continuations. If two continuations receive the same label, they are assigned a preference of 0. If the first continuation is rated higher than the second, a the pair (first, second) is assigned a score of +1 and the pair (second, first) a score of -1. All analyses comparing multiple decoding methods use this methodology.

Even with the precautions above, care is needed to ensure repeatable results. To measure this, we performed an "A/A" experiment prior to data collection. This experiment consists of having the same tasks rated by two different pools of raters. Identical analyses are performed on both rating results, and the experimental setup is deemed valid if conclusions are consistent. To achieve this, we constructed 150 tasks[3] using a subset of the context sequences and decoding methods from our primary experiment. We artificially split the qualified worker pool in two by sending the same tasks for evaluation at midnight and at noon.[4] We submit the same set of tasks to both rater pools. An analysis of results from both sets of ratings (Figure 5) reveals a statistically consistent preference of top-p over top-k and (local) temperature sampling, and a severe disapproval of random sampling from the model. These results are also consistent with the same statistics gathered in the full-scale experiment presented in the main text and another experiment described below.

To further validate the reliability of our methodology, we explicitly measure inter-rater agreement on the same set of 150 tasks in a follow-up experiment after large-scale data collection. In this experiment, we ask each task be rated by five distinct raters. We measure Fleiss's Kappa, a measure inter-rater agreement, on the resulting pairwise ratings. We obtain a score of 0.1964 – an indication that a correlation between raters exists but that the task is far from unambiguous. While this may initially appear concerning, we argue that this is an indication of the task's difficulty. Unlike image classification, for example, a universally agreeable criteria for text quality does not exist. A measure of Cohen's Kappa on the A/A experiment above produces a score of 0.19578 – nearly identical to the inter-rater agreement experiment described here. The similarity of these two statistics gives evidence that the proposed experimental design is repeatable in spite of the task's ambiguity. These reuslts underscore the importance of large-scale, repeatable studies like that presented here. We conclude by measuring rater preference between each pair of sampling method and hyperparameter on the five-raters-per-task inter-rater agreement experiment described above. Results, as shown in Figure 7, indicate that the same trends presented in the full-scale experiment (Figure 2a) hold.

[1] News articles are sourced from GPT-2's WebText dataset. https://github.com/openai/gpt-2-output-dataset

[2] Raters which incorrectly labeled at most one continuation with a label at most one level off (e.g. if the correct answer is "Bad", acceptable errors are "Passable" and "Terrible") are counted as "nearly correct".

[3] The large-scale experiment includes 1,930 tasks.

[4] All tasks within each experiment were rated within 4 hours and 1.5 hours, respectively.

Context	Continuation	$\log p(x)$	Classification
The Atlanta Falcons have started the 2015 season 4-0 under new head coach Dan Quinn. Quarterback Matt Ryan has the ...	... mental Tough O'Rourke Tough apology assessment category of virtue from Boser' Blog here. It's got letters and images on it and is utterly ...	-177	Nonsense
	... team afloat and looks closer to the 2010 Atlanta Falcons. Starting cornerback Desmond Trufant was one of the top players on the 2014 ...	-74	Reasonable
	... team in the thick of the NFC South race. The Atlanta Falcons have started the 2015 season 4-0 under new head coach Dan Quinn. Quarter...	-14	Repetition
They have changed the phone menu to try to deflect us to email, but you can still get a live ...	... answer from a female administratoria llallushoss@rahpx Sandra PJ Jenniea nightiopq HamidF daroyqg S') ...	-229	Nonsense
	... message or call on line, so I suppose they are just using that as an excuse. Yet they are still telling people to change their telephone number...	-86	Reasonable
	... link to a phone number here. They have changed the phone menu to try to deflect us to email, but you can still get a live link to...	-23	Repetition

Table 1: Examples of sentences at various model likelihoods. Sentences with very low $\log p_{\text{model}}$ generate nonsense, while sentences that have high likelihood under the model often devolve into extreme repetition. Nonsense and repetition classifications shown here are only for illustrative purposes. Crowdworkers simply rated sentences for overall quality.

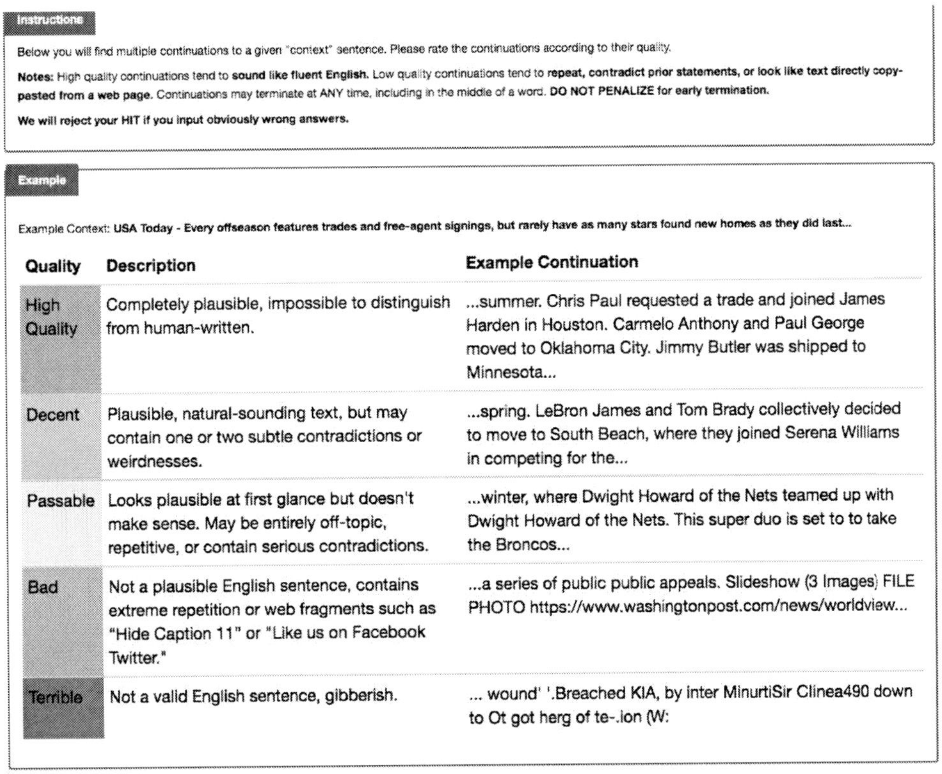

Figure 3: Instructions for the crowdworker task. Each sentence continuation is labeled on a scale from "Terrible" to "High Quality". A description of each label and an example continuation that fits each each is provided before each task. Exact example used may vary.

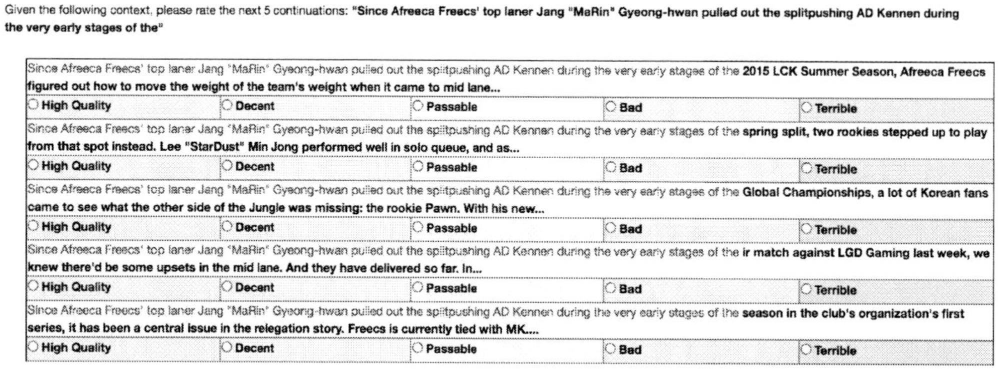
Given the following context, please rate the next 5 continuations: **"Since Afreeca Freecs' top laner Jang "MaRin" Gyeong-hwan pulled out the splitpushing AD Kennen during the very early stages of the"**

Since Afreeca Freecs' top laner Jang "MaRin" Gyeong-hwan pulled out the splitpushing AD Kennen during the very early stages of the **2015 LCK Summer Season, Afreeca Freecs figured out how to move the weight of the team's weight when it came to mid lane...**				
High Quality	Decent	Passable	Bad	Terrible
Since Afreeca Freecs' top laner Jang "MaRin" Gyeong-hwan pulled out the splitpushing AD Kennen during the very early stages of the **spring split, two rookies stepped up to play from that spot instead. Lee "StarDust" Min Jong performed well in solo queue, and as...**				
High Quality	Decent	Passable	Bad	Terrible
Since Afreeca Freecs' top laner Jang "MaRin" Gyeong-hwan pulled out the splitpushing AD Kennen during the very early stages of the **Global Championships, a lot of Korean fans came to see what the other side of the Jungle was missing: the rookie Pawn. With his new...**				
High Quality	Decent	Passable	Bad	Terrible
Since Afreeca Freecs' top laner Jang "MaRin" Gyeong-hwan pulled out the splitpushing AD Kennen during the very early stages of the **ir match against LGD Gaming last week, we knew there'd be some upsets in the mid lane. And they have delivered so far. In...**				
High Quality	Decent	Passable	Bad	Terrible
Since Afreeca Freecs' top laner Jang "MaRin" Gyeong-hwan pulled out the splitpushing AD Kennen during the very early stages of the **season in the club's organization's first series, it has been a central issue in the relegation story. Freecs is currently tied with MK....**				
High Quality	Decent	Passable	Bad	Terrible

Figure 4: Sample crowdworker task used for the main evaluation results. Raters assign a label on a scale from "Terrible" to "High Quality" to each of five continuations sharing a common context of twenty words. Each continuation is generated by a different sampling method and hyperparameter.

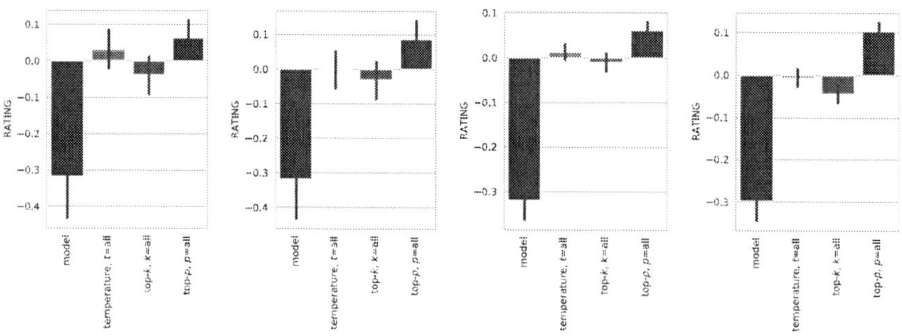

(a) A/A, midnight (b) A/A, noon (c) Full-scale (d) Inter-rater

Figure 5: Average Human judgement scores for each sampling method, aggregated across sampling method hyperparameters. In spite of being collected by different raters on different sets of tasks and different points in time, rater preference remains consistent.

Experiment	Num Ratings	Kappa
A/A	2,968	0.1957 (Cohen's)
Five-Rater	14,760	0.1964 (Fleiss's)

Figure 6: Inter-rater agreement between pairwise preference ratings as measured in a preliminary A/A experiment and an explicit, five-raters-per-task inter-rater agreement experiment. While agreement is low, Kappa is strongly consistent between both experiments.

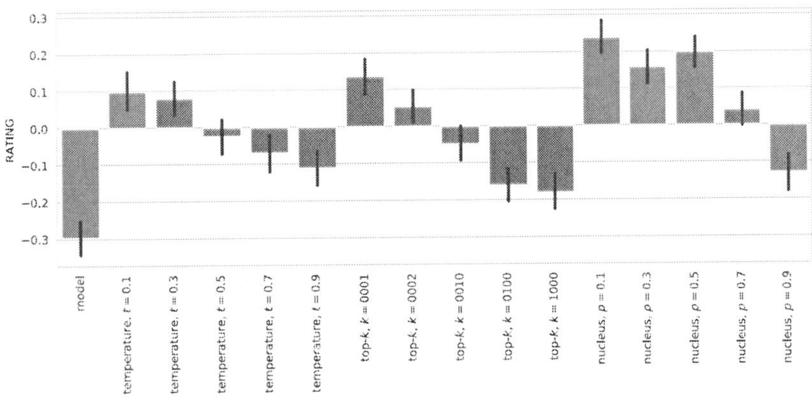

Figure 7: Human judgement scores for each decoding algorithm and hyperparameter choice, as measured in the inter-rater agreement experiment. Preference between sampling methods remains consistent with large-scale experiment shown in Figure 2a in spite of using only decodes generated by a subset of context sequences.

Towards Document-Level Human MT Evaluation: On the Issues of Annotator Agreement, Effort and Misevaluation

Sheila Castilho
Adapt Centre
School of Computing
Dublin City University
sheila.castilho@adaptcentre.ie

Abstract

Document-level human evaluation of machine translation (MT) has been raising interest in the community. However, little is known about the issues of using document-level methodologies to assess MT quality. In this article, we compare the inter-annotator agreement (IAA) scores, the effort to assess the quality in different document-level methodologies, and the issue of misevaluation when sentences are evaluated out of context.

1 Introduction

The use of machine translation (MT) has now become widespread in many areas thanks to improvements in neural modelling (Sutskever et al., 2014; Bahdanau et al., 2015; Vaswani et al., 2017). Accordingly, researchers have attempted to integrate discourse into neural machine translation (NMT) systems. As a consequence, document-level human evaluation of MT has raised interest in the community as it enables a more detailed assessment of suprasentential context. However, the definition of document-level, in terms of how much of the text needs to be shown, is still unclear. Moreover, although a few works have looked into document-level evaluation (Läubli et al., 2018; Toral et al., 2018; Barrault et al., 2019; Castilho et al., 2020), little is known about the issues of using document-level methodologies to assess MT quality.

The present research attempts to shed light on the differences in inter-annotator agreement (IAA) when evaluating MT with different methodologies, namely random single sentences, sentences in context, and full document scores. We also look into perceived effort from translators when evaluating the translations in the different methodologies. Results have shown a good level of IAA with a methodology where translators are able to assess individual sentences within the context of a document compared to a methodology with random sentence assessments, while a methodology where translators give a single score per document yields low IAA. Furthermore, we note that misevaluation cases recur in the random single sentences evaluation scenario.

2 Related Work

Document-level machine translation evaluation has been raising interest in the MT field, however, only a few works have attempted to use document-level boundaries for MT evaluation. Scarton et al. (2015) asked participants to post-edit and tag single sentences and full paragraphs in terms of cohesion and coherence. Their results showed that more post-editing was performed in paragraphs which suggests several issues could only be solved with paragraph-wide context. The authors reported Spearman's rank correlation for agreement which showed mixed to low agreement.

Toral et al. (2018) used consecutive single sentences to rank translations (in terms of preferred translation) of two MT systems and a human reference. They found that, when provided with more context, evaluators were better able to assess the translations, and moreover, IAA between professional translators was higher than that between non-experts. However, this methodology did not allow access to the full documents, as sentences were given one by one in order shown in the document.

Läubli et al. (2018) used pairwise rankings of fluency and adequacy to evaluate the quality of MT against human translation (HT) for document-level texts. The methodology consisted of translators choosing the 'best' translated documents in terms of i) adequacy and ii) fluency, that is, instead of choosing on a scale of how fluent or adequate the translations are, the raters just chose the 'best' one. The authors reported some IAA scores in the appendix of that work, showing that for fluency,

Proceedings of the Workshop on Human Evaluation of NLP Systems (HumEval), pages 34–45
Online, April 19, 2021. ©2021 Association for Computational Linguistics

document-level set-up had higher IAA than sentence set-up, but that the opposite was the case for adequacy. However, this evaluation methodology can only be used when comparing two different translations.

Castilho et al. (2020) tested the context span for the translation of 300 sentences in three different domains (reviews, subtitles, and literature) in a survey with native speakers. The results showed that over 33% of the sentences tested were found to require more context than the sentence itself to be translated or evaluated, and from those, 23% required more than two previous sentences to be properly evaluated. The most common issues found to hinder translation were ambiguity, terminology, and gender agreement. Their results show that cohesion and coherence errors types cannot be recognised at sentence-level at times.

In 2019, the Fourth Conference for Machine Translation (WMT19)[1] attempted document-level human evaluation for the *news* domain for the first time (Barrault et al., 2019). Their direct-assessment (DA)[2] task asked crowdworkers to give a score (0-100) regarding the accuracy of the translated sentence, for one MT output. They asked raters to rate i) full documents, ii) single consecutive segments in original sequential order and iii) single random sentences. WMT20 (Barrault et al., 2020) modified the methodology and extended the context span to entire documents, asking raters to score individual segments whilst seeing the entire document, and also to judge the translation of the entire document. However, conventional Kappa cannot be used with DA to measure IAA, and so consistency is measured instead, where raters have to pass some quality control criteria.

In light of this, a comparison of IAA between quality assessments on sentence- and document-level set-ups is needed in order to determine which set-up results in the most reliable evaluation. This study is a follow-up of results presented in Castilho (2020) where we present a small-scale comparison on the differences in IAA between judgements given in isolated random sentences and entire documents. In the present study, we compare the IAA in evaluation of i) random single sentences, ii) evaluation of individual sentences while translators have access to the full source and MT output, and iii) evaluation of full documents. To the best of our knowledge, this is the first paper to compare IAA for random single sentence vs individual sentences in a document-level set-up using the state-of-the-art MT evaluation metrics, namely fluency and adequacy scales,[3] error mark-up and pairwise ranking, (Castilho et al., 2018) along with reporting effort indicators.

3 Methodology

3.1 Evaluation Design

Professional English (EN) to Brazilian Portuguese (PT-BR) translators were hired to perform the evaluation in terms of fluency, adequacy, error mark-up, and pairwise ranking using a spreadsheet. The evaluation was carried out in two scenarios:

1. **Sentence-level**: where translators give one score per random single sentence, henceforth *Random-Sentence score* - RSs.
2. **Document-level**: where translators give:
   - **A**: one score per individual sentence while having access to the full text. Henceforth, *Sentence-in-Context score* - SCs;
   - **B**: one general score for the full document, henceforth *Document score* - Ds. This evaluation was performed immediately after 2A.

This methodology is used to reflect the results of the first stage of this work (Castilho, 2020) and the context-span necessary for translation as seen in Castilho et al. (2020).

3.2 Corpus

Fourteen short documents (513 sentences) from various sources were selected: News from the WMT newstest 2019, Ted Talk from OPUS Corpus (Tiedemann, 2012), excerpts from two books, and product reviews.[4] These texts were selected because they consist of relatively short documents so it was possible to display the whole documents to translators. The two books were chosen because they were both

[1]WMT is running since 2006 and had always performed evaluation solely at the sentence level until 2019 (http://www.statmt.org/wmt19/).

[2]Direct assessment started in 2016 and was performed solely on single sentences until 2019.

[3]It is important to notice that Läubli et al. (2018) used pairwise ranking of fluency and adequacy instead of the standard Likert scale, while WMT uses direct assessments.

[4]The excerpts from both books were found freely available online: The Girl on the Train (www.bookbrowse.com) and The Fault in Our Stars (www.penguin.com). Product reviews were collect on the Amazon.com website.

narrated by female characters, which is important for translation of gender. Regarding user reviews, some were chosen because they do not contain information about the reviewer's gender, or about the product. Moreover, a few documents in the WMT News had the gender modified, for example, in a document where the politician was male, it was changed to female. These characteristics were selected to add challenging gender translations to the test set (Castilho et al., 2020).

3.3 Tools and MT systems

The collected corpus was translated from EN into PT-BR using Google Translate and DeepL. This language pair was selected because, as it is the researcher's mother tongue, it makes it possible to analyse the results more carefully and see possible patterns in the process. Additionally, as Portuguese is a romance language, it is possible that the results of this pilot can be extended to the language family.

While Google Translate was used for all the tasks, DeepL was used for a second translation for the ranking task. As we are mainly interested in finding out the best document-level methodology and annotator agreement as opposed to the quality of the translation, we believe that these two freely available MT system were adequate.

The tasks were set up on a spreadsheet since it proved to be the best tool where translator can see the full text at once (or most of it) and be able to judge fluency, adequacy and error at the same time.

3.4 Human Evaluation Metrics

We used the state-of-the-art MT evaluation metrics for this comparison, namely fluency and adequacy scales, error mark-up and pairwise ranking.

Adequacy was assessed for each scenario, RSs, SCs and Ds. Translators answered the question *"How much of the meaning expressed in the source appears in the translation?"* on a Likert scale from 1 to 4, where 1. None of it, 2. Little of it, 3. Most of it, 4. All of it.

Fluency was also assessed for each scenario, RSs, SCs and Ds. Translators answered the question *"How fluent was the translation?"* on a Likert scale from 1-4, where 1. No fluency, 2. Little fluency, 3. Near native, 4. Native.

Error mark-up - Translators were asked to select from a drop-down menu the types of errors found in the MT output. As we are only interested in the agreement level between translators (as opposed to finding out the quality of the MT system), we decided to use a simple taxonomy that consisted of four error categories: Mistranslation, Untranslated, Word Form, and Word Order. Translators could also select "No errors" where the sentence/document did not contain any errors. Each sentence or document could be annotated with more than one error category, and each error category could be assigned more than once.

Translators	**Group 1**		**Group 2**	
	T1/T5	T2/T6	T3/T7	T4/T8
Test Set 1	S_1	S_2	D_1	D_2
Test Set 2	D_2	D_1	S_2	S_1

Table 1: Distribution of tasks where S is sentence-level scenario (RSs) and D is document-level scenarios (SCs and Ds), and 1 and 2 are the order of the tasks.

Pairwise Ranking was performed with translation from Google Translate and DeepL online MT systems. The systems' outputs were randomly mixed in each scenario so translators would see different outputs while ranking the translations. Translators were asked to rate their preferred translation, and ties were allowed.

3.5 Translators

Eight professional translators took part in the evaluation.[5] Their professional experiences range from 4 to 10+ years, and half of them have had previous experience with translation evaluation. Detailed guidelines on how to rate adequacy and fluency, tag errors and rank translations were made available and translators could ask for clarification for any doubts about the tasks. In order to avoid translators evaluating the same source twice, documents and scenarios were randomised. Each translator evaluated 513 sentences, 258 in scenario 1 (test set1- TS1) and 254 in scenario 2 (test set2 -TS2). Table 1 shows the distribution of the tasks for each translator, where Group 1 is made up of translators T1/T2/T5/T6, and Group 2, translators T3/T4/T7/T8.

3.6 Post-task Questionnaire

The post-task questionnaire consisted of 10 statements for the RSs and SCs scenarios. These were assessed on a scale from 1 to 6, where 1 is a negative answer (very difficult (statements 1-7) / very tiring (statement 8) / strongly disagree (statements 9-10)) and 6 is an affirmative answer (very easy/not tiring at all/strongly agree). Two additional statements for the assessment of fluency,

[5]Ethical approval has been obtained from the Dublin City University Research Ethics Committee.

Coeficients	Chance Correction	Weighted	# Raters	Measurement
Inter-rater reliability (IRR)	no	no	any	percentage
Cohen's Kappa	yes	no	2	interval 0-1
Weighted Cohen's Kappa	yes	yes	2	interval 0-1
Fleiss' Kappa (version of Scott's)	yes	no	any	interval 0-1
Krippendorff's Alpha	yes	yes	any	interval 0-1

Table 2: Inter-annotator coefficients comparison

adequacy and ranking were displayed for the Ds scenario (shown immediately after the statements for the SCs scenario). The statements for scenarios RSs and SCs were the following:

1. Understanding the meaning of the source [in the random sentences/in each sentence, with access to the full document] in general was
2. Understanding the meaning of the translated [in the random sentences/in each sentence, with access to the full document] in general was
3. Recognising the adequacy problems [in the random sentences/in each sentence, with access to the full document] in general was
4. Recognising fluency problems [in the random sentences/in each sentence, with access to the full document] in general was
5. Spotting errors [in the random sentences/in each sentence, with access to the full document] in general was
6. Choosing the best of two translations [in the random sentences/in each sentence, with access to the full document] was
7. In general, assessing the translation quality on a [sentence/document] level was (difficulty)
8. For me, assessing the translation quality on a [sentence/document] level was (fatigue)
9. I was confident with every assessment I provided for the [sentence/document] level evaluation tasks
10. I could have done a more accurate assessment if I [had had access to the full text/was assessing random sentences]

The additional statements for the Ds scenario were the following (note that statements including 'best target' and 'worst target' were only displayed for the ranking assessment):

1 Giving a general (adequacy / fluency / ranking) score for the full text was: (1 very difficult - 6 very easy)
2 In order to give a general (adequacy / fluency / ranking) score for each text, I had to re-read the full text:

Yes, both source and target texts
Yes, but only the target text
Yes, but only the best target text
Yes, but only the worst target text
No, I haven't re-read the full text(s). I remember it so I gave a general score according to my feeling of the translation

3.7 Inter-annotator agreement (IAA)

We compute IAA with some of the most common statistics for IAA in the field of computational linguistics (Artstein and Poesio, 2008). We compute IAA with some of the most common statistics for IAA in the field of computational linguistics (Artstein and Poesio, 2008). We compute **Cohen's Kappa** (Cohen, 1960)[6] both non-weighted and weighted versions.[7] We also use **Fleiss' Kappa** (Fleiss, 1971) which accounts for more than two raters, and **Krippendorff's Alpha reliability** (Krippendorff, 2011) which also applies to multiple coders, and allows for different magnitudes of disagreement. Fleiss Kappa and Krippendorff's Alpha are also used for the aggregated judgements within each condition. In addition to that, we compute a simple measure of percentage of agreement (we call it **inter-rater agreement - IRR**) calculated as the number of agreements, divided by the total number of assessments.[8] Table 2 summarises the features of each agreement coefficient.

The purpose of using Kappa-like coefficients for this study is to determine whether the assessments capture some kind of observable reality (Artstein and Poesio, 2008). Moreover, it is important to note that a discussion on the interpretation of the value of Kappa-like coefficients is beyond the scope of

[6]As Cohen's Kappa is designed for measuring the agreement between only two raters, when computing it for multiple raters, one can report the average of the Kappa statistics computed from each possible pair of raters (Mitani et al., 2017).

[7]Weighted Kappa was computed for the Adequacy and Fluency scores as they are assessed using a Likert scale, while non-weighted Kappa was computed for ranking and error tasks.

[8]All metrics were computed with Kappa built-in in SPSS software

Adequacy	RSs	SCs	Ds
Test set 1	**Group1**	**Group2**	**Group2**
Weighted κ (av)	0.40	0.41	0.30
Fleiss κ	0.32	0.29	0.13
Krippendorff α	0.50	0.51	0.28
IRR	70%	55%	68%
Test set 2	**Group2**	**Group1**	**Group1**
Weighted κ (av)	0.31	0.31	0.31
Fleiss κ	0.23	0.22	0.06
Krippendorff α	0.38	0.36	0.18
IRR	59%	59%	47%

Table 3: IAA for adequacy assessments for random single sentences (RSs), individual sentences in document context (SCs), and one score per document (Ds) scenarios.

Adequacy	RSs	SCs	Ds
Fleiss κ	0.10	0.10	-0.02
Krippendorff α	0.16	0.18	0.19

Table 4: Aggregated IAA scores for adequacy assessments.

this paper.

The comparison of the scenarios (1 - sentence *vs* 2 - document) is calculated between the test sets (Test Set 1 & Test Set 2) for a more detailed evaluation of the IAA scores, and scores are also generalised for each methodology. Due to the exploratory nature of this research, along with the small number of participants which is known to hinder the effectiveness of statistical analysis, we interpret the results gathered with these evaluations from a qualitative perspective.

4 Results

4.1 Adequacy

Results for adequacy in Table 3 show that, in general, the RSs scenario has higher IAA than the document-level scenarios (SCs and Ds) for both test sets. Interestingly, if we look at IAA within each group, we note that group 2 has higher κ and α in the SCs scenario, even though the IRR is lower. The Ds scenario has the lowest IAA scores (apart from weighted κ for group 1). The aggregated scores in Table 4 show that Rs and SCs have the same Fleiss κ, while Ds shows negative scores. Interestingly, higher α is shown for the Ds scenario, followed by the Sc scenario. Nonetheless, we observe from the IAA scores that RS and SC methodologies seem to yield similar IAA scores, higher than the Ds scenario.

4.2 Fluency

Results for the fluency assessment in Table 5 show that for Test set 1, the RSs scenario has higher IAA than both-document level scenarios, SCs and Ds. However, the SCs scenario shows slight higher IAA for Test Set 2. Within each group, we observe that group 2 has higher weighted κ and α in the SCs than in the RSs scenario, even though IRR is lower for the SCs scenario. The Ds scenario, in general, show lower IAA scores than RSs and SCs methodologies. The aggregated scores in Table 6 also confirms that the Ds scenario yields a lower IAA, and the RSs scenario shows slight higher IAA than SCs.

Fluency	RSs	SCs	Ds
Test set 1	**Group1**	**Group2**	**Group2**
Weighted κ (av)	0.40	0.41	0.00
Fleiss κ	0.28	0.16	-0.03
Krippendorff α	0.46	0.27	0.07
IRR	69%	49%	47%
Test set 2	**Group2**	**Group1**	**Group1**
Weighted κ (av)	0.31	0.31	0.31
Fleiss κ	0.16	0.19	-0.20
Krippendorff α	0.26	0.29	-0.19
IRR	56%	61%	27%

Table 5: IAA for adequacy assessments for RSs, SCs, and Ds scenarios.

Fluency	RSs	SCs	Ds
Fleiss κ	0.09	0.05	-0.05
Krippendorff α	0.14	0.10	-0.06

Table 6: Aggregated IAA scores for fluency assessments.

4.3 Error

Error mark-up results were divided into *binary*, when raters agree there was an error (any type) or no errors in the sentence/document, and *type*, when raters agree on the exact error type found in the sentence/document. Note that for the error mark-up task we decided not to ask translators to tag errors per document (Ds), for two main reasons: i) as it was proven to be hard for translators in our previous work (Castilho, 2020) and ii) as Ds scenario was evaluated immediately after RSs scenario, translators could just copy and paste the errors they have found in RSs into Ds.

Results in Table 7 show that IAA is higher for all assessments in the RSs scenario. However, we note that IAA scores for SCs, especially in Group 2, are closer to the ones in the RSs scenario. Moreover, the aggregated results in Table 8 show IAA for the SCs is similar to the RSs for the binary category, suggesting that a document-level methodology where translators can tag errors for each sentence with access to the full document can lead to

Error		RSs	SCs
Test Set 1		Group1	Group2
Cohen κ	binary	0.29	0.27
	type	0.28	0.25
Fleiss κ	binary	0.28	0.22
	type	0.27	0.24
α	binary	0.28	0.22
	type	0.27	0.24
IRR	binary	68%	63%
	type	65%	55%
Test Set 2		Group 2	Group 1
Cohen κ	binary	0.22	0.21
	type	0.25	0.21
Fleiss κ	binary	0.27	0.15
	type	0.25	0.16
α	binary	0.26	0.15
	type	0.24	0.16
IRR	binary	62%	60%
	type	58%	55%

Table 7: IAA for error mark-up assessments for RSs and SCs scenarios.

Error		RSs	SCs
Fleiss κ	binary	0.09	0.08
	type	0.10	0.86
α	binary	0.09	0.09
	type	0.10	0.08

Table 8: Aggregated IAA scores for error mark-up assessments.

better IAA.

4.4 Ranking

Results in Table 9 show that the RS scenario presents higher IAA compared to both document-level scenarios, while in test Set 2, it is the SC scenario which shows higher IAA. Interestingly, when looking within each group, we can see that the IAA scores are very close in the RSs and SCs scenarios. Moreover, the IAA scores when full texts were ranked (Ds) are largely lower compared to IAA scores where translators rank individual sentences with access to full texts (SCs). The aggregated scores in Table 10 confirm the low IAA when the Ds scenario is used, and close IAA for RSs and SCs.

4.5 Effort

The effort spent on assessment was calculated via a post-task questionnaire. Translators answered the questions (see full statements in Section 3) after they finished all tasks in all scenarios. Table 11 shows the average results for each statement for RS and SC scenarios.

We observe positive answers for the SC scenario for all statements which indicates that translators found it easier to understand both source (statement

Ranking	RSs	SCs	Ds
Test Set 1	Group 1	Group 2	Group 2
Cohen κ	0.41	0.37	-0.03
Fleiss κ	0.40	0.36	-0.12
Krippendorff α	0.45	0.39	-0.13
IRR	61%	58%	35%
Test Set 2	Group 2	Group 1	Group 1
Cohen κ	0.38	0.43	0.14
Fleiss κ	0.38	0.42	0.09
Krippendorff α	0.43	0.47	0.19
IRR	60%	62%	44%

Table 9: IAA for pair-wise ranking evaluation assessments for RSs, SCs, Ds scenarios.

Ranking	RSs	SCs	Ds
Test Set 1	Group 1	Group 2	Group 2
Fleiss κ	0.18	0.17	0.02
Krippendorff α	0.23	0.19	0.02

Table 10: Aggregated IAA for pair-wise ranking evaluation assessments.

1) and translation (2) when assessing sentences in context. Translators found it easier to recognise adequacy (3) and fluency (4) problems, as well as spotting errors (5) and choosing the best translation (6) when having access to full texts. Moreover, they found it easier to assess the quality in general (7) and less tiring (8) when having full texts, being more confident with their assessment (9). Overwhelmingly, translators think they give more accurate assessments when having access to full texts (10).

We also asked translators about the effort of giving one single score to the full texts (Ds). Table 12 shows the result for the statement "*Giving a general (adequacy / fluency / ranking) score for the full text was (1 very difficult - 6 very easy)*", while Table 13 show the result for the statement "*In order to give a general (adequacy / fluency / ranking) score for each text, I had to re-read the full text*".

We note that adequacy was the hardest assessment to be performed when translators are asked to give one score per document. One translator mentioned that both texts "*had lots of mistakes so I had to score based on quantity and quality of the mistakes, it took some calculations*. Another translator mentioned that "*Occasionally, a text would have some great individual sentences translation, but then would have missed some key words with mistranslations. So it was hard to think which factor should play a bigger role into the score*".

Regarding the question about re-reading the texts in order to assign one score for a full document, we see in Table 13 that for adequacy and fluency, while

Statements	RSs	SCs
1- Understand SOURCE	4.37	5.75
2- Understand TARGET	3.87	5.12
3- Recognise ADEQUACY	4.12	5.25
4- Recognise FLUENCY	4.62	4.87
5- Spot ERRORs	4.5	5.12
6- Choose BEST translation	4.12	4.87
7- Difficulty in assessing	4	5
8- Tiredness	3.75	4.62
9- Confidence	4.12	4.62
10- Preference	5.12	1.37

Table 11: Post-questionnaire results (average) for RSs and SCs scenarios. Scale range from 1 to 6, where 1 is very difficult/very tiring/strongly disagree and 6 is very easy/not tiring at all/strongly agree.

Statement	Adequacy	Fluency	Ranking
Difficulty level	4	4.37	4.5

Table 12: Average scores for assessing sentences in the Ds scenario, where 1 is "very difficult" and 6 is "very easy".

two translators re-read both source and target, 3 re-read the target only and 3 did not re-read the texts. For the ranking task, the majority of translators did not need to re-read any of the texts.

5 Towards a better human evaluation methodology for document-level

The recent interest in document-level MT evaluation has raised a few questions in the area. For example, it is still not clear how much context needs to be shown in a document-level evaluation set-up. This is important as we need to understand whether there is a pattern regarding how much context is required (in cases when full texts cannot be fully displayed or when they are not available) in order to have a reliable quality assessment and to avoid misevaluation issues. Some studies have used consecutive sentences (showing one at time) (Toral et al., 2018), and a few have used full short texts(Läubli et al., 2018; Barrault et al., 2019).

Castilho et al. (2020) have shown that for a great number of sentences, their successful translation and their MT evaluation requires more than sentence pairs and sometimes even full texts. Corroborating these findings, we also observe the need for a wider context in order to solve ambiguities in the evaluation. Figure 1 shows examples of context span needed when evaluating translations from EN→PT-BR.[9]

To evaluate sentence 105, the translators need

[9]The full speech can be found in the appendix I

Re-read (Y/N)	Adequacy	Fluency	Ranking
Source and target	2	2	2
Target only	3	3	1
Best target only	-	-	0
Worst target only	-	-	0
No	3	3	5

Table 13: Responses for the statement: *In order to give a general score for each text, I had to re-read the full text* displayed in the Ds scenario. Note that Best and Worst target only was only shown for the ranking assessment.

to identify the gender of the speaker in order to know whether "thank you" will be translated into the feminine (*obrigad**a***) or masculine (*obrigad**o***). For sentences 103 and 104, the translators need to know whether the pronoun "you" refers to singular or plural (*você/vocês*). Moreover, in sentence 104, because of the verb "love", some syntax constructions would need to have the gender of the pronoun "you" determined (***as** amamos -f, **os** amamos- m*).[10]

The issue of gender in 104 might be solved with sentence 102 with the use of the term "young women", as they are the ones who need "to stand up and take the reins", and the speaker knows that "you can do it" ("to stand up and take the reins"). This might imply that the "you" is also female and unlikely to be male, i.e.:

And we need strong, smart, confident young women to stand up and take the reins.
We know you can do it, Paul. ×
We know you can do it, Mary. ✓

Before sentence 102, it is only in sentence 52 that "you" is clearly identified as "women". Regarding number (singular/plural), however, it is still not possible to affirm whether "you" in sentence 104 and 103 refers to singular or plural, with the context of sentence 102, because the one being talked to could still be singular, i.e.:

And we need strong, smart, confident young women to stand up and take the reins.
We know you can do it, girls. ✓
We know you can do it, Mary. ✓

It is only with Sentence 99 that the number of "you" is solved with the term "every single one of you", which indicates that the speaker is talking to more than one person. Before that, it is only with sentences 52 and 54 that "you" is again identified as plural.

Regarding the gender issue in sentence 105, one can claim that sentence 95 "My husband works in

[10]It is also possible to translate the sentence "we love you" with the gender-neutral pronoun "vos" (nós vos amamos). However, as this is an old Portuguese construction, it is not considered by any of the translators.

1	Speaking at a London **girls' school**, **Michelle Obama** makes a passionate, personal case for each student to take education seriously.
2-25	...
26	I am an example of what's possible when girls from the very beginning of their lives are loved and nurtured by the people around them.
27-35	...
36	And these were the same qualities that I looked for in my own husband, Barack Obama.
37-51	...
52	You are the women who will build the world as it should be.
54	Not just for yourselves, but for your generation and generations to come.
55-90	...
91	My husband works in this big office.
92-97	...
98	Because we are counting on you.
99	We are counting on every single one of you to be the very best that you can be.
100	Because the world is big.
101	And it's full of challenges.
102	And we need strong, smart, confident young women to stand up and take the reins.
103	We know you can do it.
104	We love you (you).
105	Thank you so much.

Figure 1: Examples of context span needed to solve gender and number issues in sentence 104 and 105. The parts in pink relate to the gender of the speaker, red parts relate to the number of "you" (singular/plural), orange parts relate to the gender of "you", and the green parts relate to the resolution of "it".

this big office" would indicate that the speaker is feminine, however, men can also have husbands. Even if the following sentence identifies that the "big office" is the "Oval office", it does not clearly identify that the husband that works there is the actual president. It is only with sentence 36 that we see that the speaker is Michele Obama as she names the husband as "Barack Obama", however, that requires world knowledge. Sentence 26 is the closest one to 105 that clearly identifies the speaker as a "girl".

These problems with context span show that it is still uncertain how much context translators need to see in order to identify the issues in the translation and assess translation quality accordingly. We have previously shown (Castilho, 2020) that there is a risk of misevaluation when random single sentences are used in evaluation because of the lack of context. We also observe misevaluation issues in the present study, where disagreements in the RS scenario are more often related to ambiguity and lack of context. Figure 2 shows two examples of misevaluation for sentences 104 and 105 when assessments were performed in the RS scenario.

(104) Source: We love you.
MT: Nós te amamos. (no gender/singular)
HT1: Nós **as** amamos. (feminine/plural)
HT2: Nós amamos **vocês**. (no gender/plural)

When comparing the scores assigned to sentence 104 ("We love you") in the RSs and SCs scenarios, we note that in the RS evaluation, as expected, all translators assessed the MT output as having all the meaning of the source, to be native, and free of errors. None of the translators commented on the fact that there are four possible translation for the pronoun "you" in the source (singular/masculine, singular/feminine, plural/masculine, plural/feminine) and only a wider context would determine gender and number in the sentence. Translators who assessed sentence 104 in the SC scenario were able to find that the MT was not able to keep the gender agreement in the translation,[11] even when they erroneously did not consider the whole context in order to assess the sentence, as it is the case of T5. It is interesting that the scores for adequacy in the SC are quite divergent, while the scores for fluency are more homogeneous. This corroborates findings from our previous work Castilho (2020) where we note that disagreements at the document-level are more related to adequacy errors. Misevaluation was also observed in sentence 105:

(105) Source: Thank you so much.
MT: Muito obrigad**o**. (masculine)
HT: Muito obrigad**a**. (feminine)

Similar to the previous sentence, translators assessed the MT output of sentence 105 in the RS scenario as having all the meaning of the source, to be native, and free of errors. However, this time one translator (T4) commented on the fact that only a wider context would determine the gender in the sentence. Translators who assessed sentence 105 in the SC scenario were able to find errors in the MT output. Again, we note that T5 erroneously does

[11] Note that T2 considered (erroneously) the mistranslation to be a word form error

Sentence 104 S= We love you MT= Nós te amamos	Translator	Adequacy	Fluency	Errors	Comments
Random Sentence (RS)	T3	4. All of it	4. Native	No errors	
	T4	4. All of it	4. Native	No errors	
	T7	4. All of it	4. Native	No errors	
	T8	4. All of it	4. Native	No errors	
Sentence-in-Context (SC)	T1	3. Most of	4. Native	Mistranslation	amamos vocês
	T2	2. Little of	2. Little	Word Form	
	T5	4. All of it	4. Native	No errors	should be plural from context, but nothing in the sentence by itself leads us to that
	T6	3. Most of	4. Native	Mistranslation	

Sentence 105 S= Thank you so much. MT= Muito obrigado.	Trans.	Adequacy	Fluency	Errors	Comments
Random Sentence (RS)	T3	4. All of it	4. Native	No errors	
	T4	4. All of it	4. Native	No errors	without the context we cannot be sure about the gender (obrigado/obrigada)
	T7	4. All of it	4. Native	No errors	
	T8	4. All of it	4. Native	No errors	
Sentence-in-Context (SC)	T1	3. Most of	4. Native	Mistranslation	obrigada
	T2	3. Most of	2. Little	Word Form	
	T5	4. All of it	4. Native	No errors	should be feminine from context, but nothing in the sentence by itself leads us to that.
	T6	4. All of it	4. Native	Mistranslation	

Figure 2: Examples of misevaluation and (dis)agreement among translators in the RSs and SCs scenarios.

not consider the whole context in order to assess the sentence. Similar to sentence 104, the scores for adequacy in the document-level scenario are divergent, while the scores for fluency are more homogeneous.

We speculate that the reason methodologies with random single sentences show higher IAA agreement is because raters tend to accept the translation when adequacy is ambiguous but the translation is correct, especially if it is fluent. Thus, sentences like 104 and 105 are judged as correct in a scenario where there is no context to tell the evaluator *why* the translation should be different. Therefore, higher IAA scores in RS methodologies do not necessarily mean translators agreed more because the MT output was in fact better. Moreover, since NMT systems are known to have improved fluency, these types of misevaluation as shown previously are more likely to happen in a RSs set-up.

Our results have shown that a methodology where translators are able to assess individual sentences within the context of a document (SC scenario) yields good level of IAA compared to RS scenario, while a methodology where translators give one score per document (Ds) shows very low level of IAA. Moreover, the SCs methodology avoids the misevaluation cases which proved to be quite common in the RS evaluation set-ups.

6 Conclusions and Future Work

The present work attempts to shed light on the differences in IAA when evaluating MT with different methodologies, namely random single sentences, sentences in context, and full document scores.

The main finding of this comparison is that, an evaluation methodology where translators judge single random sentences might yield a better annotator agreement at times but with a high cost of misevaluation cases. Moreover, a methodology where translators assign one score per text leads to lower IAA and a great level of effort. This corroborates the results seen in Castilho (2020) where IAA scores for document-level reaches negative levels, and the level of satisfaction of translators with that methodology is also very low. In turn, evaluating the quality of MT output with individual sentences showed in the context of a document yields not only good IAA scores but avoids the issue of misevaluation which is extremely common in random single sentence evaluation set-up. We believe that a translator will be more inclined to accept as correct an ambiguous but fluent translation. This is problematic for an accurate evaluation of MT quality since it might lead to misevaluation especially when assessing the quality of NMT systems which are known to have an improved fluency level. Therefore, we suggest that evaluation set-ups using random single sentences should be avoided.

For future work, we will investigate the differences in context span needed for different domains, as well as whether the state-of-the-art metrics for human evaluation of MT (fluency, adequacy, error, ranking) must be modified in order to capture more realistically the quality level of the systems.

Acknowledgements

This project was funded by the Irish Research Council (GOIPD/2020/69) and partially by the

European Association for Machine Translation through its 2019 sponsorship of activities programme. The ADAPT Centre for Digital Content Technology (`www.adaptcentre.ie`) at Dublin City University is funded by the Science Foundation Ireland Research Centres Programme (Grant 13/RC/2106) and is co-funded by the European Regional Development Fund.

References

Ron Artstein and Massimo Poesio. 2008. Inter-coder agreement for computational linguistics. *Comput. Linguist.*, 34(4):555–596.

Dzmitry Bahdanau, Kyunghyun Cho, and Yoshua Bengio. 2015. Neural Machine Translation by Jointly Learning to Align and Translate. In *Proceedings of ICLR*, San Diego, CA.

Loïc Barrault, Magdalena Biesialska, Ondřej Bojar, Marta R. Costa-jussà, Christian Federmann, Yvette Graham, Roman Grundkiewicz, Barry Haddow, Matthias Huck, Eric Joanis, Tom Kocmi, Philipp Koehn, Chi-kiu Lo, Nikola Ljubešić, Christof Monz, Makoto Morishita, Masaaki Nagata, Toshiaki Nakazawa, Santanu Pal, Matt Post, and Marcos Zampieri. 2020. Findings of the 2020 conference on machine translation (WMT20). In *Proceedings of the Fifth Conference on Machine Translation*, pages 1–55, Online. Association for Computational Linguistics.

Loïc Barrault, Ondřej Bojar, Marta R. Costa-jussà, Christian Federmann, Mark Fishel, Yvette Graham, Barry Haddow, Matthias Huck, Philipp Koehn, Shervin Malmasi, Christof Monz, Mathias Müller, Santanu Pal, Matt Post, and Marcos Zampieri. 2019. Findings of the 2019 Conference on Machine Translation (WMT19). In *Proceedings of the Fourth Conference on Machine Translation (WMT 19)*, pages 1–61, Florence, Italy.

Sheila Castilho. 2020. On the same page? comparing inter-annotator agreement in sentence and document level human machine translation evaluation. In *Proceedings of the Fifth Conference on Machine Translation*, pages 1150–1159, Online. Association for Computational Linguistics.

Sheila Castilho, Stephen Doherty, Federico Gaspari, and Joss Moorkens. 2018. Approaches to Human and Machine Translation Quality Assessment. In *Translation Quality Assessment: From Principles to Practice*, volume 1 of *Machine Translation: Technologies and Applications*, pages 9–38. Springer International Publishing.

Sheila Castilho, Maja Popović, and Andy Way. 2020. On Context Span Needed for Machine Translation Evaluation. In *Proceedings of the Twelfth International Conference on Language Resources and Evaluation (LREC'20)*, Marseille, France.

Jacob Cohen. 1960. A Coefficient of Agreement for Nominal Scales. *Educational and Psychological Measurement*, 20(1):37–46.

JL Fleiss. 1971. Measuring nominal scale agreement among many raters. *Psychological bulletin*, 76(5):378—382.

Klaus Krippendorff. 2011. Computing krippendorff's alpha-reliability.

Samuel Läubli, Rico Sennrich, and Martin Volk. 2018. Has Machine Translation Achieved Human Parity? A Case for Document-level Evaluation. In *Proceedings of EMNLP*, pages 4791–4796, Brussels, Belgium.

Aya A. Mitani, Phoebe E. Freer, and Kerrie P. Nelson. 2017. Summary measures of agreement and association between many raters' ordinal classifications. *Annals of epidemiology*, 27:677–685.e4.

Carolina Scarton, Marcos Zampieri, Mihaela Vela, Josef van Genabith, and Lucia Specia. 2015. Searching for context: a study on document-level labels for translation quality estimation. In *Proceedings of the 18th Annual Conference of the European Association for Machine Translation*, pages 121–128, Antalya, Turkey.

Ilya Sutskever, Oriol Vinyals, and Quoc V. Le. 2014. Sequence to Sequence Learning with Neural Networks. In *Proceedings of NIPS*, pages 3104–3112, Montreal, Canada.

Jörg Tiedemann. 2012. Parallel data, tools and interfaces in OPUS. In *Proceedings of the Eighth International Conference on Language Resources and Evaluation (LREC-2012)*, pages 2214–2218, Istanbul, Turkey. European Languages Resources Association (ELRA).

Antonio Toral, Sheila Castilho, Ke Hu, and Andy Way. 2018. Attaining the Unattainable? Reassessing Claims of Human Parity in Neural Machine Translation. In *Proceedings of WMT*, pages 113–123, Brussels, Belgium.

Ashish Vaswani, Noam Shazeer, Niki Parmar, Jakob Uszkoreit, Llion Jones, Aidan N Gomez, Lukasz Kaiser, and Illia Polosukhin. 2017. Attention is all you need. In *Proceedings of the 31st Conference on Neural Information Processing Systems (NeurIPS 2017)*, pages 5998–6008, Long Beach, CA.

A Appendices

Michelle Obama Ted Talk (Opus Corpus – Tiedemann, 2012)

1	Speaking at a London girls' school, Michelle Obama makes a passionate, personal case for each student to take education seriously.
2	It is this new, brilliant generation, she says, that will close the gap between the world as it is and the world as it should be.
3	culture,education,global issues,leadership,politics
4	Michelle Obama's plea for education
5	This is my first trip, my first foreign trip as a first lady.
6	Can you believe that?
7	And while this is not my first visit to the U.K., I have to say that I am glad that this is my first official visit.
8	The special relationship between the United States and the U.K. is based not only on the relationship between governments, but the common language and the values that we share, and I'm reminded of that by watching you all today.
9	During my visit I've been especially honored to meet some of Britain's most extraordinary women – women who are paving the way for all of you.
10	And I'm honored to meet you, the future leaders of Great Britain and this world.
11	And although the circumstances of our lives may seem very distant, with me standing here as the First Lady of the United States of America, and you, just getting through school, I want you to know that we have very much in common.
12	For nothing in my life's path would have predicted that I'd be standing here as the first African-American First Lady of the United States of America.
13	There is nothing in my story that would land me here.
14	I wasn't raised with wealth or resources or any social standing to speak of.
15	I was raised on the South Side of Chicago.
16	That's the real part of Chicago.
17	And I was the product of a working-class community.
18	My father was a city worker all of his life, and my mother was a stay-at-home mom.
19	And she stayed at home to take care of me and my older brother.
20	Neither of them attended university.
21	My dad was diagnosed with multiple sclerosis in the prime of his life.
22	But even as it got harder for him to walk and get dressed in the morning – I saw him struggle more and more – my father never complained about his struggle.
23	He was grateful for what he had.
24	He just woke up a little earlier and worked a little harder.
25	And my brother and I were raised with all that you really need: love, strong values and a belief that with a good education and a whole lot of hard work, that there was nothing that we could not do.
26	I am an example of what's possible when girls from the very beginning of their lives are loved and nurtured by the people around them.
27	I was surrounded by extraordinary women in my life: grandmothers, teachers, aunts, cousins, neighbors, who taught me about quiet strength and dignity.
28	And my mother, the most important role model in my life, who lives with us at the White House and helps to care for our two little daughters, Malia and Sasha.
29	She's an active presence in their lives, as well as mine, and is instilling in them the same values that she taught me and my brother: things like compassion, and integrity, and confidence, and perseverance – all of that wrapped up in an unconditional love that only a grandmother can give.
30	I was also fortunate enough to be cherished and encouraged by some strong male role models as well, including my father, my brother, uncles and grandfathers.
31	The men in my life taught me some important things, as well.
32	They taught me about what a respectful relationship should look like between men and women.
33	They taught me about what a strong marriage feels like: that it's built on faith and commitment and an admiration for each other's unique gifts.
34	They taught me about what it means to be a father and to raise a family.
35	And not only to invest in your own home but to reach out and help raise kids in the broader community.
36	And these were the same qualities that I looked for in my own husband, Barack Obama.
37	And when we first met, one of the things that I remember is that he took me out on a date.
38	And his date was to go with him to a community meeting.
39	I know, how romantic.
40	But when we met, Barack was a community organizer.
41	He worked, helping people to find jobs and to try to bring resources into struggling neighborhoods.
42	As he talked to the residents in that community center, he talked about two concepts.
43	He talked about the world as it is and the world as it should be.
44	And I talked about this throughout the entire campaign.
45	What he said, that all too often, is that we accept the distance between those two ideas.
46	And sometimes we settle for the world as it is, even when it doesn't reflect our values and aspirations.
47	But Barack reminded us on that day, all of us in that room, that we all know what our world should look like.
48	We know what fairness and justice and opportunity look like.
49	We all know.

Table A: Full speech by Michelle Obama's - see Figure 1

50 And he urged the people in that meeting, in that community, to devote themselves to closing the gap between those two ideas, to work together to try to make the world as it is and the world as it should be, one and the same.

51 And I think about that today because I am reminded and convinced that all of you in this school are very important parts of closing that gap.

52 You are the women who will build the world as it should be.

53 You're going to write the next chapter in history.

54 Not just for yourselves, but for your generation and generations to come.

55 And that's why getting a good education is so important.

56 That's why all of this that you're going through – the ups and the downs, the teachers that you love and the teachers that you don't – why it's so important.

57 Because communities and countries and ultimately the world are only as strong as the health of their women.

58 And that's important to keep in mind.

59 Part of that health includes an outstanding education.

60 The difference between a struggling family and a healthy one is often the presence of an empowered woman or women at the center of that family.

61 The difference between a broken community and a thriving one is often the healthy respect between men and women who appreciate the contributions each other makes to society.

62 The difference between a languishing nation and one that will flourish is the recognition that we need equal access to education for both boys and girls.

63 And this school, named after the U.K.'s first female doctor, and the surrounding buildings named for Mexican artist Frida Kahlo, Mary Seacole, the Jamaican nurse known as the black Florence Nightingale, and the English author, Emily Bronte, honor women who fought sexism, racism and ignorance, to pursue their passions to feed their own souls.

64 They allowed for no obstacles.

65 As the sign said back there, without limitations.

66 They knew no other way to live than to follow their dreams.

67 And having done so, these women moved many obstacles.

68 And they opened many new doors for millions of female doctors and nurses and artists and authors, all of whom have followed them.

69 And by getting a good education, you too can control your own destiny.

70 Please remember that.

71 If you want to know the reason why I'm standing here, it's because of education.

72 I never cut class.

73 Sorry, I don't know if anybody is cutting class.

74 I never did it.

75 I loved getting As.

76 I liked being smart.

77 I liked being on time.

78 I liked getting my work done.

79 I thought being smart was cooler than anything in the world.

80 And you too, with these same values, can control your own destiny.

81 You too can pave the way.

82 You too can realize your dreams, and then your job is to reach back and to help someone just like you do the same thing.

83 History proves that it doesn't matter whether you come from a council estate or a country estate.

84 Your success will be determined by your own fortitude, your own confidence, your own individual hard work.

85 That is true.

86 That is the reality of the world that we live in.

87 You now have control over your own destiny.

88 And it won't be easy – that's for sure.

89 But you have everything you need.

90 Everything you need to succeed, you already have, right here.

91 My husband works in this big office.

92 They call it the Oval Office.

93 In the White House, there's the desk that he sits at – it's called the Resolute desk.

94 It was built by the timber of Her Majesty's Ship Resolute and given by Queen Victoria.

95 It's an enduring symbol of the friendship between our two nations.

96 And its name, Resolute, is a reminder of the strength of character that's required not only to lead a country, but to live a life of purpose, as well.

97 And I hope in pursuing your dreams, you all remain resolute, that you go forward without limits, and that you use your talents – because there are many; we've seen them; it's there that you use them to create the world as it should be.

98 Because we are counting on you.

99 We are counting on every single one of you to be the very best that you can be.

100 Because the world is big.

101 And it's full of challenges.

102 And we need strong, smart, confident young women to stand up and take the reins.

103 We know you can do it.

104 We love you.

105 Thank you so much.

Table A: Cont. - Full speech by Michelle Obama's - see Figure 1

Is this translation error critical?: Classification-based Human and Automatic Machine Translation Evaluation Focusing on Critical Errors

Katsuhito Sudoh*, **Kosuke Takahashi, Satoshi Nakamura**
Nara Institute of Science and Technology (NAIST)
8916-5 Takayamacho, Ikoma, Nara 630-0192, Japan
*PRESTO, Japan Science and Technology Agency (JST)
{sudoh,kosuke.takahashi.th0,s-nakamura}@is.naist.jp

Abstract

This paper discusses a classification-based approach to machine translation evaluation, as opposed to a common regression-based approach in the WMT Metrics task. Recent machine translation usually works well but sometimes makes critical errors due to just a few wrong word choices. Our classification-based approach focuses on such errors using several error type labels, for practical machine translation evaluation in an age of neural machine translation. We have made additional annotations on the WMT 2015-2017 Metrics datasets with fluency and adequacy labels to distinguish different types of translation errors from syntactic and semantic viewpoints. We present our human evaluation criteria for the corpus development and automatic evaluation experiments using the corpus. The human evaluation corpus will be publicly available at https://github.com/ksudoh/wmt15-17-humaneval.

1 Introduction

Most machine translation (MT) studies still evaluate their results using BLEU (Papineni et al., 2002) because of its simple, language-agnostic, and model-free methodology. Recent remarkable advances in neural MT (NMT) have cast an important challenge in its evaluation; NMT usually generates a fluent translation that cannot always be evaluated precisely by simple surface-based evaluation metrics like BLEU.

A recent trend in the MT evaluation is to use a large-scale pre-trained model like BERT (Devlin et al., 2019). Shimanaka et al. (2019) proposed BERT Regressor based on sentence-level regression using a fine-tuned BERT model, as an extension of their prior study using sentence embeddings (Shimanaka et al., 2018). Zhang et al. (2020) proposed BERTScore based on hard token-level alignment using cosine similarity of contextualized token embeddings. Zhao et al. (2019) proposed MoverScore based on soft token-level alignment using Word Mover's Distance (Kusner et al., 2015). Sellam et al. (2020) proposed BLEURT that incorporates auxiliary task signals into the pre-training of a BERT-based sentence-level regression model. These methods aim to evaluate a translation hypothesis using the corresponding reference with a high correlation to human judgment.

The evaluation of this kind of MT evaluation, often called *meta-evaluation*, is usually based on some benchmarks. The meta-evaluation in the recent studies uses the WMT Metrics task dataset consisting of human judgment on MT results. The human judgment is given in the form of Human Direct Assessment (DA) (Graham et al., 2016), a 100-point rating scale. The Human DA results are standardized into *z-scores* (human DA scores, hereinafter) and used as the evaluation and optimization objective of regression-based MT evaluation methods. Recent MT evaluation methods achieved more than 0.8 in Pearson correlation on WMT 2017 test set[1]. However, Takahashi et al. (2020) reported a weaker correlation in low human DA score ranges. Such a finding suggests the difficulty of the MT evaluation on low-quality results.

In this work, we focus on the problem in the evaluation of low-quality translations that cause serious misunderstanding. Judging erroneous translations in the 100-point rating scale would be very difficult and unstable, because the extent of errors cannot be mapped easily into a one-dimensional space. Suppose we are evaluating a translation hypothesis, (1) *It is our duty to remain at his sides* with its reference, *It is not our duty to remain at his sides*.[2] The

[1]The correlation got worse in the newer WMT datasets (Ma et al., 2018, 2019) due to noise in human judgement (Sellam et al., 2020).

[2]This example is taken from the Metrics dataset of WMT

Proceedings of the Workshop on Human Evaluation of NLP Systems (HumEval), pages 46–55
Online, April 19, 2021.

difference in this example is just in one missing word *not* in the hypothesis, but it may cause a serious misunderstanding. Such translation errors are considered as critical ones by professional translators. There are several metrics for translation quality assessment (QA) proposed in the translators' community, such as LISA QA Metric[3] and Multidimentional Quality Metrics (MQM)[4]. These metrics use a couple of error seriousness categories (Minor, Major, Critical) in several viewpoints, such as mistranslation, accuracy, and terminology. The missing negation is a kind of critical error. Nevertheless, most existing automatic MT evaluation metrics fail to penalize such errors. Human DA is also difficult from this viewpoint. Suppose we have other translation hypotheses, (2) *He bought some bags at a duty-free store.* and (3) *Not is to duty remain it sides his at.* for the same reference. We can easily identify these hypotheses are wrong. However, evaluating them together with (1) in the same 100-point rating scale by mapping these differences into one dimension is not trivial.

This work pursues a classification-based human and automatic MT evaluation based on the multidimensional evaluation. Current NMT technologies would still be far from the level of professional human translators but are also utilized in various applications. MT in practical applications should be evaluated as same as human translations by practical metrics, not just by incremental and engineering-oriented metrics like BLEU.

We propose a classification-based MT evaluation framework motivated by the discussion about critical errors. In human evaluation, we use conventional evaluation dimensions of fluency and adequacy (LDC, 2005) and define several categories different from a conventional 1-5 Likert scale. We developed a corpus with such additional annotations on WMT Metrics dataset and found that human DA scores penalize incomprehensible and unrelated MT hypotheses more than those with other critical errors that cause serious misunderstanding and contradiction. We then implemented a classification-based automatic MT evaluation using the corpus and conducted experiments on the WMT Metrics test set.

2015.

[3]http://producthelp.sdl.com/SDL_TMS_2011/en/Creating_and_Maintaining_Organizations/Managing_QA_Models/LISA_QA_Model.htm

[4]https://www.dfki.de/en/web/research/projects-and-publications/publications-overview/publication/7717/

2 Related Work

MT evaluation has evolved along with the advance of MT technologies. White et al. (1994) reviewed some attempts of human evaluation and presented adequacy, fluency, and comprehension results in the early 1990s. The Quality Panel approach presented in their paper was motivated by the evaluation of human translations, but it was finally abandoned due to human evaluation difficulties. Callison-Burch et al. (2007) presented meta-evaluation of the MT evaluation in WMT shared tasks. According to the findings there, the WMT shared tasks had employed ranking-based human evaluation for a while. Snover et al. (2006) defined Human-targeted Translation Edit Rate (HTER) that measures the translation quality by the required number of post-edits on a translation hypothesis. Denkowski and Lavie (2010) and Graham et al. (2012) discussed the differences among those human evaluation approaches. Graham et al. (2016) proposed human DA for the MT evaluation, and DA has been used as standard human evaluation in recent WMT Metrics tasks.

There is another line of human MT evaluation studies focusing on semantics. Lo and Wu (2011) proposed MEANT and its human evaluation variant HMEANT based on semantic frames. Birch et al. (2016) proposed HUME based on a semantic representation called UCCA. This kind of fine-grained semantic evaluation requires some linguistic knowledge for annotators but enables explainable evaluation instead. However, the meaning of the sentence can be changed by small changes, as discussed later in section 3. Looking at sub-structures and using their coverage in the MT evaluation may suffer from this problem.

One recent approach has been proposed by Popovič (Popovic, 2020; Popović, 2020). Her work analyzed the differences between comprehensibility and adequacy in machine translation outputs. The human annotations in her work are major and minor errors in comprehensibility and adequacy on words and phrases. These fine-grained annotations are helpful for detailed translation error detection. The focus of our work is different; we are going to develop sentence-level MT evaluation through simpler human and automatic evaluation schemes.

In this work, we suggest revisiting the classification-based evaluation with fluency and adequacy, for *absolute* human and automatic evaluation. DA-based human evaluation is beneficial in demonstrating the correlation with automatic evaluation metrics. However, it is not very intuitive in the evaluation of different kinds of translation errors.

Our work is also related to some studies using semantic equivalence and contradiction. BLEURT (Sellam et al., 2020) employed NLI in its pretraining phase. NLI includes contradiction identification, which should also contribute to the MT evaluation. BLEURT has revealed its advantage in the example shown in Table 1. Kryściński et al. (2019) proposed a weakly-supervised method for training an abstractive summarization model using adversarial summaries to improve the factual consistency between a source document and a summary. They also focused on an NLI-like semantic classification for their adversarial training. Classification-based automatic MT evaluation models can be trained similarly, using related and adversarial data.

3 Critical Translation Errors

The main focus of this work is to penalize critical errors in translation hypotheses that cause serious misunderstanding. This kind of translation errors must be avoided, as well as possible.

Suppose we have some translation hypotheses with their reference, *The Pleiades cluster is situated 445 light-years from Earth*[5]. The translation hypotheses are artificial ones with some adversarial edits over the reference, as shown in the second column of Table 1. The hypothesis hyp1 is a paraphrase, hyp2 and hyp3 have errors on "light-years", hyp4 has a wrong negation, hyp5 to hyp7 have errors on named entities, hyp8 is a shuffled word sentence, and hyp9 would come from a completely different sentence; the hypotheses have non-trivial problems except hyp1.

We put automatic evaluation scores in the table using BLEU-4[6], chrF[7], BERTScore[8], and BLEURT[9]. hyp9 is correctly penalized by all the metrics, but the other results are mixed. BLEU-4 penalizes hyp1 and hyp3 more than the others. chrF and BERTScore penalize hyp3. BLEURT penalizes hyp4 and gives lower scores on hyp2 and hyp5-7 than BERTScore. BLEU-4, BERTScore, and BLEURT penalize hyp8, while chrF gives the same score on it as hyp3. Here, we would regard hyp4, hyp8, and hyp9 as bad translations. However, we cannot identify the other erroneous translation just using the automatic scores. These observations suggest that current evaluation metrics do not always capture these critical translation errors by one or two wrong word choices. Recent NMT sometimes generates translations competitive with human translators, so they should be evaluated as same as human translations in practice.

On the other hand, MT sometimes generates incomprehensible sentences with various kind of errors, even though NMT works much better than conventional statistical MT, especially in fluency. Such incomprehensible translations are also very problematic as well as content errors in easy-to-understand and fluent translations.

However, it is not easy to penalize both of them in a single evaluation criterion. Existing automatic evaluation methods often fail to penalize content errors, although they work well for incomprehensible and unrelated sentences, as revealed by the adversarial examples in Table 1. In this work, we aim to differentiate these errors motivated by the conventional evaluation dimensions of fluency and adequacy (LDC, 2005).

4 Human Evaluation Corpus

We have developed a new human evaluation corpus from the viewpoints of fluency and adequacy. The evaluation corpus is available at GitHub[10] under CC BY-NC-SA 4.0[11]. In this section, we present the details of the corpus. Here, the human evaluation is designed in *monolingual* way; an MT hypothesis is evaluated against only its reference, supposing the reference is semantically equivalent to the source language input.

We made a contract with a linguistic data development company to conduct the human evaluation[12] with three annotators who are native speaker

[5]This example is taken from the Metrics dataset of WMT 2017.

[6]sacrebleu fingerprint: BLEU+case.lc+numrefs.1+smooth.exp+tok.13a+version.1.4.8

[7]sacrebleu fingerprint: chrF2+case.lc+numchars.6+numrefs.1+space.False+version.1.4.8

[8]Authors' implementation `https://github.com/Tiiiger/bert_score` with fingerprint: roberta-large_L17_no-idf_version=0.3.2(hug_trans=2.8.0)-rescaled

[9]Authors' implementation `https://github.com/google-research/bleurt`

[10]`https://github.com/ksudoh/wmt15-17-humaneval`

[11]`https://creativecommons.org/licenses/by-nc-sa/4.0/`

[12]The human evaluation was conducted without formal ethical review.

ID	Hypothesis	BLEU-4	chrF	BERTScore	BLEURT
ref	The Pleiades cluster is situated 445 light-years from Earth.	1.0	1.0	1.000	0.940
hyp1	The Pleiades cluster is ~~situated~~ 445 light-years far from Earth.	0.423	0.8	0.932	0.800
hyp2	The Pleiades cluster is situated 445 years from Earth.	0.658	0.8	0.854	0.670
hyp3	The Pleiades cluster is ~~situated~~ 445 light from the Earth.	0.336	0.6	0.617	0.698
hyp4	The Pleiades cluster is not situated 445 light-years from Earth.	0.702	0.9	0.892	0.028
hyp5	The Pleiades cluster is situated 345 light-years from Earth.	0.658	0.9	0.946	0.709
hyp6	The Pleiades cluster is situated 445 light-years from Mars.	0.783	0.9	0.909	0.640
hyp7	The Hyades cluster is situated 445 light-years from Earth.	0.783	0.9	0.891	0.556
hyp8	Is Earth from Pleiades the light-years situated cluster 445.	0.071	0.6	0.393	-0.659
hyp9	Turn off the light for saving the Earth.	0.085	0.2	0.039	-1.55

Table 1: Examples of automatic MT evaluation on adversarial examples. Underlines and strikethroughs represent differences from the reference.

of English and had work experiences of translation into English. We provide a set of English sentence pairs to the annotators: translation hypotheses and the corresponding references. No specific training was conducted before the evaluation. The annotators can ask questions to a moderator in the company, and the moderator asked them to the first author. The annotators conducted the evaluation independently, referring to the evaluation criteria below.

4.1 Dataset

We chose the WMT 2015-2017 Metrics datasets to give additional annotations. The MT results in the dataset and the corresponding human DA scores have been used in many existing automatic MT evaluation studies. The total number of pairs of hypothesis and reference sentences was 9,280, consisting of 2,000 pairs from WMT 2015, 3,360 pairs from WMT 2016, and 3,920 pairs from WMT 2017 datasets.

4.2 Evaluation Criteria

We propose the following evaluation criteria in fluency and adequacy, shown in Tables 2 and 3, respectively.

4.2.1 Fluency

The fluency criteria in Table 2 extend conventional ones by LDC (2005), with a *comprehension* viewpoint in the lower range. The lowest judgment *Incomprehensible* corresponds to LDC's fluency criterion "1: Incomprehensible," but is not limited to disfluency problems. The category *Poor* means the difficulty of comprehension. The other categories are defined mainly from a fluency viewpoint.

When a sentence is incomprehensible such as hyp8 in Table 1, we cannot evaluate its contents in the adequacy evaluation. On the other hand, hyp9 is not related to the reference and should be judged as a critical error in adequacy, even though it is easy-to-understand and looks fluent. These criteria were also motivated by the *acceptability* criteria (Goto et al., 2011). By the acceptability criteria, a hypothesis that lacks important information (i.e., its adequacy is not 5 in the five-point scale) is always judged as the worst, and better labels are given according to grammatical correctness and fluency.

4.2.2 Adequacy

Our adequacy criteria in Table 3 are different from the conventional ones (LDC, 2005) that focused on the amount of important information. We defined the adequacy of a translation hypothesis focusing

Category	Explanation
Incomprehensible (F)	The sentence is not comprehensible.
Poor (D)	Some contents are not easy to understand by typographical/grammatical errors and problematic expressions
Fair (B)	All the contents are easy to understand in spite of some typographical/grammatical errors
Good (A)	All the contents are easy to understand and free from grammatical errors, but some expressions are not very fluent
Excellent (S)	All the contents are easy to understand, and all the expressions are flawless

Table 2: Evaluation criteria in *Fluency*. Labels in parentheses are the ones used in the evaluation corpus.

Category	Explanation
Incomprehensible (N)	The contents cannot be understood due to fluency and comprehension issues, so the hypothesis is not eligible for the adequacy evaluation.
Unrelated (O)	The hypothesis delivers information that is *not related* to the reference
Contradiction (C)	The hypothesis delivers information that *contradicts* the reference
Serious (F)	The hypothesis delivers information that may cause serious misunderstanding due to some content errors but does not contradict the reference
Fair (B)	The hypothesis has some problems in its contents but does not cause a serious misunderstanding
Good (A)	The hypothesis has some minor problems in its contents that do not make a misunderstanding
Excellent (S)	The hypothesis delivers information equivalent to the reference.

Table 3: Evaluation criteria in *Adequacy*. Labels in parentheses are the ones used in the evaluation corpus.

on the delivery of the correct information, based on the discussion in section 3. Our criteria put more focus on possible *misunderstanding* by a translation hypothesis; we consider a translation may cause serious misunderstanding even if most parts of the translations are correct.

First, we use the category *Incomprehensible* for such hypotheses that are also classified into *Incomprehensible* in fluency. Then, we divide critical content errors into three types: *Unrelated*, *Contradiction*, and *Serious*. *Unrelated* indicates the unrelatedness, as shown by hyp9 in Table 1. It is expected to appear in poor translations in a very low-resourced condition. The category *Contradiction* indicates the contradiction with the reference, such as a negation flip at hyp4 and a number error at hyp5 in Table 1. This label was motivated by the task of natural language inference (NLI), which has also been used for the pre-training of MT evaluation (Sellam et al., 2020). The category *Serious* covers the other kind of serious content errors such as hyp6, and hyp7 in Table 1. These hypotheses deliver somewhat related but different information compared to the reference. The intermediate categories *Fair* and *Good* are used for major and minor errors, respectively.

4.3 Analyses

We conducted some analyses on the human evaluation corpus mainly in the differences among the three annotators.

4.3.1 Annotation Bias

We analyzed annotation differences among the three annotators (named A, B, and C), especially their labeling biases. Tables 4 and 5 show the annotation distributions for the three annotators on fluency and adequacy, respectively. We can see some differences among the annotators; for example, annotator B was very strict for using the best category *Excellent* in both dimensions, and annotator C gave more bad labels (*Contradiction* and *Serious*) than the others.

On average, the translation hypotheses in the WMT Metrics dataset for 2015-2017 still include many translation errors. The error tendency would be different on newer data consisting of many recent neural MT results. It is worth investigating recent MT results in future studies.

Fluency	A	B	C	Ave.
Incomprehensible	0.098	0.099	0.111	0.103
Poor	0.167	0.220	0.181	0.189
Fair	0.356	0.406	0.222	0.328
Good	0.124	0.240	0.219	0.195
Excellent	0.254	0.035	0.266	0.185

Table 4: Annotation distributions for the three annotators (fluency).

Adequacy	A	B	C	Ave.
Incomprehensible	0.098	0.099	0.098	0.098
Unrelated	0.004	0.001	0.011	0.005
Contradiction	0.009	0.019	0.086	0.038
Serious	0.205	0.187	0.311	0.234
Fair	0.374	0.343	0.146	0.288
Good	0.233	0.296	0.271	0.267
Excellent	0.076	0.005	0.076	0.069

Table 5: Annotation distributions for the three annotators (adequacy).

4.3.2 Comparison with Human Direct Assessment Scores

We compared our human evaluation labels with the human DA scores (standardized z-scores) given in the WMT Metrics data. Tables 6 and 7 show the mean and standard deviation values of human DA scores for each human evaluation label.

The human DA score ranges of the fluency and adequacy labels had almost the same partial orders among different annotators, although they still reflect the annotation bias shown in Tables 4 and 5; annotator B had a higher standard in fluency evaluation than the others.

One important finding here is the differences among the adequacy categories *Incomprehensible*, *Unrelated*, *Contradiction* and *Serious* in Table 7. The sentences with *Unrelated* were scored the worst by the human DA. However, critical content errors suggested by the labels *Contradiction* and *Serious* were penalized less than the ones with *Incomprehensible* and *Unrelated*. Such content errors should also be identified as critical translation errors in practice.

4.3.3 Inter-annotator Agreement

We also measured pairwise agreement among the three annotators using the κ coefficient (Carletta, 1996) and label concordance rate. The results are shown in Table 8. The inter-annotator agreement was not high enough but κ values are also comparable to the previous studies on older WMT datasets (Callison-Burch et al., 2007; Denkowski and Lavie, 2010)[13]. The agreement in fluency was lower than that in adequacy, especially on A-B and B-C, due to very high fluency standard of the annotator B. The agreement would improve with careful pre-annotation training and more example-based evaluation guidelines, because the annotators gave us feedback about the difficulty in discrimination among different categories.

5 Experiments

We conducted experiments using the evaluation corpus, to investigate the performance of automatic classification-based MT evaluation.

5.1 Experimental Setup

5.1.1 Data

Among the evaluation corpus, we reserved the WMT 2017 portion (3,920 samples; 560 for each language pair — cs-en, de-en, fi-en, lv-en, ru-en, tr-en, and zh-en) for the test set, chose 536 samples randomly for the development set, and used the remained 4,824 samples for the training set.

We took agreements among the three different annotators for the experiments by the following heuristics.

- If two or three annotators gave the same label, it was used as the agreement.
- If the annotators' judgment were different from each other, the worst label was used as the agreement. The label order was *Incomprehensible* < *Poor* < *Fair* < *Good* < *Excellent* for fluency and *Contradiction* < *Serious* < *Incomprehensible* < *Unrelated* < *Fair* < *Good* < *Excellent* for adequacy[14].

Tables 9 and 10 show the label statistics on the training, development, and test sets after applying the heuristics.

5.1.2 Automatic Evaluation Method

We used a simple sentence-level automatic MT evaluation framework, which takes hypothesis and reference sentences as the input and predicts the label. Since the task in the experiments was classification, the evaluation model was trained with

[13]Note that we had three annotators who evaluated all the sentences.

[14]We used this heuristic order because of the importance of content errors suggested by *Contradiction* and *Serious*.

Fluency	A	B	C
Incomprehensible	-0.644 (0.371)	-0.692 (0.356)	-0.649 (0.378)
Poor	-0.421 (0.408)	-0.420 (0.399)	-0.400 (0.418)
Fair	-0.079 (0.478)	0.019 (0.474)	-0.129 (0.449)
Good	0.165 (0.479)	0.408 (0.485)	0.122 (0.467)
Excellent	0.428 (0.524)	0.644 (0.465)	0.427 (0.521)

Table 6: Mean (standard deviation) of Direct Assessment scores for labels by the three annotators (fluency)

Adequacy	A	B	C
Incomprehensible	-0.646 (0.369)	-0.692 (0.356)	-0.662 (0.373)
Unrelated	-0.990 (0.367)	-0.926 (0.415)	-0.963 (0.363)
Contradiction	-0.370 (0.460)	-0.366 (0.468)	-0.200 (0.501)
Serious	-0.453 (0.438)	-0.499 (0.425)	-0.279 (0.473)
Fair	-0.076 (0.435)	-0.092 (0.417)	-0.029 (0.414)
Good	0.417 (0.361)	0.414 (0.363)	0.347 (0.414)
Excellent	0.814 (0.278)	0.839 (0.294)	0.756 (0.327)

Table 7: Mean (standard deviation) of Direct Assessment scores for labels by the three annotators (adequacy)

Metric		A-B	A-C	B-C
Fluency	κ	0.2860	0.3773	0.2489
	r	0.4512	0.5113	0.4014
Adequacy	κ	0.3947	0.2684	0.2774
	r	0.5459	0.5870	0.5752

Table 8: Inter-annotator agreement in κ coefficient and label concordance rate (r) on our human evaluation corpus. The fluency metric has five categories and the adequacy metric has seven categories.

Fluency	Training	Dev.	Test
Incomprehensible	545	74	282
Poor	992	96	602
Fair	1,655	196	1,341
Good	808	80	899
Excellent	824	90	796

Table 9: Label statistics of *fluency* dataset.

the classification objective, softmax cross-entropy over the category distribution. We trained and used independent models for fluency and adequacy.

We implemented the evaluator using HuggingFace Transformers[15] and its pre-trained RoBERTa model (`roberta-large`) (Liu et al., 2019). The model was fine-tuned to predict a label through an additional feed-forward layer taking the vector for `[CLS]` token as the input, using a softmax cross-entropy loss. Due to the label imbalance shown

[15] `https://github.com/huggingface/transformers`

Adequacy	Training	Dev.	Test
Incomprehensible	617	87	350
Unrelated	15	2	19
Contradiction	93	6	40
Serious	1,161	108	717
Fair	1,433	162	1,441
Good	1,208	143	1,165
Excellent	297	28	188

Table 10: Label statistics of *adequacy* dataset.

in Tables 9 and 10, we applied a sample-wise loss scaling with weights that were inversely proportional to the number of training instances with the labels. A label weight for a category c was defined as:

$$w_c = \sqrt{\frac{\max_{c' \in C} \mathrm{count}_{c'}}{\mathrm{count}_c}}, \tag{1}$$

where C is a set of categories.

We employed the Adam optimizer (Kingma and Ba, 2015) and continued the training for 30 epochs with the initial learning rate of 1e-5. We tried different minibatch sizes (4, 8, 16) and dropout rates in the additional feed-forward layer (0.1, 0.3, 0.5, 0.75)[16], and used the ones resulting in the best classification accuracy on the development set: 4 and 0.75 for fluency, 8 and 0.5 for adequacy, respectively.

[16] The dropout rate in RoBERTa was kept unchanged from its default value of 0.1. We also tried to increase it in the pilot test, but that resulted worse.

ref\pred	Inc.	Poor	Fair	Good	Exc.
Incomprehensible	**206**	45	22	8	1
Poor	45	**266**	250	43	4
Fair	15	134	**782**	358	52
Good	2	11	187	**560**	139
Excellent	0	2	35	306	**453**

Table 11: Confusion matrix in *fluency* prediction. The **bold** numbers represent correct predictions. The overall classification accuracy was 0.578.

Fluency	Precision	Recall	F1-score
Incomprehensible	0.769	0.730	0.749
Poor	0.581	0.438	0.499
Fair	0.613	0.583	0.598
Good	0.439	0.623	0.515
Excellent	0.698	0.569	0.627
Ave.	0.620	0.589	0.598

Table 12: Precision, recall, and F1-score in *fluency* prediction.

5.2 Results

We show the statistics of the prediction results by a confusion matrices and precision/recall/F1-scores. Tables 11 and 12 are from the fluency prediction, and Tables 13 and 14 are from the adequacy prediction.

In the fluency prediction, the classification accuracy on the test set was 0.578 (2,267 correct predictions out of 3,920), and that on the training and development sets was 0.999 and 0.647, respectively. Most of the incorrect predictions were in adjacent categories, and the fraction of serious misrecognition in distant categories (*Incomprehensible* → {*Good*, *Fair*}, *Poor* → *Excellent*, *Good* → *Incomprehensible*, and *Excellent* → {*Incomprehensible*, *Poor*}) was not so large (0.43%; 17 out of 3,920).

The prediction performance in Table 12 suggests the best and worst categories (*Excellent* and *Incomprehensible*) can be predicted more accurately than the intermediate categories.

In the adequacy prediction, the classification accuracy on the test set was 0.600 (2,351 correct predictions out of 3,920), and the results on the training and development sets were 0.998 and 0.632, respectively. The prediction of less frequent categories (*Unrelated* and *Contradiction*) did not work well despite the instance weighting in training. The result suggests we should use more negative examples in training for more accurate predictions on them. The prediction performance in Table 14 suggests the hypotheses with *Incomprehensible* can be identified more accurately than the others. Predictions of the other categories were still difficult. However, 93.5% of the hypotheses with the predicted label *Excellent* were good translations labeled *Excellent* or *Good* (144 out of 154); this finding would be beneficial in practice. The most serious confusion in this result was between *Serious* (critical) and *Fair* (okay). More fine-grained discrimination is needed to judge them.

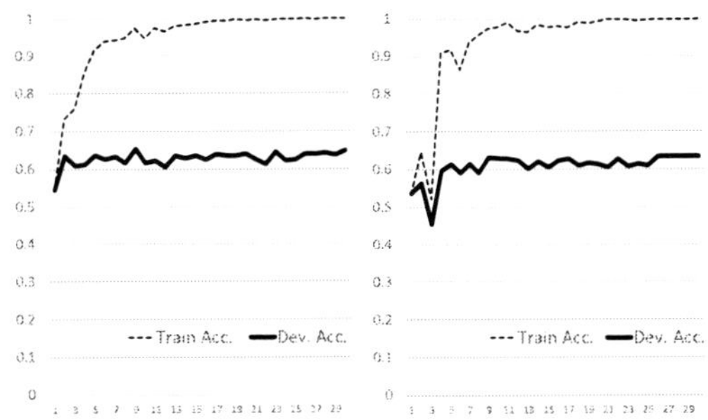

(a) Fluency (b) Adequacy

Figure 1: Learning curves in classification accuracy over training epochs.

Figure 1 (a) and (b) show the learning curves. The training set accuracy was almost saturated around 20 training epochs, but the development set accuracy was not stable until 30 epochs.

In summary, these experiments suggest our classification-based MT evaluation with absolute categories is promising, while we still need more *negative* examples. More data collections, including data augmentation, would be helpful, along with a further investigation of prediction models.

6 Conclusions

In this paper, we present our approach to classification-based human and automatic MT evaluation, focusing on critical translation errors in MT outputs. We revisited the use of fluency and adequacy metrics with some modifications on evaluation criteria, motivated by our thoughts on the critical content errors.

We developed a human evaluation corpus based on the criteria using the WMT Metrics dataset, which will be publicly available upon publication. Our corpus analyses revealed the human DA penalizes unrelated and incomprehensible hypotheses much more than contradiction and other critical errors in the content. We also conducted automatic

r\p	Inc.	Unr.	Con.	Ser.	Fair	Good	Exc.
Incomprehensible	**224**	0	0	83	38	4	1
Unrelated	0	**1**	0	13	5	0	0
Contradiction	0	0	**8**	9	13	10	0
Serious	37	0	8	**385**	242	45	0
Fair	29	0	13	237	**878**	274	10
Good	4	0	9	20	302	**771**	59
Excellent	0	0	0	1	6	97	**84**

Table 13: Confusion matrix in *adequacy* prediction. The **bold** numbers represent correct predictions. The overall classification accuracy was 0.600.

Adequacy	Precision	Recall	F1-score
Incomprehensible	0.762	0.640	0.696
Unrelated	1.000	0.053	0.100
Contradiction	0.211	0.200	0.205
Serious	0.515	0.537	0.526
Fair	0.592	0.609	0.600
Good	0.642	0.662	0.652
Excellent	0.545	0.447	0.491
Ave.	0.609	0.450	0.467

Table 14: Precision, recall, and F1-score in *adequacy* prediction.

MT evaluation experiments using the human evaluation corpus and achieved around 60% classification accuracy both in fluency and adequacy.

Our future work includes further development of human evaluation corpora that are not limited to WMT Metrics data, and data augmentation methods to tackle the label imbalance problem. It is also promising to apply the classification-based automatic MT evaluation to the neural MT training.

Acknowledgments

The authors would like to thank anonymous reviewers for their comments and suggestions. This work is supported by JST PRESTO (JPMJPR1856).

References

Alexandra Birch, Omri Abend, Ondřej Bojar, and Barry Haddow. 2016. HUME: Human UCCA-based evaluation of machine translation. In *Proceedings of the 2016 Conference on Empirical Methods in Natural Language Processing*, pages 1264–1274, Austin, Texas. Association for Computational Linguistics.

Chris Callison-Burch, Cameron Fordyce, Philipp Koehn, Christof Monz, and Josh Schroeder. 2007. (meta-) evaluation of machine translation. In *Proceedings of the Second Workshop on Statistical Machine Translation*, pages 136–158, Prague, Czech Republic. Association for Computational Linguistics.

Jean Carletta. 1996. Assessing agreement on classification tasks: The kappa statistic. *Computational Linguistics*, 22(2):249–254.

Michael Denkowski and Alon Lavie. 2010. Choosing the Right Evaluation for Machine Translation: an Examination of Annotator and Automatic Metric Performance on Human Judgment Tasks . In *Proceedings of the Ninth Biennial Conference of AMTA 2010.*

Jacob Devlin, Ming-Wei Chang, Kenton Lee, and Kristina Toutanova. 2019. BERT: Pre-training of deep bidirectional transformers for language understanding. In *Proceedings of the 2019 Conference of the North American Chapter of the Association for Computational Linguistics: Human Language Technologies, Volume 1 (Long and Short Papers)*, pages 4171–4186, Minneapolis, Minnesota. Association for Computational Linguistics.

Isao Goto, Bin Lu, Ka Po Chow, Eiichiro Sumita, and Benjamin Tsou. 2011. Overview of the Patent Machine Translation Task at the NTCIR-9 Workshop. In *Proceedings of NTCIR-9 Workshop Meeting*, pages 559–578.

Yvette Graham, Timothy Baldwin, Meghan Dowling, Maria Eskevich, Teresa Lynn, and Lamia Tounsi. 2016. Is all that glitters in machine translation quality estimation really gold? In *Proceedings of COLING 2016, the 26th International Conference on Computational Linguistics: Technical Papers*, pages 3124–3134, Osaka, Japan. The COLING 2016 Organizing Committee.

Yvette Graham, Timothy Baldwin, Aaron Harwood, Alistair Moffat, and Justin Zobel. 2012. Measurement of progress in machine translation. In *Proceedings of the Australasian Language Technology Association Workshop 2012*, pages 70–78, Dunedin, New Zealand.

Diederik P. Kingma and Jimmy Ba. 2015. Adam: A Method for Stochastic Optimization. In *Proceedings of the Third International Conference on Learning Representations*.

Wojciech Kryściński, Bryan McCann, Caiming Xiong, and Richard Socher. 2019. Evaluating the Factual Consistency of Abstractive Text Summarization. *arXiv preprint arXiv: 1910:12840.*

Matt Kusner, Yu Sun, Nicholas Kolkin, and Kilian Weinberger. 2015. From Word Embeddings To Document Distances. In *Proceedings of the 32nd International Conference on Machine Learning*, volume 37 of *Proceedings of Machine Learning Research*, pages 957–966, Lille, France. PMLR.

LDC. 2005. Linguistic Data Annotation Specification: Assessment of Fluency and Adequacy in Translations Revision 1.5, January 25, 2005 . Technical report, Linguistic Data Consortium.

Yinhan Liu, Myle Ott, Naman Goyal, Jingfei Du, Mandar Joshi, Danqi Chen, Omer Levy, Mike Lewis, Luke Zettlemoyer, and Veselin Stoyanov. 2019. RoBERTa: A Robustly Optimized BERT Pretraining Approach. *arXiv preprint arXiv: 1907:11692.*

Chi-kiu Lo and Dekai Wu. 2011. MEANT: An inexpensive, high-accuracy, semi-automatic metric for evaluating translation utility based on semantic roles. In *Proceedings of the 49th Annual Meeting of the Association for Computational Linguistics: Human Language Technologies*, pages 220–229, Portland, Oregon, USA. Association for Computational Linguistics.

Qingsong Ma, Ondřej Bojar, and Yvette Graham. 2018. Results of the WMT18 metrics shared task: Both characters and embeddings achieve good performance. In *Proceedings of the Third Conference on Machine Translation: Shared Task Papers*, pages 671–688, Belgium, Brussels. Association for Computational Linguistics.

Qingsong Ma, Johnny Wei, Ondřej Bojar, and Yvette Graham. 2019. Results of the WMT19 metrics shared task: Segment-level and strong MT systems pose big challenges. In *Proceedings of the Fourth Conference on Machine Translation (Volume 2: Shared Task Papers, Day 1)*, pages 62–90, Florence, Italy. Association for Computational Linguistics.

Kishore Papineni, Salim Roukos, Todd Ward, and Wei-Jing Zhu. 2002. Bleu: a method for automatic evaluation of machine translation. In *Proceedings of the 40th Annual Meeting of the Association for Computational Linguistics*, pages 311–318, Philadelphia, Pennsylvania, USA. Association for Computational Linguistics.

Maja Popović. 2020. Informative manual evaluation of machine translation output. In *Proceedings of the 28th International Conference on Computational Linguistics*, pages 5059–5069, Barcelona, Spain (Online). International Committee on Computational Linguistics.

Maja Popovic. 2020. On the differences between human translations. In *Proceedings of the 22nd Annual Conference of the European Association for Machine Translation*, pages 365–374, Lisboa, Portugal. European Association for Machine Translation.

Thibault Sellam, Dipanjan Das, and Ankur Parikh. 2020. BLEURT: Learning robust metrics for text generation. In *Proceedings of the 58th Annual Meeting of the Association for Computational Linguistics*, pages 7881–7892, Online. Association for Computational Linguistics.

Hiroki Shimanaka, Tomoyuki Kajiwara, and Mamoru Komachi. 2018. RUSE: Regressor using sentence embeddings for automatic machine translation evaluation. In *Proceedings of the Third Conference on Machine Translation: Shared Task Papers*, pages 751–758, Belgium, Brussels. Association for Computational Linguistics.

Hiroki Shimanaka, Tomoyuki Kajiwara, and Mamoru Komachi. 2019. Machine Translation Evaluation with BERT Regressor. *arXiv preprint arXiv: 1907.12679.*

Matthew Snover, Bonnie Dorr, Richard Schwartz, Linnea, Micciulla, and John Makhoul. 2006. A Study of Translation Edit Rate with Targeted Human Annotation. In *Proceedings of the 7th Conference of the Association for Machine Translation in the Americas (AMTA-2006).*

Kosuke Takahashi, Katsuhito Sudoh, and Satoshi Nakamura. 2020. Automatic machine translation evaluation using source language inputs and cross-lingual language model. In *Proceedings of the 58th Annual Meeting of the Association for Computational Linguistics*, pages 3553–3558, Online. Association for Computational Linguistics.

John S. White, Theresa A. O'Connell, and Francis E. O'Mara. 1994. The ARPA MT evaluation methodologies: Evolution, lessons, and future approaches. In *Proceedings of the First Conference of the Association for Machine Translation in the Americas*, Columbia, Maryland, USA.

Tianyi Zhang, Varsha Kishore, Felix Wu, Kilian Q. Weinberger, and Yoav Artzi. 2020. BERTScore: Evaluating Text Generation with BERT. In *Proceedings of the Eighth International Conference on Learning Representations.*

Wei Zhao, Maxime Peyrard, Fei Liu, Yang Gao, Christian M. Meyer, and Steffen Eger. 2019. MoverScore: Text generation evaluating with contextualized embeddings and earth mover distance. In *Proceedings of the 2019 Conference on Empirical Methods in Natural Language Processing and the 9th International Joint Conference on Natural Language Processing (EMNLP-IJCNLP)*, pages 563–578, Hong Kong, China. Association for Computational Linguistics.

Towards objectively evaluating the quality of generated medical summaries

Francesco Moramarco*
Babylon Health / London, UK
University of Aberdeen / Aberdeen, UK
francesco.moramarco†

Damir Juric*
Babylon Health / London, UK
damir.juric†

Aleksandar Savkov
Babylon Health / London, UK
sasho.savkov†

Ehud Reiter
University of Aberdeen / Aberdeen, UK
e.reiter@abdn.ac.uk

†@babylonhealth.com

Abstract

We propose a method for evaluating the quality of generated text by asking evaluators to count facts, and computing precision, recall, f-score, and accuracy from the raw counts. We believe this approach leads to a more objective and easier to reproduce evaluation. We apply this to the task of medical report summarisation, where measuring objective quality and accuracy is of paramount importance.

1 Introduction

Natural Language Generation in the medical domain is notoriously hard because of the sensitivity of the content and the potential harm of hallucinations and inaccurate statements (Kryscinski et al., 2020; Falke et al., 2019). This informs the human evaluation of NLG systems, selecting accuracy and overall quality of the generated text as the most valuable aspects to be evaluated.

In this paper we carry out a human evaluation of the quality of medical summaries of Clinical Reports generated by state of the art (SOTA) text summarisation models.

Our contributions are: (i) a re-purposed parallel dataset of medical reports and summary descriptions for training and evaluating, (ii) an approach for a more objective human evaluation using counts, and (iii) a human evaluation conducted on this dataset using the approach proposed.

2 Related Work

A recent study by Celikyilmaz et al. (2020) gives a comprehensive view on different approaches to text summary evaluation. While many of these can be wholly or partly translated between different domains, the medical domain remains particularly problematic due to the sensitive nature of its data. Moen et al. (2014) and Moen et al. (2016) try to establish if there is a correlation between automatic and human evaluations of clinical summaries. A 4-point and 2-point Likert scales are used for the human evaluation. In Goldstein et al. (2017) the authors generate free-text summary letters from the data of 31 different patients and compare them to the respective original physician-composed discharge letters, measuring relative completeness, quantifying missed data items, readability, and functional performance.

Closest to our approach is the Pyramid method by Nenkova et al. (2007), which defines semantically motivated, sub-sentential units (Summary Content Units) for annotators to extract in each reference summary. SCUs are weighed according to how often they appear in the multiple references and then compared with the SCUs extracted in the hypothesis to compute precision, recall, and f-score.

3 Data

The *MTSamples* dataset comprises 5,000 sample medical transcription reports from a wide variety of specialities uploaded to a community platform website[1]. The dataset has been used in past medical NLP research (Chen et al., 2011; Lewis et al., 2011; Soysal et al., 2017) including as a Kaggle dataset[2].

There are 40 medical specialties in the dataset, such as 'Surgery', 'Consult - History and Phy.', and 'Cardiovascular / Pulmonary'. Each specialty

*Equal contribution

[1] https://mtsamples.com

[2] https://www.kaggle.com/tboyle10/medicaltranscriptions

Proceedings of the Workshop on Human Evaluation of NLP Systems (HumEval), pages 56–61
Online, April 19, 2021.

contains a number of sample reports ranging from 6 to 1103.

The reports are free text with headings, which change according to the specialty. However, all reports also have a description field, which is a good approximation of a summary of the report. The length of each report varies greatly according to the specialty, with an average of 589 words for the body of the report, and 21 words for the description. Figure 1 shows an example of MTSamples reports, inclusive of description.

Medical Specialty: Diets and Nutritions
Sample Name: Dietary Consult - 2

SUBJECTIVE: The patient's assistant brings in her food diary sheets. The patient says she stays active by walking at the mall.

OBJECTIVE: Weight today is 201 pounds, which is down 3 pounds in the past month. She has lost a total of 24 pounds. I praised this and encouraged her to continue. I went over her food diary. I praised her three-meal pattern and all of her positive food choices, especially the use of sugar-free Kool-Aid, sugar-free Jell-O, sugar-free lemonade, diet pop, as well as the variety of foods she is using in her three-meal pattern. I encouraged her to continue all of this.

ASSESSMENT: The patient has been successful with weight loss due to assistance from others in keeping a food diary, picking lower-calorie items, her three-meal pattern, getting a balanced diet, and all her physical activity. She needs to continue all this.

PLAN: Followup is set for 06/13/05 to check the patient's weight, her food diary, and answer any questions.

DESCRIPTION: The patient has been successful with weight loss due to assistance from others in keeping a food diary, picking lower-calorie items, her three-meal pattern, getting a balanced diet, and all her physical activity.

Figure 1: An MTSamples clinical report of specialty 'Diets and Nutritions'. Note the reference Description at the bottom.

Given the brevity of some descriptions, we discard reports with descriptions shorter than 12 words and consider a dataset of 3242 reports. By examining the dataset, we note that descriptions are mostly extractive in nature, meaning they are phrases or entire sentences taken from the report. To quantify this we compute n-gram overlap with Rouge-1 (unigram) and Rouge-L (longest common n-gram) (Lin, 2004) precision scores, which are 0.989 and 0.939 respectively.

We split the dataset into 2 576 reports for training (80%), 323 for development (10%) and 343 for testing (10%). We perform the split separately for each medical specialty to ensure they are adequately represented and then aggregate the data.

The dataset, models, and evaluation results can be found on Github[3].

4 Experimental Setup

For our experiment, we consider one baseline and three SOTA automatic summarisation models (extractive, abstractive, and fine-tuned on our training set respectively). More specifically:

- **Lead–3** — this is our baseline. Following Zhang et al. (2018), this model selects the first three sentences of the clinical report as the description;
- **Bert–Ext** — the unsupervised extractive model by Miller (2019) [4];
- **Pegasus–CNN** — an abstractive model by Zhang et al. (2019) trained on the CNN/Daily mail dataset and used as is;
- **Bart–Med** — an abstractive model by Lewis et al. (2020), which we fine-tune on our MTSamples training set.

We generate descriptions with these 4 models using the entire clinical report text as input.

5 Human Evaluation Protocol

We select 10 clinical reports and summary descriptions from our MTSamples test set. Our subjects are three general practice physicians. They are employed at Babylon Health and have experience in AI research evaluation. The task is implemented with the Heartex Annotation Platform[5], which lets researchers define tasks in an XML language and specify the number of annotators. It then generates each individual task and collates the results.

The task involves (i) reading the clinical report, (ii) reading the reference description (supplied by the dataset, see Figure 1), (iii) then evaluating 4 generated descriptions by answering 5 questions (for a total of 40 generated descriptions). We ask the evaluators to count the "medical facts" in each generated description and to compare them against those in the reference. Initially, we considered listing the types of facts to be extracted, as done by Thomson and Reiter (2020), but the sheer diversity in the structure and content across the specialties

[3] https://github.com/babylonhealth/medical-note-summarisation

[4] https://pypi.org/project/bert-extractive-summarizer/

[5] https://www.heartex.ai/

in our dataset made this approach impractical. Instead, we give evaluators instructions containing two examples and ask them to extrapolate a process for fact extraction. Figure 2 shows the instructions we give them.

> The evaluation consists of reading a clinical report and a number of short descriptions, then quantifying how many "medical facts" were correctly reported. We understand that the definition of a "medical fact" is vague, and so it's up to your interpretation. As an example, in the following description:
>
> `2-year-old female who comes in for just rechecking her weight, her breathing status, and her diet.`
>
> There are (arguably) 4 facts:
> - 2 year old female
> - coming to recheck her weight
> - coming to recheck her breathing status
> - coming to recheck her diet
>
> Here's another example:
>
> `The patient had a syncopal episode last night. She did not have any residual deficit. She had a headache at that time. She denies chest pains or palpitations.`
>
> Here there are (arguably) 5 facts:
> - had a syncopal episode last night
> - no residual deficit
> - headache
> - no chest pains
> - no palpitations

Figure 2: Instructions to evaluators.

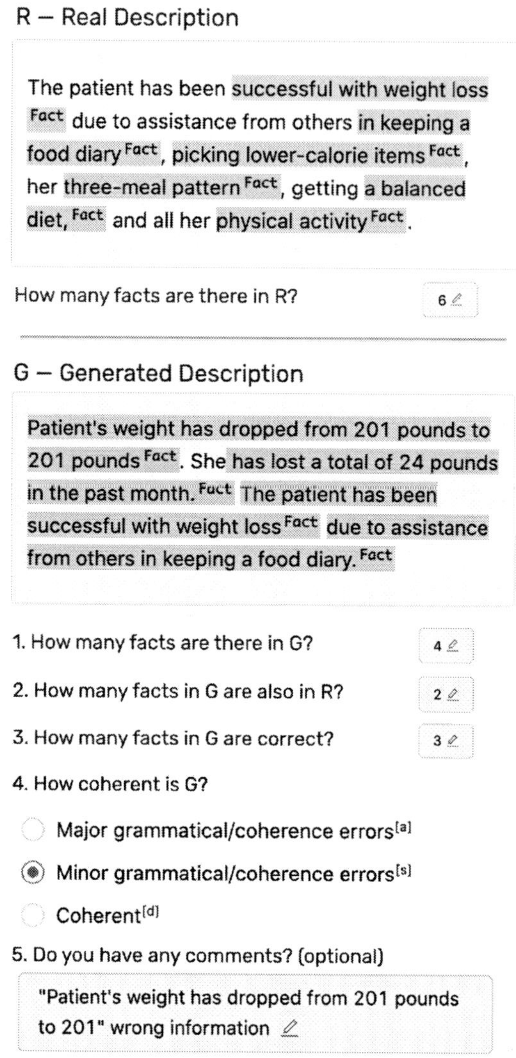

Figure 3: A completed task. *Real Description* is the reference.

The evaluators are asked to read the clinical report (as shown in Figure 1), then to analyse the reference description by reporting the number of facts. To aid them in the task, they can optionally select the facts in the text using an in-built Heartex feature. Next, they are shown four generated descriptions (one per model) and asked to count facts and answer 5 questions. Figure 3 shows the reference, generated descriptions, and questions for a given task, and gives an example annotation from one of the evaluators. When answering question 3 (How many facts in G are correct?) they refer to the clinical report as a ground truth.

Based on this set of questions, we gather the following raw counts:

- R: facts in the reference description
- G: facts in the generated description
- $R\&G$: facts in common
- C: correct facts in the generated description

We use these raw counts to compute four derived metrics:

- **Precision**, calculated as $\frac{R\&G}{G}$
- **Recall**, calculated as $\frac{R\&G}{R}$
- **F-Score**, calculated as $2 \cdot \frac{Precision \cdot Recall}{Precision + Recall}$
- **Accuracy**, calculated as $\frac{C}{G}$

For *Coherence*, we take Chen et al. (2020) and Juraska et al. (2019) definition: "*whether the generated text is grammatically correct and fluent, re-*

Model	Metric	Eval 1	Eval 2	Eval 3	Avg
Lead-3	Precision	0.42	0.43	0.46	0.44
	Recall	0.64	0.60	0.73	0.66
	F-Score	0.49	0.45	0.51	0.48
	Accuracy	1.0	1.0	1.0	**1.0**
	Coherence	0.95	0.95	0.90	0.93
Bert-Ext	Precision	0.58	0.48	0.48	0.51
	Recall	0.62	0.61	0.60	0.61
	F-Score	0.59	0.52	0.51	0.54
	Accuracy	1.0	1.0	1.0	**1.0**
	Coherence	1.0	0.95	1.0	**0.98**
Pegasus-CNN	Precision	0.29	0.36	0.31	0.32
	Recall	0.43	0.50	0.50	0.47
	F-Score	0.34	0.40	0.36	0.37
	Accuracy	0.97	0.97	0.98	0.97
	Coherence	1.0	1.0	0.95	**0.98**
Bart-Med	Precision	0.65	0.58	0.55	**0.59**
	Recall	1.0	0.96	0.97	**0.98**
	F-score	0.77	0.70	0.68	**0.72**
	Accuracy	1.0	1.0	1.0	**1.0**
	Coherence	1.0	0.75	0.95	0.90

Table 1: Derived metrics for each model and each evaluator, aggregated across tasks.

gardless of factual correctness" and ask evaluators to choose between three options (Coherent, Minor Errors, Major Errors) and convert these into continuous numbers with Coherent = 1.0, Minor Errors = 0.5, and Major Errors = 0.0.

6 Results and Discussion

Table 1 shows the results for all derived metrics, calculated on the raw counts from the evaluators. Expectedly, Bart-Med, the model trained on the MTSamples training set, scores highest in all metrics (except Coherence).

Interestingly, all four models score almost-perfect accuracy, meaning they don't hallucinate medical facts. This is not a surprise for Lead-3 and Bert-Ext, which are extractive in nature. As for Pegasus-CNN and Bart-Med, while the models are abstractive, we notice they tend to mostly select and copy phrases or entire sentences from the source report. The only hallucination the evaluators found is a numerical error, reported by Pegasus-CNN in the following generated description:

```
Patient's weight has dropped from 201
pounds to 201 pounds. She has lost a
total of 24 pounds in the past month.
```

Whereas, the source report states:

	Metric	E1–E2–E3	E1–E2	E1–E3	E2–E3
Raw Counts	R facts	0.25	0.44	0.27	0.01
	G facts	0.33	0.50	0.26	0.12
	G&R facts	0.55	0.74	0.50	0.40
	G acc facts	0.34	0.51	0.27	0.13
	Coherence	0.40	0.14	0.56	0.49
Der. Metrics	Precision	0.87	0.84	0.88	0.88
	Recall	0.90	0.93	0.89	0.89
	F-Score	0.89	0.88	0.91	0.87
	Accuracy	0.87	0.79	0.96	0.84

Table 2: Krippendorff Alpha for each metric, where *R* is reference, *G* the generated description, *G acc facts* the count of accurate facts in the generated description, *E1-E2-E3* the agreement of all three evaluators, and *Ex-Ey* the agreement between Evaluator x and Evaluator y.

```
Weight today is 201 pounds, which is
down 3 pounds in the past month. She
has lost a total of 24 pounds.
```

6.1 Agreement

To validate the human evaluation task, we compute inter-annotator agreement for each derived metric, as well as on the raw counts. We use Krippendorff Alpha (Hayes and Krippendorff, 2007) as we are dealing with continuous values. Table 2 includes overall agreement and a breakdown for each pair of evaluators.

Looking at the *E1-E2-E3* column, we note a clear divide between the low agreement on raw counts and the high agreement on the derived metrics. We investigate this by comparing the facts selected by each annotator and notice a degree of variability in the level of granularity they employed. Consider the description:

```
An 83-year-old diabetic female presents
today stating that she would like dia-
betic foot care.
```

Table 3 shows the facts selected by the three evaluators.

We compute pairwise agreement in Table 2 and notice that two of the evaluators (E1 and E2) share a similar (more granular) approach to fact selection, whereas E3 is less granular.

We also investigate the low agreement for Coherence and discover that it's due to a strong imbalance of the three classes (Coherent, Minor Errors, and Major Errors) where Coherent appears 91.67% of cases, Minor Errors 6.67% and Major Errors 1.67%. While this causes a low Krippendorff Alpha, we count the number of times all three

E	Count	Selected Facts
E1	2	- 83-year-old diabetic female - would like diabetic foot care
E2	5	- 83-year-old - diabetic - female - presents today - would like diabetic foot care
E3	3	- 83-year-old female - diabetic - would like diabetic foot care

Table 3: Example of evaluators disagreement in fact selection.

evaluators agree on a generated description being Coherent and find it to be 82.5%.

Finally, for all derived metrics the agreement scores are very high. This shows a robustness of these metrics even with different granularity in fact selection, and that the three evaluators agree on the quality of a given generated description. In other words, the evaluators agree on the quality of the generated descriptions even though they don't agree on the way of selecting medical facts.

7 Future Work

In this paper we presented an evaluation of the quality of medical summaries using fact counting. The results of this study help us to identify a number of insights to guide our future work:

- We could work on better defining a medical fact (as in Dušek and Kasner (2020)) and to prompt agreement on the level of granularity, for instance by instructing evaluators to split a description into the highest number of facts that are meaningful;
- Our evaluation focused on the quality of the generated descriptions and did not evaluate their usefulness in the medical setting. Such extrinsic evaluation would be very valuable;
- We could compare our approach of fact counting with the more common Likert scales.

References

Asli Celikyilmaz, Elizabeth Clark, and Jianfeng Gao. 2020. Evaluation of text generation: A survey. *arXiv preprint arXiv:2006.14799*.

Elizabeth Chen, Sharad Manaktala, Indra Sarkar, and Genevieve Melton. 2011. A multi-site content analysis of social history information in clinical notes. *AMIA Annual Symposium Proceedings*, 2011:227–36.

Zhiyu Chen, Harini Eavani, Wenhu Chen, Yinyin Liu, and William Yang Wang. 2020. Few-shot NLG with pre-trained language model. In *Proceedings of the 58th Annual Meeting of the Association for Computational Linguistics*, pages 183–190, Online. Association for Computational Linguistics.

Ondřej Dušek and Zdeněk Kasner. 2020. Evaluating semantic accuracy of data-to-text generation with natural language inference. In *Proceedings of the 13th International Conference on Natural Language Generation*, pages 131–137.

Tobias Falke, Leonardo FR Ribeiro, Prasetya Ajie Utama, Ido Dagan, and Iryna Gurevych. 2019. Ranking generated summaries by correctness: An interesting but challenging application for natural language inference. In *Proceedings of the 57th Annual Meeting of the Association for Computational Linguistics*, pages 2214–2220.

Ayelet Goldstein, Yuval Shahar, Efrat Orenbuch, and Matan J Cohen. 2017. Evaluation of an automated knowledge-based textual summarization system for longitudinal clinical data, in the intensive care domain. *Artificial intelligence in medicine*, 82:20–33.

Andrew F Hayes and Klaus Krippendorff. 2007. Answering the call for a standard reliability measure for coding data. *Communication methods and measures*, 1(1):77–89.

Juraj Juraska, Kevin Bowden, and Marilyn Walker. 2019. ViGGO: A video game corpus for data-to-text generation in open-domain conversation. In *Proceedings of the 12th International Conference on Natural Language Generation*, pages 164–172, Tokyo, Japan. Association for Computational Linguistics.

Wojciech Kryscinski, Bryan McCann, Caiming Xiong, and Richard Socher. 2020. Evaluating the factual consistency of abstractive text summarization. In *Proceedings of the 2020 Conference on Empirical Methods in Natural Language Processing (EMNLP)*, pages 9332–9346.

Mike Lewis, Yinhan Liu, Naman Goyal, Marjan Ghazvininejad, Abdelrahman Mohamed, Omer Levy, Veselin Stoyanov, and Luke Zettlemoyer. 2020. BART: Denoising sequence-to-sequence pre-training for natural language generation, translation, and comprehension. In *Proceedings of the 58th Annual Meeting of the Association for Computational Linguistics*, pages 7871–7880, Online. Association for Computational Linguistics.

Neal Lewis, Daniel Gruhl, and Hui Yang. 2011. Extracting family history diagnosis from clinical texts. pages 128–133.

Chin-Yew Lin. 2004. Rouge: A package for automatic evaluation of summaries. In *Text summarization branches out*, pages 74–81.

Derek Miller. 2019. Leveraging bert for extractive text summarization on lectures. *arXiv preprint arXiv:1906.04165*.

Hans Moen, Juho Heimonen, Laura-Maria Murtola, Antti Airola, Tapio Pahikkala, Virpi Terävä, Riitta Danielsson-Ojala, Tapio Salakoski, and Sanna Salanterä. 2014. On evaluation of automatically generated clinical discharge summaries. In *PAHI*, pages 101–114.

Hans Moen, Laura-Maria Peltonen, Juho Heimonen, Antti Airola, Tapio Pahikkala, Tapio Salakoski, and Sanna Salanterä. 2016. Comparison of automatic summarisation methods for clinical free text notes. *Artificial Intelligence in Medicine*, 67:25 – 37.

Ani Nenkova, Rebecca Passonneau, and Kathleen McKeown. 2007. The pyramid method: Incorporating human content selection variation in summarization evaluation. *TSLP*, 4.

Ergin Soysal, Jingqi Wang, Min Jiang, Yonghui Wu, Serguei Pakhomov, Hongfang Liu, and Hua Xu. 2017. CLAMP – a toolkit for efficiently building customized clinical natural language processing pipelines. *Journal of the American Medical Informatics Association*, 25(3):331–336.

Craig Alexander Thomson and Ehud Reiter. 2020. A gold standard methodology for evaluating accuracy in data-to-text systems. In *Proceedings of the 13th International Conference on Natural Language Generation*.

Jingqing Zhang, Yao Zhao, Mohammad Saleh, and Peter J. Liu. 2019. Pegasus: Pre-training with extracted gap-sentences for abstractive summarization.

Xingxing Zhang, Mirella Lapata, Furu Wei, and Ming Zhou. 2018. Neural latent extractive document summarization. In *Proceedings of the 2018 Conference on Empirical Methods in Natural Language Processing*, pages 779–784.

A preliminary study on evaluating Consultation Notes with Post-Editing

Francesco Moramarco*
Babylon Health / London, UK
University of Aberdeen / Aberdeen, UK
francesco.moramarco†

Alex Papadopoulos Korfiatis*
Babylon Health / London, UK
alex.papadopoulos†

Aleksandar Savkov
Babylon Health / London, UK
sasho.savkov†

Ehud Reiter
University of Aberdeen / Aberdeen, UK
e.reiter@abdn.ac.uk

†@babylonhealth.com

Abstract

Automatic summarisation has the potential to aid physicians in streamlining clerical tasks such as note taking. But it is notoriously difficult to evaluate these systems and demonstrate that they are safe to be used in a clinical setting. To circumvent this issue, we propose a semi-automatic approach whereby physicians post-edit generated notes before submitting them. We conduct a preliminary study on the time saving of automatically generated consultation notes with post-editing. Our evaluators are asked to listen to mock consultations and to post-edit three generated notes. We time this and find that it is faster than writing the note from scratch. We present insights and lessons learnt from this experiment.

1 Introduction

In modern EHR (Electronic Health Records) systems, at the end of a medical consultation the physician is required to file a consultation note detailing symptoms, examination, and treatment discussed. This is a pain point for physicians, who, according to a US study in 2017-2018 (Arndt et al., 2017) spend up to 44.2% of their time on clerical tasks, and this is a major contributor to physician burnout (Medscape, 2018).

A number of recent studies (Kazi and Kahanda, 2019; Molenaar et al., 2020; Krishna et al., 2020) propose to use summarisation systems to automatically generate the consultation note from the transcript of the consultation. Yet there is limited work on how to properly evaluate such a system so that it may be used in the clinical setting. Intrinsic evaluation metrics through Likert scales or ranking methods may help select the best model, but they don't ensure the model will never hallucinate information or miss key items when generating the consultation note.

In this study we propose to evaluate generated consultation notes with an extrinsic measure based on post-editing time. We ask our evaluators (primary healthcare physicians) to listen to a consultation, write a consultation note, and post-edit a number of generated notes. We then compare the timings of each task to determine whether post-editing a note is faster than writing one from scratch.

We focus on post-editing time because (i) it's simple to measure, and (ii) it provides a gate for adoption of the technology (i.e. post-editing a note should be faster than writing it from scratch). There are other extrinsic metrics which we intend to investigate in the future, such as patient satisfaction, doctor cognitive load, doctor-patient engagement, and usefulness for the next doctor accessing the note.

2 Related Work

Post-editing has a long history in Machine Translation (MT) (Chander, 1994; Carl et al., 2015; Graham et al., 2017; Koponen, 2016; De Sousa et al., 2011), with a number of production systems and tools using a semi-automatic approach to fix errors and check the output of the system before it is shown to the users (Dowling et al., 2016; Aziz and Specia, 2012).

Outside of MT, Sripada et al. (2005) carry out a study on post-editing an NLG system for generating weather forecast from data.

As an evaluation metric, Allman et al. (2012) define *Productivity* as "the quantity of text an experienced translator could translate in a given period of time [compared] with the quantity of text gen-

*Equal contribution

Proceedings of the Workshop on Human Evaluation of NLP Systems (HumEval), pages 62–68
Online, April 19, 2021. ©2021 Association for Computational Linguistics

erated by [the system] that the same person could edit in the given time."

To the best of our knowledge, post-editing is not widely used in document summarisation. We speculate this is partly because a post-editor of document summaries would need to read the entire document in order to accurately post-edit the summary, and this may minimise the benefit of having a generated summary compared to writing it from scratch. This is not the case, however, with consultation note generation, whereby the physician in charge of writing the note is the same physician who has conducted the consultation. Here post-editing may be very valuable in saving physician time.

3 Data

We partner with a UK healthcare provider, Babylon Health, which gives us access to a dataset of 800 proprietary consultation transcripts (automatically transcribed) and notes. The consultations span various topics within primary healthcare and are 10 minutes long on average. The notes are written by the physician who carried out the consultation and are in patient-friendly format, meaning they are in the same language the doctor used while talking to the patient and don't contain any abbreviations or acronyms. Each note is made up of three sections: *History & Examination*, *Diagnosis*, and *Management*.

For our evaluation, we design a dataset of 57 mock consultations produced in a similar manner. We ask five Babylon Health physicians working in primary healthcare to act as doctors and a number of lay people (employees at Babylon) to act as patients. Participation is entirely voluntary and all participants sign a consent form explaining what the study would involve and the intended use of the data produced. They are given the choice to withdraw consent at any point.

We give each patient a case card, prepared by a physician, that contains the condition they need help with and a list of medical details and symptoms. We record the audio of each mock consultation and ask the doctor to write a patient-friendly note as described above. Figure 1 shows a mock patient-friendly note.

We then employ a transcription agency to transcribe the recordings on an utterance level. Figure 2 shows a transcript snippet from the same consultation.

For the evaluation reported here, we only use 3 out of the 57 consultations; we are planning to publish the whole dataset at a later stage.

HISTORY & EXAMINATION
You developed lower abdominal pain 2 days ago. The pain came on gradually, is burning in nature, constant and is worsening. You have no bowel symptoms or pain on urination, but have noticed a pink colour to your urine. You have not noticed and blood in your urine. You feel some nausea, but have not vomited. You feel hot and sweaty. You are sexually active with a long term partner. Your last sexual health check-up was 6 months ago. You last had unprotected sex 2 days ago. Your last period was 2 weeks ago. You have no other symptoms. You have no past medical history, but use implanon for contraception.
DIAGNOSIS: Urinary Tract Infection. Must rule out pregnancy
MANAGEMENT
Take a pregnancy test. Give urine sample for a urine dip and to check for bacteria. Treat with antibiotics. Regular paracetamol for pain. Review in 1 - 2 days if no improvement, or earlier if symptoms are worsening.

Figure 1: Mock consultation note written by a locum doctor, from our evaluation dataset.

4 Experimental Setup

We use the proprietary dataset of 800 consultations to finetune two automatic summarisation models based on BART (Lewis et al., 2020). We feed the transcripts as inputs and the consultation notes as outputs.

We then apply the models on the mock consultation dataset, using them to generate the *History & Examination* section of the consultation note. For our experiment, we consider the generated notes from these two models (Model A, Model B) together with the original reference note (Ref). We shuffle these for each task and tell the evaluators that all three notes are generated.

The task is presented to the evaluators using Heartex (Tkachenko et al., 2020), a configurable annotation platform that allows us to customise the design of the evaluation task.

Our evaluators are three primary healthcare physicians. They are employed at Babylon Health

[...]
Doctor: Hello? Good morning, Tim. Um, how can I help you this morning?
Patient: Um, so I'm having some, some pain, uh, in my tummy, like the lower part of my tummy. Um and I've just been feeling, quite, hot and sweaty.
Doctor: OK. Right, I'm sorry to hear that. When, when did your symptoms all start?
Patient: About two days ago.
Doctor: OK. And whereabouts in your tummy is the pain, exactly?
Patient: Uh, like below my belly button, it's like quite, sore when I press on it.
Doctor: OK. Did the pain come on quite suddenly, or was it more gradual?
Patient: it hasn't been, it's more gradual and it's just, it is getting a bit worse now.
Doctor: OK, OK. And can you describe the pain to me? [...]

Figure 2: Sample transcript from the mock dataset.

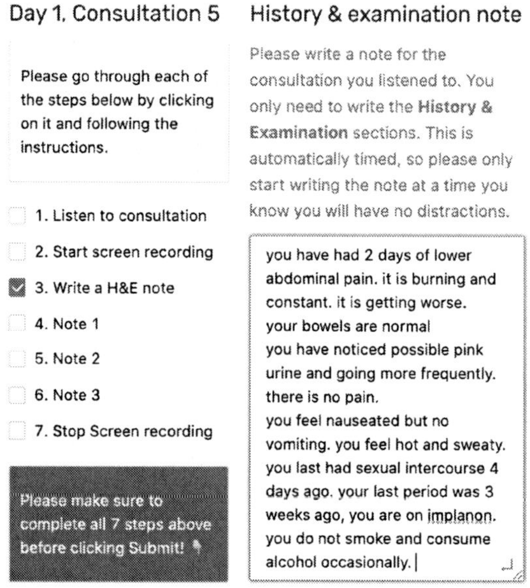

Figure 3: Heartex Annotation interface for writing the History&Examination section of the consultation note.

and have experience in AI research annotation. The task we submit to them consists of the following steps:

1. **Listen to the audio of a mock consultation.** We let evaluators note down any key symptoms on a piece of paper as they would normally do during a consultation.

2. **Write the *History & Examination* sections of the consultation note (this is timed).** Just as they would in the clinical setting, after having listened to a consultation recording we ask them to write the first section of the consultation note. Figure 3 shows an example.

3. **Post-edit three generated notes (this is timed).** The evaluators are presented with the three generated notes (Model A, Model B, Ref, in random order) for the given consultation and are asked to edit incorrect statements and to add missing statements.

   We then present a number of questions to evaluate the quality of the given note. Our criteria are *Correctness*, *Completeness* (Goldstein et al., 2017), and *Coherence*. We agreed these criteria with the lead physician, who drafted definitions and a scoring guidance for the evaluators (Figure 4). Figure 5 shows the questions we ask for scoring these criteria and a sample annotation.

We also ask evaluators to record their screen for the duration of the task. We use these recordings to calculate how long they took to write the note (step 2) and to edit each generated note (step 3). We use the difference of these two timings as our extrinsic measure to check whether editing a generated note is faster than writing one from scratch.

5 Results and Discussion

For this experiment, we run our evaluation on 3 of the 57 mock consultations. Table 2 gives a breakdown of the time it took to edit each note and write one from scratch. Here are some observations:

- In almost all cases, post-editing an existing note is faster than writing a note from scratch;
- As expected, post-editing the reference note (written by the consulting physician) is in general faster than post-editing the notes generated by either model. However, there are a number of instances (across all evaluators) where this isn't the case;
- Note-taking style and length is very different amongst physicians (Cohen et al., 2019), and this can be seen in our results as well. Doctor A tends to write shorter, terser notes and only

Scoring Guidance

We are scoring the quality of the note based on:

Correctness: you will be asked to identify the number of incorrect statements in the note.

Completeness: you will be asked to identify the number of major and minor omissions from the note. If an omission is negligible, please do not include it in the omission count. Here's a description of each omission type:

- **Major** = any edit that would be needed before the consultation notes are completed (if not corrected, it would render the note unsatisfactory from a medico-legal and quality perspective) e.g. features of chest pain
- **Minor** = any edit that would be preferable before the notes are completed (satisfied from a medico-legal point of view but deficient from a quality point of view) e.g. alcohol, smoking hx
- **Negligible** = any edit if missed would not pose any issues but if included would improve the quality of the notes (this is information that you may tend not to record but if you had more time, you might record if you remember) e.g. medication hx which is already recorded elsewhere in the record

Coherence: you will be asked if the note makes sense, regardless of the content.

Figure 4: Scoring guidance drafted by the lead physician.

	Incorrect			Major Omissions			Minor omissions			Coherence		
Source	**Dr A**	**Dr B**	**Dr C**	**Dr A**	**Dr B**	**Dr C**	**Dr A**	**Dr B**	**Dr C**	**Dr A**	**Dr B**	**Dr C**
Ref	0.67	2	1.67	0.33	0.67	1	0.33	3	0.67	2	2	1.67
Model A	1.67	2.33	1.33	0.67	3.67	3.33	1	4.67	0	2	1	1
Model B	1.67	2.33	0.67	1.67	3.33	3.33	0.33	5	1	1.67	1.67	1.33

Table 1: Aggregated scores for each evaluator, each criterion, and each note. For a full breakdown along tasks, please refer to Table A1 in the Appendices.

Task	Eval	Write	Mod A	Mod B	Ref
1	**Dr A**	2:14	1:26	0:55	1:03
	Dr B	4:02	4:30	4:16	2:44
	Dr C	3:51	1:43	2:35	1:45
2	**Dr A**	4:02	0:38	1:04	0:50
	Dr B	3:19	2:31	2:51	1:43
	Dr C	2:26	1:10	1:16	0:42
3	**Dr A**	4:17	1:59	2:15	0:45
	Dr B	4:21	4:04	3:32	4:17
	Dr C	3:53	-	-	-

Table 2: A breakdown of the time taken by the evaluators to write the note from scratch and post-edit each of the generated notes (Mod A, Mod B, Ref). The timings are in M:ss for minutes and seconds taken.

edits the generated notes when there are substantial issues. Doctor B on the other hand is more meticulous and edits the generated notes extensively. This is reflected in both their edit times and their note scoring (see Table 1). We report a detailed view of this disagreement in Figure A1 in the Appendices;

- While it's not feasible to compute correlation between post-editing times and note scores given our sample size, there does seem to be a connection between the two: notes that are scored as containing more omissions and/or incorrect statements take longer to edit. For example, both Dr. B's aggregated scores (Table 1) and edit timings (Table 2) are higher than the other two doctors.
- In one instance, one physician was so frustrated by the quality of a specific generated note that they decided to copy the note they wrote from scratch and paste it instead of trying to edit the generated one. This is why we have missing values in Table 2;
- The first task each physician completed took 36 minutes on average, while subsequent tasks were quicker (23 minutes on average).

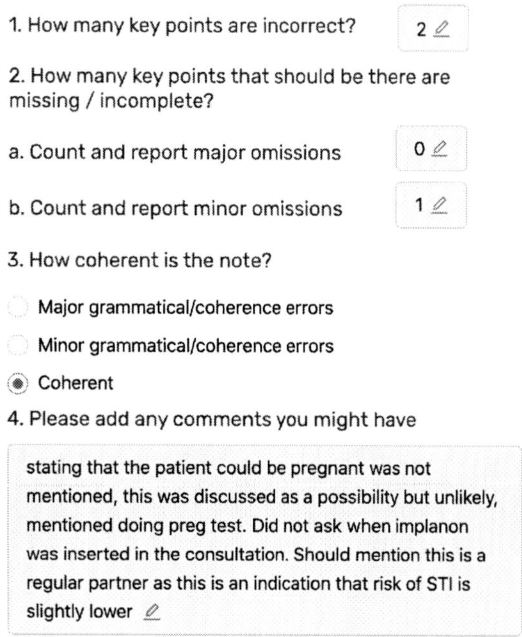

Figure 5: Heartex interface for scoring a generated note.

After watching the recordings and collecting the results, we asked the three evaluators for qualitative feedback regarding the task, the annotation platform, and the generated notes. Here are the key insights we gathered:

- Unlike post-editing, scoring is hard and time-consuming. This is partly due to the interface, which currently doesn't highlight the evaluators' edits on the generated note;
- Familiarity with the interface is key. We shadowed 2 of the 3 physicians through their first few tasks, and that reduced confusion and sped up their work. The physician we did not shadow expressed more difficulty in the evaluation task;
- Our evaluation setup — with physicians asked to listen to a consultation before writing the note — doesn't exactly reproduce the reality of the clinical setting, where they are actually conducting the consultation;
- One physician expressed the worry that even though post-editing a generated note might take less time than writing a note from scratch, it however requires a higher cognitive load. This is because the physician needs to critically read, understand and evaluate the generated note in order to correct it.
- In our experiment, we always ask the evaluators to first write a note from scratch, and then post-edit the generated notes. This specific order may bias our timings. The evaluators may be faster in post-editing after having written the note, or they may be slower if the generated note doesn't follow their style of writing. We plan to address this by shuffling the order of these two tasks.

6 Future work

In this paper, we presented our preliminary evaluation study of consultation note generation with post-editing. Based on the insights from this study, we plan to:

- Extend the evaluation to the entire mock consultation dataset and calculate agreement between the evaluators. It would also be interesting to compute agreement between the scores (Correctness, Completeness) and the time taken to post-edit;
- Evaluate the usefulness of auto-generated notes in a live clinical setting;
- Investigate and compare the cognitive load of post-editing notes with that of writing them.

If the issues described in this paper are addressed, we believe post-editing time can be a metric that is both valuable for evaluating model performance and relevant for use in production systems.

Finally, it is important to mention that while automation of medical note taking might help reduce physician burnout and allow the doctors to spend more time with the patients, there are ethical considerations associated to the use of such a technology. For example, time pressures or unwarranted trust in an automated system could potentially result in doctors not properly reviewing and editing the automated notes. Also, post-editing is a very different cognitive task from writing a note from scratch, and that might put extra strain on doctors' already cognitively demanding workflows. In order to mitigate the above concerns in a production system, user experience design, system evaluation, and clinician on-boarding and training are crucially important.

References

Tod Allman, Stephen Beale, and Richard Denton. 2012. Linguist's assistant: A multi-lingual natural language generator based on linguistic universals, typologies, and primitives. In *INLG 2012 Proceedings of the Seventh International Natural Language Generation Conference*, pages 59–66, Utica, IL. Association for Computational Linguistics.

Brian G Arndt, John W Beasley, Michelle D Watkinson, Jonathan L Temte, Wen-Jan Tuan, Christine A Sinsky, and Valerie J Gilchrist. 2017. Tethered to the ehr: primary care physician workload assessment using ehr event log data and time-motion observations. *The Annals of Family Medicine*, 15(5):419–426.

Wilker Aziz and Lucia Specia. 2012. Pet: a tool for post-editing and assessing machine translation. *LREC*.

Michael Carl, Silke Gutermuth, and Silvia Hansen-Schirra. 2015. Post-editing machine translation. *Psycholinguistic and cognitive inquiries into translation and interpreting*, 115:145.

Ishwar Chander. 1994. Automated Postediting of Documents. In *AAAI-94 Proceedings*, pages 779–784.

Genna R Cohen, Charles P Friedman, Andrew M Ryan, Caroline R Richardson, and Julia Adler-Milstein. 2019. Variation in physicians' electronic health record documentation and potential patient harm from that variation. *Journal of general internal medicine*, 34(11):2355–2367.

Sheila CM De Sousa, Wilker Aziz, and Lucia Specia. 2011. Assessing the post-editing effort for automatic and semi-automatic translations of dvd subtitles. In *Proceedings of the International Conference Recent Advances in Natural Language Processing 2011*, pages 97–103.

Meghan Dowling, Teresa Lynn, Yvette Graham, and John Judge. 2016. English to irish machine translation with automatic post-editing. In *Proceedings of the second Celtic Language Technology Workshop*, Paris, France.

Ayelet Goldstein, Yuval Shahar, Efrat Orenbuch, and Matan J Cohen. 2017. Evaluation of an automated knowledge-based textual summarization system for longitudinal clinical data, in the intensive care domain. *Artificial intelligence in medicine*, 82:20–33.

Yvette Graham, Qingsong Ma, Timothy Baldwin, Qun Liu, Carla Parra Escartín, and Carolina Scarton. 2017. Improving evaluation of document-level machine translation quality estimation. In *Proceedings of the 15th Conference of the European Chapter of the Association for Computational Linguistics: Volume 2, Short Papers*, pages 356–361.

Nazmul Kazi and Indika Kahanda. 2019. Automatically generating psychiatric case notes from digital transcripts of doctor-patient conversations. In *Proceedings of the 2nd Clinical Natural Language Processing Workshop*, pages 140–148.

Maarit Koponen. 2016. Is machine translation post-editing worth the effort? a survey of research into post-editing and effort. *The Journal of Specialised Translation*, 25:131–148.

Kundan Krishna, Sopan Khosla, Jeffrey P Bigham, and Zachary C Lipton. 2020. Generating soap notes from doctor-patient conversations. *arXiv preprint arXiv:2005.01795*.

Mike Lewis, Yinhan Liu, Naman Goyal, Marjan Ghazvininejad, Abdelrahman Mohamed, Omer Levy, Veselin Stoyanov, and Luke Zettlemoyer. 2020. BART: Denoising sequence-to-sequence pre-training for natural language generation, translation, and comprehension. In *Proceedings of the 58th Annual Meeting of the Association for Computational Linguistics*, pages 7871–7880, Online. Association for Computational Linguistics.

Medscape. 2018. Medscape national physician burnout depression report 2018.

Sabine Molenaar, Lientje Maas, Verónica Burriel, Fabiano Dalpiaz, and Sjaak Brinkkemper. 2020. Medical dialogue summarization for automated reporting in healthcare. In *International Conference on Advanced Information Systems Engineering*, pages 76–88. Springer.

Somayajulu Sripada, Ehud Reiter, and Lezan Hawizy. 2005. Evaluation of an nlg system using post-edit data: Lessons learnt. In *Proceedings of the Tenth European Workshop on Natural Language Generation (ENLG-05)*.

Maxim Tkachenko, Mikhail Malyuk, and Nikolai Liubimov. 2020. Heartex: Data labeling platform for machine learning.

A Appendices

Task & Source		incorrect Dr A	Dr B	Dr C	major omissions Dr A	Dr B	Dr C	minor omissions Dr A	Dr B	Dr C	coherence Dr A	Dr B	Dr C
	ref	2	2	1	1	0	1	0	4	1	2	2	2
1	model A	1	2	1	0	3	4	2	6	0	2	1	2
	model B	0	1	1	2	4	4	0	6	1	2	1	1
	ref	0	2	3	0	1	0	0	3	0	2	2	1
2	model A	1	2	1	0	3	2	0	5	0	2	1	1
	model B	2	1	1	0	3	2	1	5	0	2	2	1
	ref	0	2	1	0	1	2	1	2	1	2	2	2
3	model A	3	3	2	2	5	4	1	3	0	2	1	0
	model B	3	5	0	3	3	4	0	4	2	1	2	2

Table A1: Scores table.

Evaluator 2	Evaluator 3
You have been having some problems with your left ear for 3 weeks Your hearing is muffled on the left side You noticed that your face has been feeling a bit numb on the left side of your face, around the ear and the jawline You have no weakness or numbness in the rest of the body. You have not had any difficulty speaking or swallowing. You have noticed no problems with your vision. The numbness is present on the left side of your face. ~~You have used Cochran spray to clean your ears.~~ ~~You do not have any other illnesses.~~ No recent fever You have been told you had polyps in your nose in the past and occasionally use a prescribe nasal spray to relieve symptoms. You have occasional heart burn for which you take over the counter medication. You have had labyrinthitis in the past You are a jockey You get a ringing in your left ear and feel a bit dizzy which has been affecting your work You live alone with your partner and have no pets at home. Your brother has neurofibromatosis You are allergic to latex	You have been having some problems with your left ear for the last few days. You noticed that your face has been feeling a bit numb. You have no weakness or numbness in the rest of the body. You have not had any difficulty speaking or swallowing. ~~You have noticed no problems with your vision.~~ The numbness is present on the left side of your face. You have used Cochran spray to clean your ears. You do not have any other illnesses. You have been told you had polyps in your nose and labyrinthitis in the past and occasionally get some kind of funny feeling. You are a jockey but sometimes you get a ringing and feel a bit dizzy. Currently this has limited your time in your job. You live alone and have no pets at home.

Figure A1: Disagreement in editing and scoring a generated note. **Red** marks incorrect statements, orange major omissions, and **blue** minor omissions.

The Great Misalignment Problem in Human Evaluation of NLP Methods

Mika Hämäläinen
University of Helsinki and Rootroo Ltd
mika.hamalainen@helsinki.fi

Khalid Alnajjar
University of Helsinki and Rootroo Ltd
khalid.alnajjar@helsinki.fi

Abstract

We outline the Great Misalignment Problem in natural language processing research, this means simply that the problem definition is not in line with the method proposed and the human evaluation is not in line with the definition nor the method. We study this misalignment problem by surveying 10 randomly sampled papers published in ACL 2020 that report results with human evaluation. Our results show that only one paper was fully in line in terms of problem definition, method and evaluation. Only two papers presented a human evaluation that was in line with what was modeled in the method. These results highlight that the Great Misalignment Problem is a major one and it affects the validity and reproducibility of results obtained by a human evaluation.

1 Introduction

There has been a lot of academic discussion recently about different evaluation methods used and their validity (Novikova et al., 2017; Reiter, 2018; Howcroft et al., 2020; van der Lee et al., 2019). Reproducibility is an important problem in our field of science and it is not currently archived in human evaluation, as some researches have found that trying to reproduce a human evaluation gives different results (Hämäläinen et al., 2020; Mieskes et al., 2019).

However important reproducibility is, we have identified an even more severe problem in human evaluation. We call this problem *the Great Misalignment Problem* that is a mismatch between a problem statement, a proposed model and a proposed evaluation method.

It is typical in the field of NLP to work with ill-defined problems. For instance, many machine translation papers (Roest et al., 2020; Chen et al., 2020; Talman et al., 2019) do not extensively define what they mean by translation, a topic that has multiple definitions in translation studies (Hermans, 1985; Reiss, 1989; Lederer, 2003), but merely take it for granted and focus on proposing systems that achieve high scores in an automatic evaluation metric such as BLEU (Papineni et al., 2002).

For as long as you work with a problem the solution of which you can objectively measure by automated metrics, the role of a problem definition is not that important. The situation changes, however, when your main evaluation method is a subjective human evaluation. The reason for this is simple: only when you have defined the problem clearly, can you derive the questions and methods for a human evaluation (c.f. Alnajjar and Hämäläinen 2018; Jordanous 2012). When one does not have a clear understanding of the problem one seeks to solve, the evaluation is usually not representative of the problem, thus they are misaligned.

The Great Misalignment Problem is not just about the misalignment between the problem definition and the evaluation, but also the proposed solution, let it be rule-based, algorithmic or a machine learning model. We can often see that the solution itself has very little to do with the human evaluation methods used.

In this paper, we study the Great Misalignment Problem (alignment of a problem definition, method and human evaluation) by surveying papers published in ACL 2020 that use human evaluation. We focus on ACL since it is supposed to be the most prestigious conference in the field. For courtesy reasons, we anonymize the papers surveyed, except Paper 3 (Mohankumar et al., 2020) which was the only paper that did not exhibit the Great Misalignment Problem. We do not want single anyone out with our critique as that is not the goal of our paper.

Proceedings of the Workshop on Human Evaluation of NLP Systems (HumEval), pages 69–74
Online, April 19, 2021. ©2021 Association for Computational Linguistics

	Definition	Method in line with the definition	Evaluation in line with the definition	Evaluation in line with the method	Evaluation in line with the topic
Paper 1	Theoretical	No	No	No	No
Paper 2	Absent	No	No	**Yes**	**Yes**
Paper 3	ML	**Yes**	**Yes**	**Yes**	**Yes**
Paper 4	Absent	No	No	No	No
Paper 5	Absent	No	No	No	**Yes**
Paper 6	Absent	No	No	No	No
Paper 7	Math	**Yes**	No	No	No
Paper 8	Theoretical	**Yes**	No	No	**Yes**
Paper 9	Absent	No	No	No	No
Paper 10	Absent	No	No	No	No

Table 1: The Great Misalignment Problem in the papers surveyed.

2 Surveying the Great Misalignment Problem

We filter all papers that have the words "human" and "evaluat*" or "judge*" in their abstract. This way, we can find papers mentioning human evaluation, human evaluators and so on. We include all papers published in the ACL 2020[1] (excluding workshops) in the search. We sort these papers (79 in total) at random and take the first 10 papers that actually have used human evaluation, as some of the papers mentioned human and evaluation, but did not conduct a human evaluation. We did not consider papers that suggested automated evaluation metrics based on correlation with human evaluation as their main contribution. Human evaluation is most common in natural language generation as 8 out of 10 papers deal with NLG.

The papers, we considered for evaluation in terms of human evaluation, presented automatic evaluation metrics in addition to human evaluation. For all the 10 papers, we looked at the following questions:

- How is the problem defined and narrowed down?
- Is the proposed method in line with the definition?
- Is the evaluation in line with the definition?
- Is the evaluation in line with what was modeled by the method?
- Is the evaluation in line with the overall topic of the paper?

As an example, if a paper proposes a model for poem generation and does not define what is meant by poem generation, we consider the definition to be absent. A simple statement of the topic is not enough as there are nuances to poem generation such as rhyme, meter, metaphors, symbolism, personification and so on. If a paper presents a more narrowed-down definition and this definition is followed in the method proposed, we consider the two to be in line.

Evaluation is in line with the definition, if the evaluation questions reflect the different aspects that were defined important in the problem definition. For the evaluation to be in line with the model, it should evaluate what the model was designed to do. If for example, a poem generator model takes meter and rhyme into account, but it is evaluated based on fluency and poeticness, the method and the evaluation are not in line. For them to be in line, meter and rhyme should have been evaluated. The evaluation can be in line with the overall topic of the paper: for example, evaluating poeticness is in line with poem generation.

The results of our survey can be seen in Table 1. As we can see, almost all papers had the Great Misalignment Problem except for one paper, Paper 3. Unlike the rest of the papers surveyed, this particular paper did not try to solve an NLP problem per se, but rather focused on studying the attention models used in LSTM neural networks. Therefore its problem definition, method and human evaluation focused on the attention models rather than any NLP problems.

Paper 7 presented a very explicit mathematical statement for the problem they were to solve in the paper. Although, this is very specific to the implementation the authors had, it is still better than a completely absent definition as seen in the majority of papers that took an abstract level topic

[1] https://www.aclweb.org/anthology/events/acl-2020/

# of Samples	N
Less than 20	1
100-500	5
500-1000	2
1000-1500	2

Table 2: Number of samples produced by the method that were evaluated.

Judges per sample	N
Not Given	2
1-3	2
4-5	3
6-10	2
Above 10	1

Table 3: Number of human evaluators used per sample produced by the method.

for granted and solved it with some method.

Paper 1 and Paper 8 used an existing theory to narrow down the topic. Paper 8 did this in a good way, as their implementation followed exactly the notions defined by the theory they used. However, Paper 1 merely mentioned a theory for their definition, completely ignoring it in the implementation of the method and in the evaluation.

Papers 2, 4-6 and 9-10 do not provide any definition for the problem they are trying to solve, but rather take the definition for granted. Therefore their evaluation cannot be in line with the definition either, as no definition was provided, but in some cases the evaluation was at least in line with the overall topic of the paper, although this was not always the case.

Only Paper 3 had their evaluation in line with the definition and only Paper 3 and Paper 2 had their evaluation in line with what was modeled in the method. This is very concerning, as it highlights how little the evaluation questions used had to do with what was actually done in the papers. On a more positive note, Papers 2, 3, 5 and 8 at least have their evaluation in line with the topic of the paper, however this means that are 6 papers the evaluation of which is not in line with the topic.

Table 2 show how many samples (different outputs by a system) were evaluated. We can see that there is a lot of variety in this respect in the papers surveyed, but half of the papers have evaluated from 100 to 500 samples. The situation gets even more complicated when we look at the results reported in Table 3. Here, we can see that there is a lot of variety in how many human evaluators evaluated each sample. Two of the papers did not report this at all.

3 Discussion

A direct implication of the Great Misalignment Problem is that the results of any human evaluation cannot be reproducible as they are measuring something else than what was modeled in the proposed solution. Therefore, any results obtained by the human evaluation can only be due to some other variable such as the data used in training, a bias in the often too small evaluation sample or a bias in the often too few evaluators.

Furthermore, many factors affect the quality of the human evaluation. For instance, forcing the evaluators to provide answers to questions that they do not know how to answer without giving them the possibility to skip such questions could introduce noise in the evaluation data. On the contrary, some unfaithful evaluators (scammers) might abuse such an opportunity to finish the survey effortlessly and in a short time by submitting valid answers, i.e. "I do not know".

Some surveying platforms support defining criteria to discard scammers, such as test questions or a minimum response time. Test questions are greatly useful to enhance the quality of answers. However, when used for evaluating subjective tasks they would add a bias as evaluators must share the same opinions of the authors or, else, they will be rejected from continuing the survey. The minimum response time is there to eliminate scammers who answer promptly without even reading the questions.

Other similar criteria exist, e.g., language and geographical restrictions that might aid in finding competent evaluators, the ordering of samples when presented side by side, and the bias of providing a single answer consistently to different questions (Veale and Alnajjar, 2015). This just to show that many factors regarding the human evaluation setup contribute massively to the quality of the evaluation. There is no one fixed or correct way to conduct all human evaluations, but researchers in the field should consider such biases and aim towards reducing them in addition to revealing the full details of the evaluation setup and the intuition behind it to the reader to allow reproducibility of the scientific work. Unfortunately, none of the papers surveyed described the human evaluation conducted in a clear fashion, where different biases or threats to the validity of the results would have been made clear.

Our field is very often focused on gaining the

state of the art performance from our models. However, when the human evaluation metrics used have little to nothing to do with the problem or the method, knowing what truly is the state of the art becomes less clear. Each system, regardless of their final evaluation score, will have a lot of advantages and disadvantages that do not become evident if the problem they are used to solve is ill-defined. This leads to the problem that evaluation scores are the only way of showcasing the superiority of your system, no matter how unrelated the evaluation scores were to the problem or to your method.

The problem that comes from not evaluating what you have modeled in your method is that you cannot say whether what you modeled actually works as intended. This is especially problematic in the case of NLG, which represents a majority of papers surveyed. Nowadays generating good sounding text is no longer an issue as very generic models such as GPT-2 (Radford et al., 2019) can be used to generate many different kinds of text. This leads to the problem that if no clear definition is provided, any method that spits out text will satisfy the requirements, and if the evaluation does not capture anything about how the method was implemented, then it is impossible to tell whether your system actually improved anything but the very surface of the text.

In our own experiments (Hämäläinen and Alnajjar, 2019a) with human evaluation, we have found that questions that do not measure what has been modeled make it very difficult to say what should be improved in the system and how, although such an evaluation makes the end results look impressive. As Gervás (2017) puts it, any feature not modeled in a generative system that happens to be in the output can hardly be a merit of the system, but is in the result due to mere serendipity. To complicate the things, Veale (2016) points out that people are willing to read more content into the output of a system than what the system had planned.

To solve these problems, we decided to follow an approach where we defined exactly what we need our system to be able to produce in its output (humorous headlines). In our first paper (Alnajjar and Hämäläinen, 2018), we believed we had solved the problem, only to realize in our follow-up paper (Hämäläinen and Alnajjar, 2019c) that the human evaluation results contradicted our own impression of the output produced by the different systems. As it turns out, the evaluation questions were too abstract and left enough room for people to read more into the output.

While our latest trial in solving the issue has been using concrete evaluation questions (Hämäläinen and Alnajjar, 2019b) that measure exactly what the system was designed to do in order to reduce subjectivity, such an evaluation practice cannot be embraced if there is no alignment between the definition, solution and evaluation. No matter how concrete the evaluation questions are or how sound the evaluation method is in terms of forming a good quantitative questionnaire, an evaluation that neither evaluates the method nor the problem can hardly be meaningful.

All in all, we have had good experiences when conducting human evaluation in person by printing out questionnaires and presenting them to people. It is not at all difficult to find test subjects who are willing to participate. This way, one can avoid the problem of paid online questionnaires where the motives and skills of the human evaluators is difficult to assess. Furthermore, conducting evaluation this way, opens the evaluation up for criticism and it is easy to get direct feedback from the participants on the test design and its difficulty.

4 Conclusions

In this paper, we have described a fundamental issue in human evaluation in the field of NLP. Our initial survey results show that the issue can be found extensively in the papers published in our field. The Great Misalignment Problem makes it impossible to critically assess the advancements in the field, as usually problems papers are trying to solve, are not defined well enough to be thoroughly evaluated by human judges. In addition, if the method proposed does not align well with the problem nor the evaluation, any human evaluation results can hardly be a merit of the method.

There are several uncontrolled variables involved and based on our survey results, human evaluation is not conducted in the same rigorous fashion as in other fields dealing with human questionnaires such as in social sciences (c.f. Babbie 2015) or fields dealing with evaluation of computer systems such as design science (c.f. Hevner et al. 2004). There is a long way for our field to go from here in order to establish more sound and reproducible human evaluation practices.

Narrowing the problem definition down from an abstract definition such as "poem generation" or "diverse dialog generation" not only helps in understanding the problem from the point of view evaluation, but also makes it possible to ask more meaningful questions while proposing a solution. Such an ideology can be useful also in domains where evaluation is conducted automatically in order to critically assess the validity of the approach and the evaluation method used.

The results presented in this paper are based on only 10 papers published in ACL 2020. The sample seems representative to the general feel of the state of human evaluation in the field, but it is important in the future to survey a larger sample of papers to better understand the problem. While conducting our survey, we also paid attention to other issues in human evaluation such as the fact that the evaluation methods are not usually adequately described in terms of presentation of the evaluation questions (many papers did not report the questions at all), selection of human judges, task instructions and so on. There were huge differences also in the number of human judges from only 3 to 30 judges, and also in the number of samples evaluated.

Our field does not have an established methodology for human evaluation, but at the current stage, the validity of many human evaluation methods is questionable. This is problematic as our field clearly has problems that rely on human evaluation. We do not believe that removing human evaluation altogether in favor of objective evaluation methods is the optimal solution either, as automatic evaluation metrics come with their own problems and biases. In order to reach to better human evaluation practices, a study of human evaluation itself is needed. From our experiences with human evaluation, we can say that it is certainly not a straight forward problem due to a variety of different reasons, the largest of them being subjective interpretation and limited understanding the human evaluators have of the evaluation task, questions and the actual output that is to be evaluated.

References

Khalid Alnajjar and Mika Hämäläinen. 2018. A master-apprentice approach to automatic creation of culturally satirical movie titles. In *Proceedings of the 11th International Conference on Natural Language Generation*, pages 274–283.

Earl R Babbie. 2015. *The basics of social research*. Nelson Education.

Kehai Chen, Rui Wang, Masao Utiyama, and Eiichiro Sumita. 2020. Content word aware neural machine translation. In *Proceedings of the 58th Annual Meeting of the Association for Computational Linguistics*, pages 358–364, Online. Association for Computational Linguistics.

Pablo Gervás. 2017. Template-free construction of rhyming poems with thematic cohesion. In *Proceedings of the Workshop on Computational Creativity in Natural Language Generation (CC-NLG 2017)*, pages 21–28, Santiago de Compostela, Spain. Association for Computational Linguistics.

Mika Hämäläinen and Khalid Alnajjar. 2019a. Generating modern poetry automatically in Finnish. In *Proceedings of the 2019 Conference on Empirical Methods in Natural Language Processing and the 9th International Joint Conference on Natural Language Processing (EMNLP-IJCNLP)*, pages 5999–6004, Hong Kong, China. Association for Computational Linguistics.

Mika Hämäläinen and Khalid Alnajjar. 2019b. Let's face it. finnish poetry generation with aesthetics and framing. In *Proceedings of the 12th International Conference on Natural Language Generation*, pages 290–300.

Mika Hämäläinen and Khalid Alnajjar. 2019c. Modelling the socialization of creative agents in a master-apprentice setting: The case of movie title puns. In *Proceedings of the 10th International Conference on Computational Creativity*, pages 266–273, Portugal. Association for Computational Creativity. International Conference on Computational Creativity ; Conference date: 17-06-2019 Through 21-06-2019.

Mika Hämäläinen, Niko Partanen, Khalid Alnajjar, Jack Rueter, and Thierry Poibeau. 2020. Automatic dialect adaptation in finnish and its effect on perceived creativity. In *11th International Conference on Computational Creativity (ICCC'20)*. Association for Computational Creativity.

Theo Hermans. 1985. *The manipulation of literature (routledge revivals): Studies in Literary Translation*. Routledge.

Alan R Hevner, Salvatore T March, Jinsoo Park, and Sudha Ram. 2004. Design science in information systems research. *MIS quarterly*, pages 75–105.

David M. Howcroft, Anya Belz, Miruna-Adriana Clinciu, Dimitra Gkatzia, Sadid A. Hasan, Saad Mahamood, Simon Mille, Emiel van Miltenburg, Sashank Santhanam, and Verena Rieser. 2020. Twenty years of confusion in human evaluation: NLG needs evaluation sheets and standardised definitions. In *Proceedings of the 13th International Conference on Natural Language Generation*, pages 169–182, Dublin, Ireland. Association for Computational Linguistics.

Anna Jordanous. 2012. A standardised procedure for evaluating creative systems: Computational creativity evaluation based on what it is to be creative. *Cognitive Computation*, 4(3):246–279.

Marianne Lederer. 2003. *Translation: The interpretive model*. Routledge.

Chris van der Lee, Albert Gatt, Emiel van Miltenburg, Sander Wubben, and Emiel Krahmer. 2019. Best practices for the human evaluation of automatically generated text. In *Proceedings of the 12th International Conference on Natural Language Generation*, pages 355–368, Tokyo, Japan. Association for Computational Linguistics.

Margot Mieskes, Karën Fort, Aurélie Névéol, Cyril Grouin, and Kevin B Cohen. 2019. Nlp community perspectives on replicability. In *Recent Advances in Natural Language Processing*.

Akash Kumar Mohankumar, Preksha Nema, Sharan Narasimhan, Mitesh M. Khapra, Balaji Vasan Srinivasan, and Balaraman Ravindran. 2020. Towards transparent and explainable attention models. In *Proceedings of the 58th Annual Meeting of the Association for Computational Linguistics*, pages 4206–4216, Online. Association for Computational Linguistics.

Jekaterina Novikova, Ondrej Dusek, Amanda Cercas Curry, and Verena Rieser. 2017. Why we need new evaluation metrics for nlg. In *2017 Conference on Empirical Methods in Natural Language Processing*, pages 2231–2242. Association for Computational Linguistics.

Kishore Papineni, Salim Roukos, Todd Ward, and Wei-Jing Zhu. 2002. Bleu: a method for automatic evaluation of machine translation. In *Proceedings of the 40th annual meeting of the Association for Computational Linguistics*, pages 311–318.

Alec Radford, Jeffrey Wu, Rewon Child, David Luan, Dario Amodei, and Ilya Sutskever. 2019. Language models are unsupervised multitask learners. *OpenAI blog*, 1(8):9.

Katharina Reiss. 1989. Text types, translation types and translation assessment. *Readings in translation theory*, 19771989.

Ehud Reiter. 2018. A structured review of the validity of BLEU. *Computational Linguistics*, 44(3):393–401.

Christian Roest, Lukas Edman, Gosse Minnema, Kevin Kelly, Jennifer Spenader, and Antonio Toral. 2020. Machine translation for English–Inuktitut with segmentation, data acquisition and pre-training. In *Proceedings of the Fifth Conference on Machine Translation*, pages 274–281, Online. Association for Computational Linguistics.

Aarne Talman, Umut Sulubacak, Raúl Vázquez, Yves Scherrer, Sami Virpioja, Alessandro Raganato, Arvi Hurskainen, and Jörg Tiedemann. 2019. The university of Helsinki submissions to the WMT19 news translation task. In *Proceedings of the Fourth Conference on Machine Translation (Volume 2: Shared Task Papers, Day 1)*, pages 412–423, Florence, Italy. Association for Computational Linguistics.

Tony Veale. 2016. *3. The shape of tweets to come: Automating language play in social networks*, pages 73–92. De Gruyter Mouton.

Tony Veale and Khalid Alnajjar. 2015. Unweaving the lexical rainbow: Grounding linguistic creativity in perceptual semantics. In *Proceedings of the Sixth International Conference on Computational Creativity*, pages 63 – 70, United States. Brigham Young University.

A View From The Crowd: Evaluation Challenges for Time-Offset Interaction Applications

Alberto M. Chierici and **Nizar Habash**
Computational Approaches to Modeling Language (CAMeL) Lab
New York University Abu Dhabi, UAE
{alberto.chierici, nizar.habash}@nyu.edu

Abstract

Dialogue systems like chatbots, and tasks like question-answering (QA) have gained traction in recent years; yet evaluating such systems remains difficult. Reasons include the great variety in contexts and use cases for these systems as well as the high cost of human evaluation. In this paper, we focus on a specific type of dialogue systems: Time-Offset Interaction Applications (TOIAs) are intelligent, conversational software that simulates face-to-face conversations between humans and pre-recorded human avatars. Under the constraint that a TOIA is a single output system interacting with users with different expectations, we identify two challenges: first, how do we define a 'good' answer? and second, what's an appropriate metric to use? We explore both challenges through the creation of a novel dataset that identifies multiple good answers to specific TOIA questions through the help of Amazon Mechanical Turk workers. This 'view from the crowd' allows us to study the variations of how TOIA interrogators perceive its answers. Our contributions include the annotated dataset that we make publicly available and the proposal of Success Rate @k as an evaluation metric that is more appropriate than the traditional QA's and information retrieval's metrics.

Interrogator: Hi

Avatar: Hey!

Interrogator: What's your name

Avatar: My name is Margarita.

Interrogator: Nice to meet you

Avatar: Nice to see you, too!

Interrogator: How old are you?

Avatar: I am 22.

Interrogator: Do you study or work?

Avatar: I just graduated from New York University Abu Dhabi!

Interrogator: Cool, and what do you plan to do next?

Avatar: I will be working in Tax, Transfer Pricing, at PwC starting August 2019!

Interrogator: How long ave you been in Abu Dhabi?

Avatar: So I came here four years ago, but because of all the traveling probably two years in total.

Interrogator: Wow where have you been?

Avatar: I've been to Buenos Aires and New York for a semester each and I've done to January terms in Shanghai and Paris.

Interrogator: Which one did you prefer

Avatar: Music completes this artistic and techie side of me because I studied composition and sound engineering, but economics fulfilled my social and analytical side, because I wanted to learn about how to make an impact in the world and I love math.

Interrogator: Did you prefer New York or Buenos Aires?

Avatar: My favorite place ever is New York. I hope to get back there at some point. I just love how vibrant the city is and there's always something to do and people are just the right amount of polite and minding their own business.

Figure 1: Initial ten turns of a casual dialogue between an interrogator and a TOIA avatar using our best performing retrieval model.

1 Introduction

Time-Offset Interaction Applications (TOIAs) (Artstein et al., 2015) are a sort of chatbot applications that lie between Question Answering (QA) and Information Retrieval (IR). They differ from QA in that a TOIA's task is **not** about demonstrating comprehension of a text span (Rajpurkar et al., 2016; Reddy et al., 2019) but selecting a single (one-shot) appropriate answer from a restricted set of answers, a problem also known as Answer Retrieval (AR) or retrieval-based dialogue (Boussaha et al., 2019).

Ideal TOIA interactions are expected to mirror a dialogue with a real person, including all the possible directions it may take — which naturally has great ramification on evaluation: when two people meet and engage in casual conversation, questions may range over different topics and depending on the answer to a specific question, different conversational question-answer threads may unravel. Also, not unexpected, different answers to a specific question can be acceptable and not cause a change in the overall conversational flow. So, how can we answer the question *what is a 'good' (i.e., 'right', 'correct' or 'relevant') answer?*

We explore this question using a publicly available dataset that was manually annotated by its avatar maker – the Margarita Dialogue Corpus (MDC) (Chierici et al., 2020). The best performing

Proceedings of the Workshop on Human Evaluation of NLP Systems (HumEval), pages 75–85
Online, April 19, 2021. ©2021 Association for Computational Linguistics

IR model we could produce had a low Recall@1 – 24% on the development (dev) set and just below 10% on the test set. When trying to interact with this avatar, one would expect to get a wrong answer about 1/4th of the times or less. However, when chatting with the avatar using the best performing model (Figure 1), we could see that the system wasn't so bad in entertaining and holding a conversation. Hence we asked a 'crowd' of human annotators to give their opinion, and we learned that the task to define the correct answers isn't straightforward, primarily due to misaligned expectations about answer relevance. We explore a number of metrics and single out Success Rate @k (SR@k) as the most pertinent metric for optimizing TOIAs. Our contributions include the annotated dataset that we make publicly available, and the introduction of SR@k as the best metric for evaluating TOAIs.

We present previous work on TOIAs and related datasets in Section 2. Sections 3, 4, and 5 introduce the corpus, retrieval models, and annotation process we used, respectively. We present our results and analysis in Section 6, and discuss further in Section 7. In Section 8, we share how to apply this work's conclusions to develop better avatars.

2 Related Work

We present a number of recent TOIAs, and data sets relevant for their study and development. While most of the related work focuses on large corpora, working with small datasets and addressing evaluation issues of TOIAs are interesting, practical problems both for the IR (what is 'relevant'?) and the NLP communities (transfer learning and low resources corpora).

2.1 Recent TOIAs

TOIAs have applications in a number of practical scenarios. For example, they are used for keeping historical memories (Traum et al., 2015b), job interview practice for young adults with developmental disabilities,[1] and building digital humans across different industries.[2,3] The most recent TOIAs involve significant production costs, they are mainly used as museum attractions or training prototypes for the army, and they require recording about 2,000 answers for building an avatar (Nishiyama et al., 2016; Jones, 2005). While these works focus more on the overall system architecture, components and the avatar creation methodologies, their evaluation has seldom been addressed. Furthermore, research into time-offset interactions needs to generalize and streamline the avatar development process. A first attempt made by Abu Ali et al. (2018) goes towards this direction and includes the possibility to chat with the avatars in different languages. We develop our TOIA using their open-sourced architecture. Building and democratizing access to this technology is an interesting problem, and defining the right evaluation setup is a critical step forward.

2.2 The Evaluation Problem

Traum et al. (2015a) report that their TOIA gives relevant direct answers to 60-66% of user utterances, and that seems to be good enough from "informal impressions from current testing at a museum." However, we don't have to date a rigorous study about how multiple users of TOIAs evaluate such interactions. Regarding the evaluation task in adjacent fields such as IR and QA, this is often criticized and remains an open problem (Liu et al., 2016). IR systems focus on the relevance of a set of documents retrieved and 'relevance' itself is a notion not exempt from criticism (Manning et al., 2008). The evaluation metrics mostly reported are the Mean Average Precision (MAP) and the Mean Reciprocal Rank (MRR). Applying these metrics to question-answer (q-a) retrieval makes it difficult to compare systems. In the context of TOIAs, we only care about the single retrieved answer as the most relevant. Moreover, MAP and MRR are influenced by how many relevant q-a pairs exist or are retrieved by the system (more on this in Section 7) so it's difficult to compare results across different datasets or annotation methodologies of the same dataset. Other metrics like Recall@k also depend on the number of relevant q-a pairs. For example Lowe et al. (2015) report Recall@k by picking the right answer and 10 randomly sampled distractors, rather than computing a relevance score between a question and all the possible answers available in the knowledge base. This way Recall@10 would always give 100%, making it difficult to judge how good the system would be from a user perspective in a practical implementation.

QA system evaluation is not necessarily relevant for TOIAs as the QA task is more about reading comprehension than the ability to retrieve an answer from a knowledge base and engage in a free-

[1] `https://ict.usc.edu/prototypes/vita/`
[2] `www.soulmachines.com`
[3] `www.storyfile.com`

form dialogue format. Moreover, such systems often use text generation models which we didn't use in our TOIA. Text generation methodologies are usually evaluated with n-gram based metrics (Merdivan et al., 2020) such as BLEU (Papineni et al., 2002), ROUGE (Lin, 2004) and METEOR (Banerjee and Lavie, 2005), which are often criticized for their poor alignment with human judgement (Chen et al., 2019). Across all these works as well as the datasets presented for study free-form conversations, there is a gap in addressing the question of what is a 'good' answer. This is an important question to address not only for evaluating the relevant NLP tasks, but also for defining an annotation methodology.

2.3 Relevant Dialogue Data

Conversational questions have challenging phenomena not present in existing reading comprehension datasets. Recent datasets that focus on free-form human dialogues and include human annotations are CoQA (Reddy et al., 2019) and HUMOD (Merdivan et al., 2020). CoQA is a large scale reading comprehension dataset that improves a dataset like SQuAD (Rajpurkar et al., 2016) by including questions that depend on conversation history and by ensuring the naturalness of answers in a conversation. HUMOD instead takes inspiration from the Cornell's movie dialogue corpus (Danescu-Niculescu-Mizil and Lee, 2011) by adding human annotations to it. The Douban Conversation Corpus (Wu et al., 2016) contains dialogues between people sampled from Douban, a popular social network in China. The dataset is public and open domain — people chat about movies, books, music, etc. These datasets are both large scale and address different tasks, whereas TOIAs usually involve much smaller datasets. A system like Traum et al. (2015b)'s has a Knowledge Base (KB) of about 2,000 answers. We used the Margarita Dialogue Corpus (MDC) made available by Chierici et al. (2020), which has a KB of 431 answers, as well as a set of complete annotated dialogues.

2.4 Deep Retrieval-Based Dialogue Systems

State-of-the-art results have been achieved very recently on Answer-Retrieval tasks using deep learning architectures (Wu et al., 2016; Humeau et al., 2019; Roller et al., 2020). We used more straightforward techniques for this work as we want to focus on human evaluation rather than AR techniques. Moreover, the data size for the TOIA we use – and for TOIAs in general – is too small for deep learning. We manage to overcome this limitation for a sentence similarity model (more on this in the next section) and plan to leverage transfer learning in future work.

3 The Margarita Dialogue Corpus

Chierici et al. (2020) recorded twenty dialogues with twenty different interrogators who were each instructed to engage in a 15-minute conversation with a TOIA's avatar maker. They then used ten randomly picked dialogues to define the training set (in the original data, these dialogues are labeled as 'train' but here we call them 'development' or 'dev' set as we use them as such). They used these dialogues as the inspiration for defining the KB of q-a pairs the avatar maker recorded in the TOIA. The MDC comprises conversations 'on-topic' and 'wild': half of the conversations are about the university attended by the avatar maker and half did not have a set topic – the interrogator was instructed to get to know the avatar maker as one would do when meeting a person for the first time. For the original dialogues and KB statistics, we point to the original MDC paper tables. Here we limit ourselves to mention a few highlights. The KB is not in dialogue format. There are 431 unique answers and 758 unique questions. The answers in the KB correspond to the videos the avatar maker recorded for powering the TOIA. Some questions have more than one possible answer, and some answers have more than one possible question. In total, the MDC KB comprises 892 self-contained q-a pairs. In addition to the KB, the MDC includes dev and test dialogues comprising 340 and 319 q-a pairs, respectively. Each dialogue has 33 turns on average.

Figure 2 shows the distribution of frequent tri-gram prefixes for the MDC's KB questions and answers, and for the dialogues dev set. Because of the free-form nature of questions, we have a richer variety of questions in the dialogues than the KB. While nearly half of the KB questions are dominated by 'what' questions, the dev questions are distributed across multiple question types. Several sectors indicated by prefixes *I, that, so,* and *it* are frequent in the dev set but are completely absent in the KB. This indicates that dialogues are highly conversational whereas the KB is not, and while a large portion of questions in the dev set are *do, I,* and *what* type of questions, an equally large number are made of different types of questions.

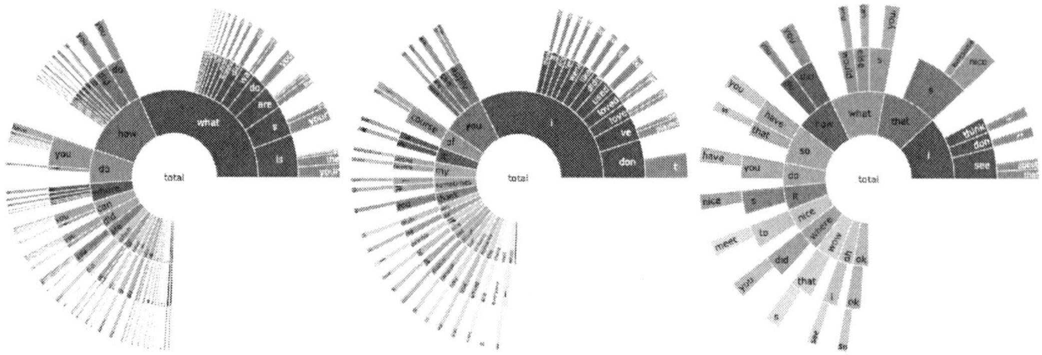

(a) KB Questions (b) KB Answers (c) Dev dialogues set questions

Figure 2: Distribution of trigram prefixes of questions and answers in the Margarita Dialogue Corpus' KB (a, b), and questions in the MDC's dialogue sets (c).

4 Retrieval Models

We used five models for retrieving answers for the questions in the MDC dialogue dataset, and for shortlisting the top candidate responses for the 'crowd' annotation task.

(1) TF-IDF q-Q: Let q be a query from a user (in our case, a question in the MDC dialogue dataset), and Q a question annotated in the MDC KB. We vectorized q and Q using a TF-IDF vectorizer trained on the KB, and computed the shortest distance between q and Q with cosine similarity. We used the sci-kit learn Python library for the TF-IDF vectorizer (Pedregosa et al., 2011).

(2) Okapi BM25 q-Q: Okapi BM25 (Trotman et al., 2014) is a bag-of-words retrieval function that ranks a set of documents based on the query terms appearing in each document. We used the Rank-BM25 implementation in Python.[4] Since BM25 was the worst performing approach, we do not report on it further due to limited space.

(3) BERT q-Q: BERT is a large deep learning model architecture, and one of 2018's breakthroughs in NLP (Devlin et al., 2018). We computed the sentence embedding for each q and Q by taking the mean of BERT pre-trained layers. The cosine similarity between embeddings gives us the ranking function for computing how close a query in the dialogues is to a question in the KB.

(4 and 5) Fine-tuned BERT q-A: We fine-tuned BERT on answer selection as a classification task. Let A be an answer in the KB. For every Q-A pairs in the KB, we labeled them as 1's to indicate a relevant match. We then sampled a number of irrelevant (or 'wrong') matches for every question, and labeled them as 0's. We tried different sampling ratios, namely drawing one wrong match for every correct one (1:1), ten wrong ones (1:10), a hundred (1:100) and using all the available utterances (1:All). To increase the data size further and better generalize for questions phrased differently, we augmented the train data by sampling synthetic questions using the methodology proposed by Wei and Zou (2019) and their Python implementation.[5] We fine-tuned BERT for 3 more epochs (we chose a few epochs as advised by Dodge et al. (2020)) using Wolf et al. (2019)'s Transformers library. We only report on **BERT q-A 1:100** and **BERT q-A 1:All** as they were the best performing.

5 Crowd Annotations

We developed a web interface (Figure 3) for collecting the annotations from the 'crowd' using the crowdsourcing platform Amazon Mechanical Turk (AMT). Full anonymity of the users were maintained and the ERB review of the host institution didn't raise ethical concerns.

For each question in the MDC dialogue dataset, we took the union of the top-10 answers retrieved by the five different retrieval techniques described above. On average, each question has about 24 selected answers. Using a sliding window on all the dialogue questions, we selected three conversation turns, and appended the prediction as a fourth turn (interrogator-avatar-interrogator-predicted avatar response) without specifying who was whom, and

[4] `https://pypi.org/project/rank-bm25/`

[5] `https://github.com/jasonwei20/eda_nlp`

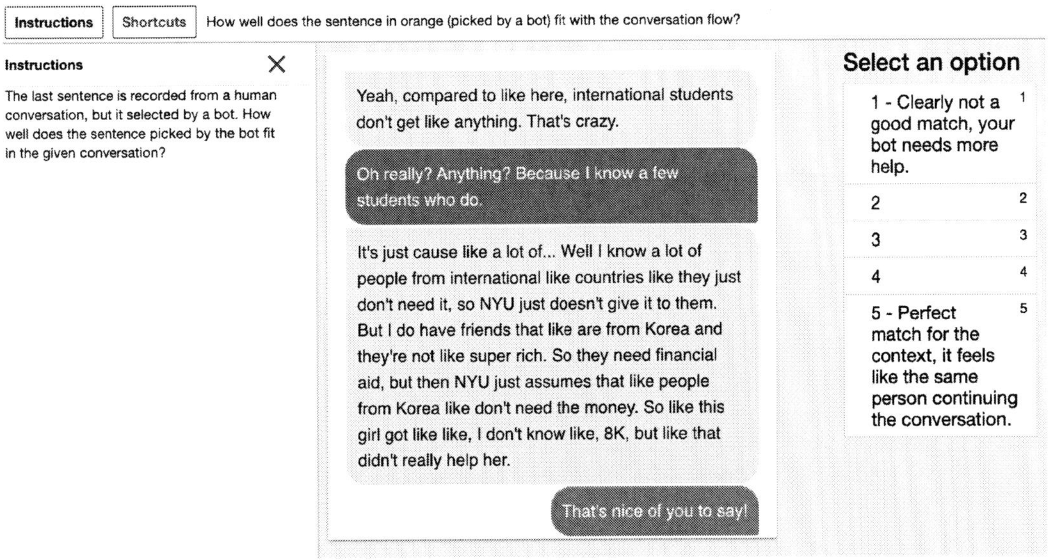

Figure 3: Annotation interface displayed to the human annotators.

always starting the dialogue snippet from an interrogator's question and ending with the avatar's answer. We chose four turns because it seems to give an optimal context size by looking at the annotations performed on the HUMOD dataset (Merdivan et al., 2020). So we have 339 dialogue snippets for the dev set and 341 for the test set. Each human annotator could rate as many snippets as they wanted in one task. On average, they rated 23 sampled dialogue conversations. They were asked to rate the last reply of the dialogue snippet on a 1–5 scale according to the dialogue context (where 1: Clearly not a good match; 5: Perfect match for the context). Each dialogue–reply pair is rated by three different annotators. For each dialogue context, there are on average 72 annotated answers (24 times 3), resulting in a total dataset size of 24,291 annotations for the dev dialogues and 24,555 for the test dialogues. In order to maintain high quality responses in the data, we defined a blacklist of annotators who gave poor quality annotations as follows. We forced each annotator to give a rating for the 'gold answer' given by the avatar maker in the dialogues data. If the annotator gave a rating lower than 4 (i.e., 1, 2 or 3) to the gold answer, we removed them from the annotations. While this blacklisting methodology is quite restrictive (we lose about 36% annotations), we have a large enough number of annotations left for our purposes.

Rater 1 vs Rater 2	**κ (dev)**	**κ (test)**
Closest two ratings	0.51	0.50
Lowest two ratings	0.23	0.20
Highest two ratings	0.07	0.11
Random two ratings	0.10	0.04

Table 1: Inter-annotator agreement computed using Cohen's kappa score (κ) for the dev set and the test set.

6 Results and Analysis

We analyze our annotations in terms of interannotator agreement and the relationship between the crowd's opinion and the best retrieved answers by the models. We then report the IR metrics on the models we decided to study.

6.1 Inter-annotator Agreement

We computed the weighted Cohen's kappa score (Cohen, 1968) between human ratings to compute inter-annotator agreement excluding the blacklisted annotations. Following the approach of Merdivan et al. (2020), we calculated the weighted kappa score for different configurations of three ratings for each different context-predicted answer pair. We calculated weighted kappa score for the closest two (as a majority voting) ratings, the highest two ratings, the lowest two ratings, and on a random selection of two ratings from the three ratings of each predicted answer. For example, if a dialogue snippet is rated 1, 2 and 5, we keep the closest two

	Gold	TF-IDF q-Q	BERT q-Q	BERT q-A 1:100	BERT q-A 1:All
			dev		
Average	4.53	4.03	3.99	4.17	4.01
%Gold		89.0	88.2	92.1	88.5
Rank		2	4	1	3
			test		
Average	4.59	3.01	2.98	3.47	3.25
%Gold		65.6	64.9	75.7	70.9
Rank		3	4	1	2

Table 2: Average ratings assigned to the gold and top retrieval model choices in dev and test sets. %Gold specifies the ratio of model average rating to gold average rating. Rank specifies the performance rank of the retrieval model.

(1 and 2) and randomly assigned them to **Rater 1** and **Rater 2**. Table 1 shows the results of each combination for the MDC's dialogue dev set and test set. The inter-annotator agreement seems consistent between the test and dev set apart for the highest two ratings and the random two ratings scenarios. However, both scenarios register quite a low agreement between annotators. Though representing moderate agreement, the highest is between the closest two ratings, showing that the 'crowd' seems more in agreement on a majority vote than on the lowest two ratings, highest two, or random two ratings. Moreover, agreeing on the worst answers (lowest two ratings) seems easier than agreeing on the best answers (highest two ratings). As our analysis points out, the poor level of agreement between annotators isn't about the quality of the annotations. It rather shows the difficulty of defining what is a good answer for a TOIA's interrogator.

6.2 Crowd Ratings of Retrieval Top Choices

Next we consider the average rating given by the AMT workers to the gold answer, and to the top retrieved reply by our four models. We include the ratings to all snippets excluding blacklisted annotations for both dev and test. We drop 35% of the annotations for the top retrieved answers due to blacklisting, consistently with the overall drop reported above. See Table 2 for the averages, percentage of the gold answer (i.e. how close to the gold answer is a model), and model ranking. The standard deviation of the average ratings for the gold answer is 0.35 in dev and 0.39 in test (because of blacklisting, we only keep ratings 4 and 5 for the gold answer).[6] The standard deviation of the retrieval models ranges from 1.17 to 1.33 in dev and 1.20 to 1.38 in test.

Retrieval	ρ (dev)	ρ (test)
TF-IDF q-Q	0.25	0.10
BERT q-Q	0.16	0.08
BERT q-A 1:100	0.30	0.13
BERT q-A 1:All	0.29	0.15

Table 3: Spearman's Rank Correlation Coefficient (ρ) between each retrieval model and the human ratings for the dev set and the test set.

The results indicate that, although the crowd disagrees, they generally give high ratings to the best retrieved answers. So, annotators may disagree on many instances, but when the models retrieve sensible answers, these are recognized by the annotators. For this reason we decide not to resolve the annotator's disagreements, and in the analysis that follows we use the average rating between the three (or less because of blacklisting) scores given by the crowd for each dialogue context-predicted reply pair. According to the crowd, the model with the best top choice is BERT q-A 1:100, and the model with the worst top choice is BERT q-Q.

6.3 Correlations Between Models and Annotations

We also computed the Spearman's Rank Correlation Coefficients between the rankings produced by four of the models used for answer retrieval and the annotators ratings (always excluding the blacklisted annotations). The results are displayed in Table 3. While the correlations are weak (yet statistically significant as all the p-values approached 0), we can notice a mixed behavior. The models performing better (See Table 4) do not necessarily correlate more with human ratings. This is a ranking correlation. So the crowd may rank differently than the models' answers but agree on the top ranked replies as we have seen earlier. Furthermore, on the 24 answer presented for each dialogue snippet on average, few ones are the top ranked by the models and the majority are 'negative' examples, where it's easier to disagree or rank differently.

[6]For reference, the average of all ratings of the gold answers (i.e. without blacklisting) is 3.96 for dev and 3.76 for test, with corresponding standard deviation of 0.71 and 0.74 respectively.

	Avatar Maker's Annotations						Crowd's Annotations					
Metric	Rand	TF-IDF q-Q	BERT q-Q	BERT q-A 1:100	BERT q-A 1:All	Crowd	Rand	TF-IDF q-Q	BERT q-Q	BERT q-A 1:100	BERT q-A 1:All	Crowd
R@1	0.0	23.4	22.9	**24.0**	21.0	9.1	0.1	6.5	3.9	**7.5**	6.6	20.9
R@2	0.2	29.5	28.0	**33.3**	29.5	15.5	0.2	9.6	6.3	**10.8**	9.6	40.4
R@10	1.1	38.2	42.0	**55.2**	43.1	34.0	1.3	21.5	**24.7**	24.0	18.7	98.4
MRR	2.6	69.1	60.5	70.1	**81.8**	48.0	7.0	49.4	49.1	53.6	**63.4**	97.3
MAP	2.4	66.5	69.1	**90.3**	59.6	18.8	4.5	33.6	**35.7**	28.8	17.6	97.3
SR@1	0.0	32.4	31.8	**33.2**	29.1	12.6	0.3	36.6	36.0	**42.3**	36.9	97.3
SR@2	0.3	40.6	38.2	**45.0**	40.9	20.9	0.9	50.6	48.8	**55.4**	52.4	97.3
SR@10	1.5	49.1	51.5	**66.8**	57.1	43.5	5.6	75.3	80.7	**82.4**	79.5	97.3

Table 4: Information Retrieval metrics on the **dev** dialogues set for all the models, including a random selection model and using the crowd ratings as a retrieval model. On the left the models are assessed against the original annotations made by the avatar maker. On the right the models are assessed against the annotations from the crowd.

6.4 Versatile Questions and Answers

Excluding random noise or poor quality annotations, one hypothesis is that the more volatile (or the higher the disagreement in) the ratings for a given q-a pair, the more difficult it is to assign a 'ground truth' value to an annotation. To validate this hypothesis, we computed a more practical proxy of disagreement. The Coefficient of Variation (CoV) is defined as the standard deviation of the three ratings given on the same q-a pairs divided by their average. The CoV quantifies the variability of the ratings with respect to the average rating for a given q-a pair.

Let A be the set of questions with a CoV higher than the 75th percentile (0.50) and B the set of questions with a CoV lower than the median (0.25). A has 167 utterances, B has 239 and their intersection has 133. Set A less the intersection defines the 'versatile' questions, i.e. utterances that go well with many answers and generate high disagreement. Set B less the intersection represents 'one-sided' questions, i.e. questions that don't go well with many answers, hence generate low disagreement. To confirm this expected behavior, we re-computed the Weighted Cohen's kappa on the two versatile and one-sided questions. The uplift in agreement or disagreement confirmed our interpretation. E.g., for the one-sided questions, the inter-annotator agreement doubles on the highest two ratings, it improves by a few points for the closest two ratings and the lowest two ratings, while κ becomes negative for the one-sided questions. It seems that there are less versatile questions (34) than one-sided ones (106) in the dev dialogues.

	Avatar Maker		Crowd	
Metric	BERT q-Q	BERT q-A 1:100	BERT q-Q	BERT q-A 1:100
SR@1	7.8	**11.9**	13.5	**25.2**
SR@2	12.2	**19.7**	23.3	**35.5**
SR@10	22.6	**36.1**	**75.8**	68.2

Table 5: SR@k metrics on the **test** set only for the best performing models on SR@1 and SR@10.

Repeating the same analysis on the answers, we have 152 versatile, 237 one-sided, and 118 in the intersection.

6.5 IR Metrics

Given that a TOIA's ability to engage in a conversation depends critically on retrieving a correct answer from the knowledge base, we focus on models (and hence metrics) used for Information Retrieval. The IR metrics we use to evaluate the answer retrieval ability of our TOIA are Recall@k (Lowe et al., 2015), Mean Average Precision (MAP), Mean Reciprocal Rank (MRR), and we include the Success Rate (SR@k) inspired by the work of Sakata et al. (2019). Success Rate is the fraction of questions for which at least one correct answer is ranked among the top k.

Table 4 summarizes the retrieval metrics for four of the models we worked with. We added two benchmarks: a model that randomly picks any answer from the KB, and we used the average crowd ratings' as a 'retrieval' model. When we compare the avatar maker's annotations vs. the crowd's annotations, we label an answer as 'correct' for the

Question (*redacted*) I think it's somewhere in California. Basically people are no longer afraid of being caught with meth. So like the whole city is like a capital of meth. So what do you feel about that? Does that change what you previously said?

Avatar Maker No.	**BERT** Kind of.

Question So would you feel the same way about like meth, heroin, coke because technically those...?

Avatar Maker (Can you ask me something else?, I'd rather talk about something else, sorry.)	**BERT** Sure.

Question(*redacted*) How about like your perception of like religion, like are you religious or?

Avatar Maker I am sure something bigger than us exists, but I don't follow any specific book or rituals.	**BERT** I started questioning my beliefs when I was a teenager after watching lots of documentaries and talking to agnostics alike.

Question (*redacted*) How is your romantic life.

Avatar Maker I like to keep things like this private.	**BERT** Relationships are harder to maintain because of all the study-aways. Also, the campus is a bit isolated from the city so it's not as lively.

Question Yeah, that's fascinating. So no toilet in your granny house?

Avatar Maker No.	**BERT** Sure.

Question Bye!

Avatar Maker Goodbye!	**BERT** See you later!

Figure 4: Examples in the dev set where the BERT q-A 1:100 system choice differs from the Avatar Maker's.

crowd, if it received an average rating $>= 3.5$. The metrics consistently show that the best retrieval model looks like the fine-tuned BERT on the q-A relevance task with a training set ratio of 1:100 between correct and wrong Q-A pairs. We can now notice why Recall@k, MRR and MAP may not be adequate for the context of TOIAs (and for the wider task of q-a retrieval from a KB).

One would expect that AMT raters would be more generous in classifying answers as 'relevant' for a given question. In fact, there are often cases where a sensible answer gets retrieved by a model (Figure 4), but the avatar maker did not deem it as appropriate. Other utterances like yes/no, sure, and OK answers are relevant for many questions, but, as expected, the avatar maker would be more selective to choose which one between a yes or a no is an appropriate answer. However, the Recall@k, MAP and MRR look lower in the case where the models are assessed against the crowd annotated data. This is partly due to the models trained on the data annotated by the avatar maker, but mostly because the crowd is indeed more generous and the examples of relevant q-a pairs increased vs. the avatar maker's annotations. Moreover, MRR is highly influenced by the number of documents retrieved by a model. In fact, the trivial model retrieving all possible answers in the KB would give a 100% MRR. MRR is the only metrics for which it seems that the BERT q-A model with the 1:All sampling ratio performs better than the 1:100 ratio but, in reality, this is due to the model with the 1:All ratio retrieving more documents.

Including the SR@k metrics makes things easier to assess. SR@k's for models evaluated on the crowd's annotations are consistently higher than the respective models assessed on the avatar maker's annotations with the only exception of the best model. BERT q-A (1:100) gives SR@k's that are higher than R@k's when evaluated on the data annotated by the avatar maker. The difference is even steeper on the data annotated by the crowd.

We evaluated the retrieval models versus the data with combined annotations, i.e. both by the AMT workers and the avatar maker. The results have negligible differences with respect to the assessment against the data annotated by the crowd, suggesting that the avatar-maker annotations are mostly included in the crowd annotations.

7 Discussion

7.1 Accurate vs Plausible Answers

Models that produce state-of-the-art results in other domains seem to not perform as well in the context of a TOIA. While a model like BERT q-A 1:100 retrieves *plausible* answers, the avatar maker's *accurate* answers differ (Figure 4, Table 2). This is also shown by the weak correlation between the IR models and the human annotators, and by the poor results the 'crowd model' generates on the data annotated by the avatar maker (Figure 4). For some answers, it seems that the avatar maker missed them when annotating the dialogues set due to human error. In fact, she had to manually go through 431 answers for 659 questions for a total of 284,029 look-ups. On the other hand, many questions require affirmative or negative answers, which both makes sense when evaluating a dialogue snippet but only one type of answer is correct for the avatar.

7.2 Viable Metrics for TOIA Evaluation

A TOIA is a single-output system, where the best answer should be retrieved as the top ranked document, and there may be more than one answer that suits perfectly within a conversation turn. This makes traditional IR metrics unsuitable for optimizing time-offset systems, so we identified SR@1 as the metric that gives the best indication for the ability of the system to retrieve a 'good' answer. For $k > 1$, SR@k gives us more insight into how to improve a model. For instance, the best performing model can retrieve a good answer in the top 10 ranked retrieved utterances in more than 80% of the cases. This information can be used to improve the system, e.g. by retrieving the top 10 answers using BERT q-A 1:100 and fine-tuning a re-ranking methodology that pushes on top the best answers. Table 5 shows the SR@k metrics for the test set, and it's interesting to notice that BERT q-Q yields a better SR@10 on the crowd's annotations than the BERT q-A 1:100 model.

7.3 Limitations

We limited the study to a retrieval problem and we did not leverage the conversational format of the dialogues set. There are some turns where we can observe co-reference (a few examples can be seen in Figures 1 and 4). We manually annotated co-references in a sample of 100 dialogue turns and these happen in about 5% of the dialogues. So while the IR techniques produce some errors due to the conversational structure, this is not as material as to invalidate this study. Regarding the annotation methodology, a 'fairer' way to annotate the answers might have been to ask the AMT workers to give a rating for every question in the KB paired with every dialogue snippets in the dialogue sets. So when we use the crowd ratings as a model (Table 4), we are limited to the the answers that were rated by the human annotators. Rating all answers for every single question would be unpractical and picking the union of the top 10 retrieved answers from our models makes sure that the human raters could see an answer annotated by the avatar-maker for at least 66.8% of the questions (SR@10 of the best performing model, Table 4).

8 Conclusion and Future Work

We explored the challenge of defining what a 'good' answer is in the context of a TOIA by annotating a dataset used for creating an avatar, and evaluating human-avatar dialogues. We learned that the perceived 'right' answer for avatar interrogators differs from the avatar maker expectations partly because some questions and answers are too versatile, i.e., they go well with many answers and questions, respectively. Additionally, yes and no answers are equally perceived as relevant by users interrogating an avatar but would be right or wrong for a given avatar maker. We make all the human annotations we collected available to the research community. We challenged classical retrieval metrics and proposed that TOIA's dialogue managers should optimize Success Rate @1. Success Rate @k for different levels of k can help identify how to improve retrieval techniques.

Our future work includes recognizing versatile questions and answers, designing methods to elicit more precise answer recordings at the avatar creation stage, and forcing yes/no answers with acceptable degrees of confidence. We plan to use transfer-learning and one-shot learning for leveraging state-of-the-art results of deep neural models in the context of a TOIA. Addressing misaligned expectations between different user needs and picking the right metric are essential to improving the design, usability, and answer retrieval methodology of time-offset interaction applications.

Acknowledgments

The first author was supported by the New York University Abu Dhabi Global PhD Student Fellowship program. The support and resources from the High Performance Computing Center at New York University Abu Dhabi are gratefully acknowledged. We thank NYUAD's CAMeL Lab member Bashar Alhafni for helpful discussions.

References

Dana Abu Ali, Muaz Ahmad, Hayat Al Hassan, Paula Dozsa, Ming Hu, Jose Varias, and Nizar Habash. 2018. A bilingual interactive human avatar dialogue system. In *Proceedings of the 19th Annual SIGdial Meeting on Discourse and Dialogue*, pages 241–244.

Ron Artstein, Anton Leuski, Heather Maio, Tomer Mor-Barak, Carla Gordon, and David Traum. 2015. How many utterances are needed to support time-offset interaction? In *The Twenty-Eighth International Flairs Conference*.

Satanjeev Banerjee and Alon Lavie. 2005. Meteor: An automatic metric for mt evaluation with improved correlation with human judgments. In *Proceedings of the acl workshop on intrinsic and extrinsic evaluation measures for machine translation and/or summarization*, pages 65–72.

Basma El Amel Boussaha, Nicolas Hernandez, Christine Jacquin, and Emmanuel Morin. 2019. Deep retrieval-based dialogue systems: a short review. *arXiv preprint arXiv:1907.12878*.

Anthony Chen, Gabriel Stanovsky, Sameer Singh, and Matt Gardner. 2019. Evaluating question answering evaluation. In *Proceedings of the 2nd Workshop on Machine Reading for Question Answering*, pages 119–124.

Alberto Chierici, Nizar Habash, and Margarita Bicec. 2020. The margarita dialogue corpus: A data set for time-offset interactions and unstructured dialogue systems. In *Proceedings of The 12th Language Resources and Evaluation Conference*, pages 476–484.

Jacob Cohen. 1968. Weighted kappa: nominal scale agreement provision for scaled disagreement or partial credit. *Psychological bulletin*, 70(4):213.

Cristian Danescu-Niculescu-Mizil and Lillian Lee. 2011. Chameleons in imagined conversations: A new approach to understanding coordination of linguistic style in dialogs. In *Proceedings of the Workshop on Cognitive Modeling and Computational Linguistics, ACL 2011*.

Jacob Devlin, Ming-Wei Chang, Kenton Lee, and Kristina Toutanova. 2018. Bert: Pre-training of deep bidirectional transformers for language understanding. *arXiv preprint arXiv:1810.04805*.

Jesse Dodge, Gabriel Ilharco, Roy Schwartz, Ali Farhadi, Hannaneh Hajishirzi, and Noah Smith. 2020. Fine-tuning pretrained language models: Weight initializations, data orders, and early stopping. *arXiv preprint arXiv:2002.06305*.

Samuel Humeau, Kurt Shuster, Marie-Anne Lachaux, and Jason Weston. 2019. Poly-encoders: Transformer architectures and pre-training strategies for fast and accurate multi-sentence scoring. *arXiv preprint arXiv:1905.01969*.

Karen Spärck Jones. 2005. ACL lifetime achievement award: Some points in a time. *Computational Linguistics*, 31(1):1–14.

Chin-Yew Lin. 2004. Rouge: A package for automatic evaluation of summaries. In *Text summarization branches out*, pages 74–81.

Chia-Wei Liu, Ryan Lowe, Iulian Serban, Mike Noseworthy, Laurent Charlin, and Joelle Pineau. 2016. How NOT to evaluate your dialogue system: An empirical study of unsupervised evaluation metrics for dialogue response generation. In *Proceedings of the 2016 Conference on Empirical Methods in Natural Language Processing*, pages 2122–2132, Austin, Texas. Association for Computational Linguistics.

Ryan Lowe, Nissan Pow, Iulian Serban, and Joelle Pineau. 2015. The ubuntu dialogue corpus: A large dataset for research in unstructured multi-turn dialogue systems. *arXiv preprint arXiv:1506.08909*.

Christopher Manning, Prabhakar Raghavan, and Hinrich Schutze. 2008. Introduction to information retrieval.

Erinc Merdivan, Deepika Singh, Sten Hanke, Johannes Kropf, Andreas Holzinger, and Matthieu Geist. 2020. Human annotated dialogues dataset for natural conversational agents. *Applied Sciences*, 10(3):762.

Masashi Nishiyama, Tsubasa Miyauchi, Hiroki Yoshimura, and Yoshio Iwai. 2016. Synthesizing realistic image-based avatars by body sway analysis. In *Proceedings of the Fourth International Conference on Human Agent Interaction*, pages 155–162. ACM.

Kishore Papineni, Salim Roukos, Todd Ward, and Wei-Jing Zhu. 2002. Bleu: a method for automatic evaluation of machine translation. In *Proceedings of the 40th annual meeting of the Association for Computational Linguistics*, pages 311–318.

F. Pedregosa, G. Varoquaux, A. Gramfort, V. Michel, B. Thirion, O. Grisel, M. Blondel, P. Prettenhofer, R. Weiss, V. Dubourg, J. Vanderplas, A. Passos, D. Cournapeau, M. Brucher, M. Perrot, and E. Duchesnay. 2011. Scikit-learn: Machine learning in Python. *Journal of Machine Learning Research*, 12:2825–2830.

Pranav Rajpurkar, Jian Zhang, Konstantin Lopyrev, and Percy Liang. 2016. Squad: 100,000+ questions for machine comprehension of text. *arXiv preprint arXiv:1606.05250*.

Siva Reddy, Danqi Chen, and Christopher D Manning. 2019. Coqa: A conversational question answering challenge. *Transactions of the Association for Computational Linguistics*, 7:249–266.

Stephen Roller, Emily Dinan, Naman Goyal, Da Ju, Mary Williamson, Yinhan Liu, Jing Xu, Myle Ott, Kurt Shuster, Eric M Smith, et al. 2020. Recipes for building an open-domain chatbot. *arXiv preprint arXiv:2004.13637*.

Wataru Sakata, Tomohide Shibata, Ribeka Tanaka, and Sadao Kurohashi. 2019. Faq retrieval using query-question similarity and bert-based query-answer relevance. In *Proceedings of the 42nd International ACM SIGIR Conference on Research and Development in Information Retrieval*, pages 1113–1116.

David Traum, Kallirroi Georgila, Ron Artstein, and Anton Leuski. 2015a. Evaluating spoken dialogue processing for time-offset interaction. In *Proceedings of the 16th Annual Meeting of the Special Interest Group on Discourse and Dialogue*, pages 199–208.

David Traum, Andrew Jones, Kia Hays, Heather Maio, Oleg Alexander, Ron Artstein, Paul Debevec, Alesia Gainer, Kallirroi Georgila, Kathleen Haase, et al. 2015b. New dimensions in testimony: Digitally preserving a holocaust survivor's interactive storytelling. In *International Conference on Interactive Digital Storytelling*, pages 269–281. Springer.

Andrew Trotman, Antti Puurula, and Blake Burgess. 2014. Improvements to bm25 and language models examined. In *Proceedings of the 2014 Australasian Document Computing Symposium*, pages 58–65.

Jason Wei and Kai Zou. 2019. EDA: Easy data augmentation techniques for boosting performance on text classification tasks. In *Proceedings of the 2019 Conference on Empirical Methods in Natural Language Processing and the 9th International Joint Conference on Natural Language Processing (EMNLP-IJCNLP)*, pages 6383–6389, Hong Kong, China. Association for Computational Linguistics.

Thomas Wolf, Lysandre Debut, Victor Sanh, Julien Chaumond, Clement Delangue, Anthony Moi, Pierric Cistac, Tim Rault, Rémi Louf, Morgan Funtowicz, Joe Davison, Sam Shleifer, Patrick von Platen, Clara Ma, Yacine Jernite, Julien Plu, Canwen Xu, Teven Le Scao, Sylvain Gugger, Mariama Drame, Quentin Lhoest, and Alexander M. Rush. 2019. Huggingface's transformers: State-of-the-art natural language processing. *ArXiv*, abs/1910.03771.

Yu Wu, Wei Wu, Chen Xing, Ming Zhou, and Zhoujun Li. 2016. Sequential matching network: A new architecture for multi-turn response selection in retrieval-based chatbots. *arXiv preprint arXiv:1612.01627*.

Reliability of human evaluation for text summarization: Lessons learned and challenges ahead

Neslihan Iskender, Tim Polzehl, Sebastian Möller
Technische Universität Berlin, Quality and Usability Lab
{neslihan.iskender, tim.polzehl1, sebastian.moeller}@tu-berlin.de

Abstract

Only a small portion of research papers with human evaluation for text summarization provide information about the participant demographics, task design, and experiment protocol. Additionally, many researchers use human evaluation as gold standard without questioning the reliability or investigating the factors that might affect the reliability of the human evaluation. As a result, there is a lack of best practices for reliable human summarization evaluation grounded by empirical evidence. To investigate human evaluation reliability, we conduct a series of human evaluation experiments, provide an overview of participant demographics, task design, experimental set-up and compare the results from different experiments. Based on our empirical analysis, we provide guidelines to ensure the reliability of expert and non-expert evaluations, and we determine the factors that might affect the reliability of the human evaluation.

1 Introduction

Evaluation of summarization quality plays a crucial role in the development of summarization tools since a well-executed evaluation can help to determine whether the system has adequately outperformed the existing tools in terms of quality and speed or whether the designed properties work as intended (van der Lee et al., 2018; Lloret et al., 2018). The human evaluation has been the most trusted evaluation method and used as gold standard for summarization evaluation (Gatt and Krahmer, 2018; Celikyilmaz et al., 2020). However, in recent years, some researchers have provided an extensive overview of papers with human evaluation and pointed out that there is a lack of standardized procedures leading to mostly non-comparable and non-reproducible results (van der Lee et al., 2019; Belz et al., 2020; Howcroft et al., 2020; van der Lee et al., 2021).

Howcroft et al. (2020) have reported based on the analysis 165 papers with human evaluation published in INLG and ENLG that more than 200 different terms have been used for human evaluation, which results in lack of clarity in reports and extreme diversity in approaches. van der Lee et al. (2021) have analyzed 304 research papers published in INLG and ACL conferences and reported that only 3% of 304 analyzed papers described the demographics, 6% provided the details about task design, 19% reported any inter-rater agreement score, 23% conducted a statistical analysis for human evaluation, and 32% reported the number of different evaluators per item, where 92% of the reported cases only one rating is used.

In this paper, we aim to contribute the human evaluation research as follows: 1) we conduct series of human evaluation with experts, crowd, and laboratory participants on two different data sets, 2) we report on the participant demographics, task design, and evaluation criteria 3) we demonstrate a comprehensive statistical analysis of human experiments, and 4) we provide guidelines to ensure the reliability of experts and non-experts and determine the factors affecting the human reliability grounded by the empirical evidence from our experiments. Data associated with this work is available at https://github.com/nesliskender/reliability_humeval_summarization.

2 Related Work

Human evaluation of text summarization can be conducted either by linguistic experts or non-experts such as laboratory participants or crowd workers. However, expert evaluation has been established as the gold standard in the summarization evaluation and the reliability of non-experts has been repeatedly questioned (Lloret et al., 2018).

Proceedings of the Workshop on Human Evaluation of NLP Systems (HumEval), pages 86–96
Online, April 19, 2021. ©2021 Association for Computational Linguistics

Gillick and Liu (2010) have conducted a crowd-sourcing experiment for summarization evaluation for the first time and concluded that crowd workers can not evaluate summary quality because of the non-correlation with experts. However, they did not report the number of crowd workers per summary. Fabbri et al. (2020) have compared the crowd ratings with expert ratings using five crowd workers per item. They have also reported that crowd ratings do not correlate with experts and emphasized the need for protocols for improving the human evaluation of summarization. Further, Gao et al. (2018); Falke et al. (2017); Fan et al. (2018) have used crowd workers to evaluate the quality of their automatic summarization systems without questioning the reliability of crowd workers.

When we look at the approaches used for human summarization evaluation, they can be broadly classified into two categories: intrinsic and extrinsic evaluation (Jones and Galliers, 1996; Belz and Reiter, 2006; Steinberger and Ježek, 2012). In intrinsic evaluation, the summarization output's quality is measured based on the summary itself without considering the source text. Generally, it has been carried out as a pair comparison (compared to expert summaries) or using absolute scales without showing a reference summary (Jones and Galliers, 1996). However, the extrinsic evaluation, called also *task-based evaluation*, aims to measure the summary's impact on the completion of some task based on the source document (Mani, 2001). Reiter and Belz (2009) have argued that the extrinsic evaluation is more useful than intrinsic because the summarization systems are developed to satisfy the information need from the source text in a condensed way, but van der Lee et al. (2021) have reported that only 3% of the papers presented an extrinsic evaluation.

Further, the quality criteria used in the human evaluation and the terminology used for describing these criteria had a high degree of variation, 200+ variations in terminology (Howcroft et al., 2020). Researchers have used either the same terminology but evaluated something different or used different terminology but measured the same thing (Belz et al., 2020). In most cases, they did not define the quality criteria they investigated or cite a reference for it, making it difficult to compare the results and draw conclusions across the papers. The scales for evaluation have also varied often, such as Likert (3, 4, 5, 6, 7, 10, 11-point), categorical choice (Yes or No), or rank-based scale (van der Lee et al., 2021).

So, human evaluation lacks structured, reliable evaluation practices, and the current way of reporting human evaluation in research papers generates non-comparable and non-reproducible results. We aim to contribute to human evaluation research for text summarization by determining the intrinsic and extrinsic quality in a reliable and reproducible way with our experiments in section 3.

3 Experiments

As our source documents, we used the 67 unique post-query pairs from a telecommunication company's customer service forum in German, where customers ask questions about the company's products and services such as "*Where can I find my customer number*" or "*My internet is not working*". Each query had 6-10 corresponding forum posts, including the answers from other customers to provide a solution or at least some help to the customer problem. The average word count of the posts was 571.2, the shortest one with 150 words, and the longest one with 1006 words, where the average word count of the corresponding queries was 9.1, the shortest query with three, and the longest with 23 words.

We conducted series of human experiments on this data set shown in Table 1 in chronological order. In experiment 1, crowd workers created extractive summaries for 67 post-query pairs. In experiment 2, different crowd workers evaluated the quality of crowd-generated summaries, the output from experiment 1. Because of the high cost of human evaluation, we limited our evaluation data set for further experiments based on the overall quality ratings from experiment 2. From those, we selected 50 summaries within ten distinct quality groups ranging from lowest to highest scores (lowest group [1.667, 2]; highest group (4.667, 5]), each represented by five summaries. We generated a stratified sample of the data set consisting of summaries with low, medium, and high quality. These summaries originated from 27 post-query pairs.

This new data set, 27 post-query pairs with 50 summaries in varying qualities, has been evaluated by experts in experiment 3, by crowd workers in experiment 4, and by laboratory participants in experiment 5. In these experiments, the task design and the summaries were exactly the same to compare the effect of expertise (expert vs. non-expert) and environment (lab vs. crowd) on the

Exp. No	Type	Human	Items	#Evaluator per Item	#Total Evaluator	Average Age	Gender	Payment
1	Creation	Crowd	67 post-query pair	4	76	39.43	41m, 35f	1.2 € per task
2	Evaluation	Crowd	256 summaries (output from 1.exp)	3	86	38.8	49m, 37f	1.2 € per task
3	Evaluation	Expert	Selected 50 summ. from 1.exp output	2	2	26.5	2f	30 € per hour
4	Evaluation	Crowd	Same as in 3.exp	24	46	42.47	27m, 19f	1.2 € per task
5	Evaluation	Lab	Same as in 3.exp	24	71	29.30	38m, 33f	15 € per hour
6	Creation	Expert	27 post-query pair	2	2	26.5	2f	30 € per hour
7	Evaluation	Expert	TextRank summ. of 27 post-query pair	2	2	26.5	2f	30 € per hour
8	Evaluation	Crowd	Same as in 7.exp	10	21	28.4	15m, 6f	1.2 € per task

Table 1: Overview of all human experiments

quality assessment. Further, we created machine summaries for the same 27 post-query pairs using the sumy[1] library to investigate the effect of summary generation method (human vs. machine) on the quality assessment. We applied TextRank algorithm (Mihalcea and Tarau, 2004) for machine summarization since it is one of the limited open-source German summarization algorithm and the most used unsupervised baseline in text summarization (Allahyari et al., 2017). Experts have evaluated these machine summaries in experiment 7, crowd workers evaluated the summaries in experiment 8. Here, we did not ask laboratory participants to evaluate the machine summaries' quality since the comparisons of experiments 3, 4, and 5 revealed the insights regarding the environment's effect on the quality assessment. The experts also created the gold standard summaries for these 27 post-query pairs in experiment 6.

In human evaluation experiments, we applied both intrinsic and extrinsic approaches. As the literature reveals a high degree of variation in quality criteria used in human experiments (Belz et al., 2020; Howcroft et al., 2020; van der Lee et al., 2021), we limited the intrinsic factors to six and the extrinsic factors to three. As the limitation criteria, we narrowed the scope of human evaluation from NLG to text summarization and adopted the commonly used quality metrics. Especially, we applied the criteria from the Document Understanding Conferences (DUC[2]), which have been the forum for researchers in text summarization to compare methods and results. Additionally, we used a measure for overall quality to assess the summaries' total quality. While limiting the extrinsic quality factors, we focused on quality metrics for usefulness for the task and information need because these are the most commonly used criteria in NLG as reported in (Howcroft et al., 2020).

So, we determined intrinsic quality using six different quality criteria: overall quality, defined as "responsiveness evaluation" in Louis and Nenkova (2013), and the five readability (linguistic) measures (grammaticality, non-redundancy, referential clarity, focus, and structure & coherence) defined as in Dang (2005). We evaluated the extrinsic quality using following three measures: summary usefulness defined as "content responsiveness" in Conroy and Dang (2008), source usefulness (in our case post usefulness, because our source documents are forum posts) defined as "relevance assessment" in Mani et al. (2002), and summary informativeness defined as "informativeness" in Mani et al. (2002). We conducted all our evaluations using a continuous scale, 5-point Mean Opinion Score (MOS) with the labels *very good, good, moderate, bad, very bad*, which is one of the most applied scales in subjective quality assessment (Streijl et al., 2016).

3.1 Crowdsourcing Experiments

We conducted all of the crowdsourcing experiments using Crowdee[3] platform. Before each of our crowdsourcing experiment, we had test runs with the student workers who have acted like crowd workers and gave us feedback regarding the task design and understandability. For each new crowdsourcing experiment, we did at least ten or more alterations based on the students' feedback. Further, we payed the minimum hourly wage in Germany and determined payment based on our crowdsourcing experiments' estimated work duration.

3.1.1 Crowd Worker Selection

For crowd worker selection, we developed a two-step qualification process for both crowd creation and evaluation. In the first step, crowd workers needed to pass the German language proficiency test provided by the Crowdee platform with a score

[1]https://github.com/miso-belica/sumy

[2]https://duc.nist.gov/

[3]https://www.crowdee.com/

of 0.9 and above (scale [0, 1]). In the second step, crowd workers needed to pass a semantic task-specific pre-qualification test.

In the pre-qualification test for summary creation, at first, we presented the summary creation guidelines: 1) Summary should be non-redundant, fluent, informative, and grammatically correct, 2) Summary should be readable and understandable, 3) Summary should be created by copy-pasting 3-5 sentences from forum posts, 4) Any alternation of the sentences and also writing new sentences were not allowed. We also presented an example of a good and bad summary generated for the same post-question pair. 103 out of 144 crowd workers were approved for the summary creation task. The criterion for approval was the ROUGE score of crowd workers' summaries, calculated with summaries created by linguists of the authors' team. Further, we manually evaluated the crowd worker's summaries with a low ROUGE score (ROUGE-1 < 0.4), and if the summary quality was still acceptable, their authors were approved.

In the pre-qualification test for summary evaluation, we gave a brief explanation of the summarization process, highlighting that the summaries were created by simple cutting-out sentences from forum multiple posts, and therefore may appear slightly unnatural. Crowd workers were then asked to evaluate the overall quality of four summaries (two very good, two very bad). The quality of these summaries have already been determined by the linguists of the authors' team on a 5-point MOS scale. For each exact rating match, crowd workers got 4 points, and for each point deviation, they got a point less, so deviations were linearly punished. 98 out of 150 crowd workers passed this qualification test with a point ratio $>= 0.625$.

3.1.2 Crowd Creation

In experiment 1, we instructed the crowd workers to create one extractive, 3-5 sentences long summary for each post-query pair using the same summary creation guidelines as in the pre-qualification test. To illustrate the guidelines, we presented crowd workers an example of a post-query pair and corresponding one good and one bad summary. Additionally, forum posts were shown as an itemized list of sentences in the creation process, so that each crowd worker only had to select and copy the specified sentences into a summary. Overall 76 unique crowd workers (41m, 35f, $M_{age} = 39.43$) participated in the experiment 1. Four different crowd workers per post-query pair created 256 summaries for 67 post-query pairs after eliminating cheaters. The average work duration was 458.8 seconds, and total tasks (67 x 4) were completed in 46 hours.

3.1.3 Crowd Evaluation

In experiment 2, the crowd workers evaluated the quality of 256 crowd summaries generated in experiment 1. First, a brief explanation of the summary creation process was shown with an example of a query, forum posts, and a summary to provide background information. Next, the crowd workers were asked to evaluate two summaries regarding the overall quality and the five intrinsic quality measures in the following order: 1) overall quality, 2) grammaticality, 3) referential clarity, 4) non-redundancy, 5) focus and 6) structure & coherence. Three different crowd workers evaluated each summary, and a single crowdsourcing task included the evaluation of two summaries.

The overall quality was rated first to avoid influencing it by more detailed aspects. The evaluation of each aspect was done on a separated page, which contained a definition of the particular aspect (illustrated with an example), a summary, and a 5-point MOS scale (*very good, good, moderate, bad, very bad*) as radio buttons. To have an intrinsic (summary-focused) evaluation, crowd workers did not see the corresponding original post-query pair. Overall 86 crowd worker (49m, 37f, $M_{age} = 38.8$) completed the summary evaluation task with an average work duration of 356.36 seconds within 12 days. We noticed that conducting a crowdsourcing experiment at Christmas time has slowed the total task completion duration. Further, crowd workers had the chance to give some feedback at the end of the task, and multiple crowd workers commented about the summary content, such as "I don't find the summary very informative overall, so the overall rating was worse than the individual ratings.".

Therefore, we added questions regarding the summary's content quality to experiment 4. We used the same instructions and task description as in experiment 2 and added three extrinsic quality measures showing the original corresponding post-query pair to evaluate the summary's content quality. Also, we increased the number of unique crowd workers to 24 for each summary following the recommendations of Naderi et al. (2018) for a robust crowdsourcing study. Since reading the summary and all the source text increases the reading effort, we asked crowd workers to rate the quality of one summary in one task.

After answering the same six questions explained in the above paragraphs, we asked crowd workers to evaluate the following extrinsic quality measures: 7) summary usefulness, 8) post usefulness, 9) summary informativeness. Again, the evaluation of each aspect was done on a separate page, which contained the definition of the particular aspect with an example, the post-query pair, the summary, and the answer options as the 5-point MOS scale. Overall, 46 crowd workers (19f, 27m, $M_{age} = 43$) completed the evaluation of selected 50 summary with an average work duration of 249.88 seconds. The total of 1200 tasks (50 summary x 24 crowd worker) was published in batches, and each batch was completed within one day.

In our last crowdsourcing experiment, experiment 8, we asked crowd workers to evaluate the quality of 27 TextRank summaries using the same task design as in experiment 4. Overall, 21 crowd workers (15m, 6f, $M_{age} = 26.3$) participated in experiment 8 with an average task completion duration of 287.92 seconds, completing total tasks within three days. Our analysis from experiments 3 and 4 has shown that 8-10 crowd workers per summary delivers results corresponding to laboratory experiments. Therefore, we collected evaluations from 10 different crowd workers per summary.

3.2 Laboratory Experiment

In experiment 5, we recruited participants via a local participant pool for the summary quality evaluation experiment in a controlled laboratory environment. We accepted only the native German speakers and did not perform any other pre-qualification. The experiment design and the summaries were exactly the same as in experiment 4, where 24 different laboratory participants evaluated the nine different quality aspects of 50 summaries. They also completed the task using Crowdee platform to avoid any user interface biases.

In addition to instructions of experiment 4, all the participants were also instructed in written form before the experiment start and all of the participant's questions regarding the task's understandability were answered immediately by the lab instructor. As expected, the participants were also physically present in a controlled laboratory environment during the task. The experiment duration was set to one hour, and the participants were asked to evaluate as many summaries as they can in an hour. Overall, 71 participants (38m, 33f, $M_{age} = 29.3$) completed the experiment 5, evaluating 12 summaries per hour on average within 51 days.

3.3 Expert Experiments

In experiment 3, two experts who are Masters students in linguistics evaluated the same selected 50 summaries with the same task design as in experiment 4. At first, they evaluated the summaries separately using Crowdee platform. After the first separate evaluation round, the inter-rater agreement scores, Cohen's κ, showed that the experts often diverted in their assessment. To reach consensus among experts, we followed an iterative approach similar to the Delphi method (Linstone et al., 1975) and arranged physical follow-up meetings with experts which we refer as mediation meetings.

In these meetings, experts discussed the reasons and backgrounds of their ratings for each summary in case of disagreement and eventually aligned in case of consensus. Eventually, acceptable inter-rater agreement scores were reached for nine quality measures. One should keep in mind that elaborated follow-up meetings principally lead to the increasing convergence of expert ratings. We did not test for a saturation effect with this observation, but the effort allocated in this step clearly influences the expert rating values.

In experiment 6, the same experts created gold standard summaries for the corresponding source post-query pairs of 27 TextRank summaries using the same task design as in experiment 1. Lastly, in experiment 7, the same experts evaluated the quality of 27 TextRank summaries following the same iterative approach and same task design as in experiment 3.

4 Results

Results are presented for the mean opinion scores (MOS) of overall quality (OQ), grammaticality (GR), non-redundancy (NR), referential clarity (RC), focus (FO), structure & coherence (SC), summary usefulness (SU), post usefulness (PU) and summary informativeness (SI) collected in experiments 2, 3, 4, 5, 7, and 8 (see table 1). We will refer to these measurements by their abbreviations in this section. Further, we use non-parametric statistics in our analysis because of the non-normal distribution of some measurements in these experiments.

	Before Mediation				After Mediation			
	Crowd Summ.		TextRank Summ.		Crowd Summ.		TextRank Summ.	
	Agr. in %	κ	Agr. in %	κ	Agr. in %	κ	Agr. in %	κ
OQ	54	0.228	22.2	-0.040	82	0.637	85.2	0.717
GR	42	0.078	18.5	0.086	78	0.626	88.9	0.809
NR	34	-0.012	11.1	-0.084	70	0.520	85.2	0.797
RC	56	0.381	29.6	0.013	88	0.819	92.6	0.882
FO	52	0.249	88.9	0.779	80	0.685	96.3	0.922
SC	42	0.212	22.2	0.070	82	0.743	85.2	0.783
SU	44	0.220	37	0.093	76	0.635	88.9	0.839
PU	38	0.005	48.1	0.169	70	0.469	92.6	0.856
SI	34	-0.038	40.7	0.234	78	0.565	92.6	0.886

Table 2: Raw agreement in % and Cohen's κ scores between two experts for the evaluation of crowd summaries and TextRank summaries before mediation and after mediation

4.1 Reliability of Human Evaluation

4.1.1 Expert Evaluation

In this section, we compare the results from experiment 3 with experiment 7 to analyze expert reliability. Following the recommendations of van der Lee et al. (2019), we calculated the raw agreement in percentage and Cohen's κ as inter-rater agreement scores.

Looking at Table 2, we observe that the mediation meetings increased the agreement scores enormously both for the evaluation of crowd and TextRank summaries. Only after the mediation meetings, acceptable Cohen's κ scores between experts could be achieved with all measures having substantial (0.6-0.8] or almost perfect agreement (0.80-1.0] for all measures except for NR, PU, and SI being weak in crowd summary evaluation (0.40-0.60] (Landis and Koch, 1977).

For TextRank summaries, the increase is considerably higher than the crowd summaries. Since the same experts evaluated the TextRank summaries under the same experimental conditions as in experiment 3, we can conclude that the characteristics of machine-generated summaries such as unnaturalness or non-fluency constitute a challenge even for experts before mediation. Further, the TextRank summaries included usually same kind of mistakes which made it easier for experts to agree on a specific evaluation scheme for each evaluation criteria during mediation sessions, leading to higeher agreement in comparison to crowd summaries.

The effect of mediation on the inter-rater agreement scores shows clearly that the mediation meetings are necessary for reliable expert evaluation, especially when evaluating machine-generated summaries. We plan to use the specific evaluation criteria shaped during expert mediation sessions to improve the task design in future work.

4.1.2 Crowd Evaluation

This section compares the results from experiment 2 with experiment 4 to measure the re-test reliability of crowd experiments. To do so, we calculated the Spearman correlations between the crowd evaluations from experiment 2 (3 crowd workers per item) and experiment 4 (24 crowd workers per item) for the six intrinsic measures. To have the same number of crowd workers per summary as in experiment 2, we selected the first three evaluations per summary from experiment 4. The black circles in Figure 1a show the correlation between these first three crowd evaluations from experiment 4 and crowd evaluation from experiment 2. The correlation coefficients range from 0.497 to 0.587 for all six measures, indicating a moderate re-test reliability of crowd evaluation.

However, choosing the first 3 out of 24 crowd raters for correlation analysis is neither a conscious nor reliable choice. Would we still get the same correlations if some of the remaining 21 crowd workers would have completed the task before the first three considered above? To investigate this, we randomized 100 times the order of 24 crowd evaluations and selected the first three evaluations to correlate them with the evaluation from experiment 2. Figure 1a shows the scatter plots for these correlations, ranging from weak to strong for all six measures. We see a noticeable difference between the initial correlations (black circles in Figure 1a) and randomizations. Here, we observed that the correlations ranged from 0.2 to 0.75, showing that

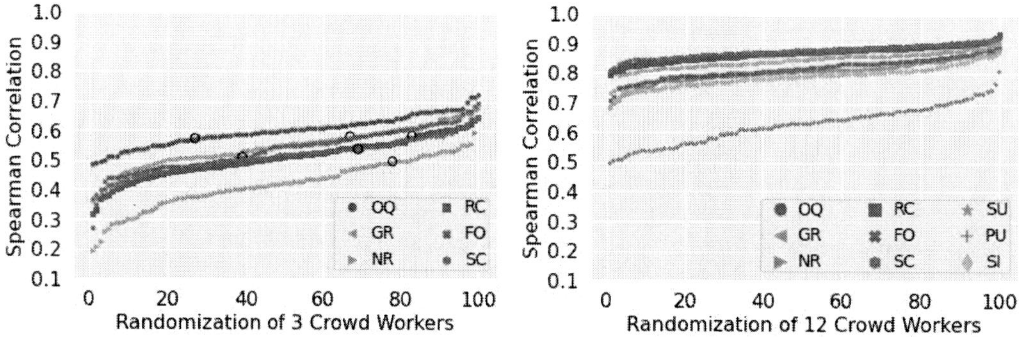

(a)

(b)

Figure 1: Spearman correlations of crowd evaluations from experiment 4 as 100 randomized groups of 3 crowd workers with crowd evaluations from experiment 2 (a) and Spearman correlations of crowd evaluations from experiment 4 as 100 randomized groups of 12 crowd workers with the remaining 12 crowd workers (b)

the crowdsourcing experiments with three crowd workers per summary still include high degree of unpredictability and can only be moderately reliable.

If we increase the number of crowd workers per item, can we overcome this unpredictability? To investigate this, we divided the existing data from experiment 4 into two random groups, two groups each with 12 crowd workers per item, and calculated Spearman correlations between them. Figure 1b shows the correlation between these two randomized groups for the nine quality measures. In comparison to Figure 1a, the slope of randomized correlations in Figure 1b is lower and the mean correlation of randomizations is very strong except for PU and SI which are strong ($\rho_{OQ} = 0.874$, $\rho_{GR} = 0.858$, $\rho_{NR} = 0.799$, $\rho_{RC} = 0.857$, $\rho_{FO} = 0.815$, $\rho_{SC} = 0.874$, $\rho_{SU} = 0.848$, $\rho_{PU} = 0.626$, $\rho_{SI} = 0.793$).

This result proves that the reliability of crowdsourcing experiments depends on the number of crowd workers per item and reliable crowdsourcing results cannot be achieved with three crowd workers per item.

4.2 Effect of Expertise and Environment

To investigate the effect of expertise and environment on the human summarization evaluation, we compare the results from experts (experiment 3), crowdsourcing (experiment 4), and laboratory (experiment 5) experiments, which are conducted on the same data set with the same task design.

Figure 2 shows the boxplots of expert, crowd, and laboratory ratings for nine quality measures. Here, we see that the experts used the upper end of the scale more often than the non-experts and gave higher ratings on average. Further, the non-expert evaluations are slightly negatively skewed using a smaller portion of the scale.

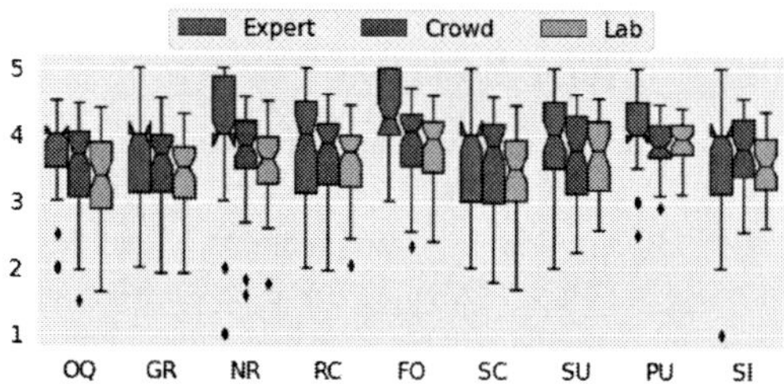

Figure 2: Boxplots of expert evaluations (blue), crowd evaluations (green) and laboratory evaluations (orange) for crowd summaries

To explore if these differences statistically significant, we calculated the non-parametric ANOVA, Kruskal-Wallis Test, between expert, crowd, and laboratory ratings. The test results revealed no significant difference between the expert and crowd evaluations except for PU and between the crowd and laboratory except for SI. However, the expert evaluations differed significantly from laboratory evaluations. Experts gave significantly higher ratings than the laboratory participants for all measures except for SU and SI. Here, we observe that significant differences exist only between the intrinsic evaluations indicating that the intrinsic evaluations require more expertise than the extrinsic evaluation.

Additionally, we calculated the Spearman correlations of expert evaluations with crowd and laboratory for all nine measures as shown in Figure 3. We found that the correlation magnitudes between ex-

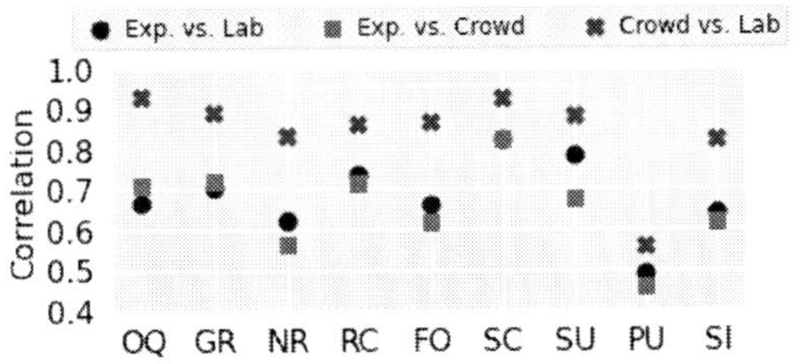

Figure 3: Spearman correlations between expert and laboratory, expert and crowd, and crowd and laboratory for the nine quality measures

pert and laboratory and between expert and crowd were very similar, ranging from moderate to very strong. However, the correlations between crowd and lab were very strong except for PU and remarkably higher than the correlations with experts. These results show that the environment does not have a significant effect on human evaluation, but the level of expertise affects the human evaluation.

4.3 Effect of Data Quality

To analyze the effect of the data quality itself on human evaluation, we compare the correlations between expert (experiment 3) and crowd (experiment 4) for crowd-generated summaries with the correlation between expert (experiment 7) and crowd (experiment 8) for TextRank-generated summaries. On average, the correlations for TextRank summaries for nine quality measures were 0.12 points lower than the crowd summaries. To determine if this is a significant difference, we applied Zou's confidence intervals test for independent variables (Zou, 2007) and found out that the differences were not statistically significant except for SC.

Further, we calculated non-parametric T-test, the Mann-Whitney U test, between crowd and expert ratings for TextRank summaries. The results revealed that the crowd workers rated OQ, RC, FO, SU, and PU of TextRank summaries significantly lower than the experts. In contrast, when evaluating crowd summaries, crowd ratings did not differ significantly from experts except for PU. This result indicates that crowd workers tend to give lower ratings than the experts for machine-generated summaries. However, the summary generation method does not affect the rank-order of their ratings, and the correlation between crowd and expert do not differ from each other significantly both for human- and machine-generated summaries.

4.4 Goodness of Automatic Metrics: With whom to compare?

The goodness of automatic summarization evaluation metrics is generally measured by their correlation to human evaluations, usually expert evaluations (Bhandari et al., 2020). In this section, we compare the correlations of commonly used automatic metrics ROUGE (Lin, 2004) and BERTScore (Zhang* et al., 2020) with expert and crowd evaluations for TextRank summaries to find out if the crowd workers can be used instead of experts.

	ROUGE-1	ROUGE-2	ROUGE-L	BERTScore
OQ_{ex}	0.636	0.680	0.675	0.582
OQ_{cr}	0.576	0.526	0.499	0.552
SU_{ex}	0.467	NS	0.397	NS
SU_{cr}	0.657	0.586	0.592	0.614
SI_{ex}	0.542	0.546	0.527	0.501
SI_{cr}	0.421	0.506	0.504	0.424

NS: Not significant

Table 3: Spearman correlations of ROUGE-1, ROUGE-2, ROUGE-L and BERTScore with expert and crowd evaluations for TextRank summaries

As human evaluation measures, we only considered the OQ, SU, and SI because the automatic metrics are content-based metrics and should rather be compared to content-based human evaluations (Lloret et al., 2013). Table 3 shows the correlations of ROUGE and BERTScore with OQ, SU, and SI measured by experts and crowd. To determine if these correlation differences are significant, we applied Zou's confidence intervals test for overlapping dependent variables and found out that there is no significant difference between any correlation. This result indicates that crowd workers can be used instead of experts to determine the goodness of automatic metrics.

5 Conclusion and Future Work

In this paper, we report a comparative analysis of series of human evaluation experiments with crowd workers, laboratory participants, and experts on two different data sets to determine the reliability of human evaluation for text summarization.

However, the research papers with expert evaluations for summarization have not reported any mediation meetings, let alone only 19 % reported the inter-rater agreement scores in the range of 0.3-0.5 (van der Lee et al., 2021). This raises the question of expert reliability, and to avoid that, we recommend having mediation meetings with experts for reliable expert evaluation based on our results in section 4.1.1. With our analysis, we showed that mediation meetings are elementary to assure the reliability of expert evaluations for all quality measures.

Further, we found out that the number of crowd workers per item determines the crowd evaluation's reliability. van der Lee et al. (2021) showed only 57 % of papers specified number of evaluators and the median was 3 among the papers which have reported the evaluator number. But our analysis in Section 4.1.2 showed that when using crowdsourcing, three crowd workers per item can only deliver moderately reliable results and around ten or more different crowd workers should evaluate each summary. This result is also inline with our previous findings in Iskender et al. (2020b,a).

While the environment (crowd vs. lab) does not affect the human evaluations, the level of expertise might have affected the human evaluation. Although there are mostly strong correlations between the experts and non-experts, their evaluations do not match 100%. Depending on the evaluation aim or the end-user group of the summarization system, the evaluator's expertise should be determined, e.g., summarization systems developed for naive end-users should be evaluated by the naive end-users rather than the experts, and expert systems should be evaluated by linguistic experts.

Additionally, the summary generation method (human vs. machine) might cause a bias in crowd assessments. Because of machine summaries' unnaturalness, the crowd workers tended to rate machine summaries lower than the experts. The feedback that the summaries were very "unnatural" and "robotic" from the crowd workers in experiment 8 also confirms this finding. But still, crowd workers can be used as a direct substitute for experts to determine the goodness of automatic evaluation metrics developed for machine summaries.

However, this paper has some limitations regarding the data set and task design. We used one task design with a single rating scale (5-point MOS scale) and the same set of definitions and explanations for our evaluation criteria in all our experiments, which were conducted on small sized data sets. In future work, we plan to include different human evaluation criteria, compare different rating scales with each other, conduct A/B testing with a second task design, which includes improved definitions of evaluation criteria based on the expert mediation sessions, and expand the data set size to increase the statistical power of our analysis. Additionally, we plan to conduct virtual mediation sessions between two or three crowd workers to find out if we can reach similar results to experts with a small number of crowd workers.

Despite the limitations of our paper, we believe that this paper makes a significant contribution to human evaluation research of text summarization. As Table 1 demonstrates, the time and organizational efforts and the cost of human experiments can be enormous. Especially, conducting laboratory and expert experiments required high organizational effort, and these experiments were completed in months while crowdsourcing experiments usually were finished in a couple of days. This shows how burdensome and time-consuming conducting human evaluation can be, which is a great challenge in a fast-moving field like summarization. Therefore, finding reliable ways of using crowdsourcing can be a promising solution and we hope to see more research in this field.

References

Mehdi Allahyari, Seyed Amin Pouriyeh, Mehdi Assefi, Saeid Safaei, Elizabeth D. Trippe, Juan B. Gutierrez, and Krys Kochut. 2017. Text summarization techniques: A brief survey. *CoRR*, abs/1707.02268.

Anja Belz and Ehud Reiter. 2006. Comparing automatic and human evaluation of NLG systems. In *11th Conference of the European Chapter of the Association for Computational Linguistics*, Trento, Italy. Association for Computational Linguistics.

Anya Belz, Simon Mille, and David M. Howcroft. 2020. Disentangling the properties of human evaluation methods: A classification system to support comparability, meta-evaluation and reproducibility testing. In *Proceedings of the 13th International Conference on Natural Language Generation*, pages 183–194, Dublin, Ireland. Association for Computational Linguistics.

Manik Bhandari, Pranav Narayan Gour, Atabak Ashfaq, Pengfei Liu, and Graham Neubig. 2020. Re-evaluating evaluation in text summarization. In *Proceedings of the 2020 Conference on Empirical Methods in Natural Language Processing (EMNLP)*, pages 9347–9359, Online. Association for Computational Linguistics.

Asli Celikyilmaz, Elizabeth Clark, and Jianfeng Gao. 2020. Evaluation of text generation: A survey.

John M. Conroy and Hoa Trang Dang. 2008. Mind the gap: Dangers of divorcing evaluations of summary content from linguistic quality. In *Proceedings of the 22nd International Conference on Computational Linguistics (Coling 2008)*, pages 145–152, Manchester, UK. Coling 2008 Organizing Committee.

Hoa Trang Dang. 2005. Overview of duc 2005. In *Proceedings of the document understanding conference*, volume 2005, pages 1–12.

Alexander R. Fabbri, Wojciech Kryściński, Bryan McCann, Caiming Xiong, Richard Socher, and Dragomir Radev. 2020. Summeval: Re-evaluating summarization evaluation.

Tobias Falke, Christian M. Meyer, and Iryna Gurevych. 2017. Concept-map-based multi-document summarization using concept coreference resolution and global importance optimization. In *Proceedings of the Eighth International Joint Conference on Natural Language Processing (Volume 1: Long Papers)*, pages 801–811, Taipei, Taiwan. Asian Federation of Natural Language Processing.

Angela Fan, David Grangier, and Michael Auli. 2018. Controllable abstractive summarization. In *Proceedings of the 2nd Workshop on Neural Machine Translation and Generation*, pages 45–54, Melbourne, Australia. Association for Computational Linguistics.

Yang Gao, Christian M. Meyer, and Iryna Gurevych. 2018. APRIL: Interactively learning to summarise by combining active preference learning and reinforcement learning. In *Proceedings of the 2018 Conference on Empirical Methods in Natural Language Processing*, pages 4120–4130, Brussels, Belgium. Association for Computational Linguistics.

Albert Gatt and Emiel Krahmer. 2018. Survey of the state of the art in natural language generation: Core tasks, applications and evaluation. *J. Artif. Int. Res.*, 61(1):65–170.

Dan Gillick and Yang Liu. 2010. Non-expert evaluation of summarization systems is risky. In *Proceedings of the NAACL HLT 2010 Workshop on Creating Speech and Language Data with Amazon's Mechanical Turk*, pages 148–151, Los Angeles. Association for Computational Linguistics.

David M. Howcroft, Anya Belz, Miruna-Adriana Clinciu, Dimitra Gkatzia, Sadid A. Hasan, Saad Mahamood, Simon Mille, Emiel van Miltenburg, Sashank Santhanam, and Verena Rieser. 2020. Twenty years of confusion in human evaluation: NLG needs evaluation sheets and standardised definitions. In *Proceedings of the 13th International Conference on Natural Language Generation*, pages 169–182, Dublin, Ireland. Association for Computational Linguistics.

Neslihan Iskender, Tim Polzehl, and Sebastian Möller. 2020a. Best practices for crowd-based evaluation of German summarization: Comparing crowd, expert and automatic evaluation. In *Proceedings of the First Workshop on Evaluation and Comparison of NLP Systems*, pages 164–175, Online. Association for Computational Linguistics.

Neslihan Iskender, Tim Polzehl, and Sebastian Möller. 2020b. Towards a reliable and robust methodology for crowd-based subjective quality assessment of query-based extractive text summarization. In *Proceedings of the 12th Language Resources and Evaluation Conference*, pages 245–253, Marseille, France. European Language Resources Association.

Karen Sparck Jones and Julia R. Galliers. 1996. *Evaluating Natural Language Processing Systems: An Analysis and Review*. Springer-Verlag, Berlin, Heidelberg.

J. Richard Landis and Gary G. Koch. 1977. The measurement of observer agreement for categorical data. *Biometrics*, 33(1):159–174.

Chris van der Lee, Albert Gatt, Emiel van Miltenburg, Sander Wubben, and Emiel Krahmer. 2019. Best practices for the human evaluation of automatically generated text. In *Proceedings of the 12th International Conference on Natural Language Generation*, pages 355–368, Tokyo, Japan. Association for Computational Linguistics.

Chris van der Lee, Bart Verduijn, Emiel Krahmer, and Sander Wubben. 2018. Evaluating the text quality, human likeness and tailoring component of PASS: A Dutch data-to-text system for soccer. In *Proceedings of the 27th International Conference on Computational Linguistics*, pages 962–972, Santa Fe, New Mexico, USA. Association for Computational Linguistics.

Chin-Yew Lin. 2004. ROUGE: A package for automatic evaluation of summaries. pages 74–81.

Harold A Linstone, Murray Turoff, et al. 1975. *The delphi method*. Addison-Wesley Reading, MA.

Elena Lloret, Laura Plaza, and Ahmet Aker. 2013. Analyzing the capabilities of crowdsourcing services for text summarization. *Language Resources and Evaluation*, 47(2):337–369.

Elena Lloret, Laura Plaza, and Ahmet Aker. 2018. The challenging task of summary evaluation: An overview. *Lang. Resour. Eval.*, 52(1):101–148.

Annie Louis and Ani Nenkova. 2013. Automatically assessing machine summary content without a gold standard. *Computational Linguistics*, 39(2):267–300.

Inderjeet Mani. 2001. Summarization evaluation: An overview.

Inderjeet Mani, Gary Klein, David House, Lynette Hirschman, Therese Firmin, and Beth Sundheim. 2002. Summac: a text summarization evaluation. *Natural Language Engineering*, 8(1):43–68.

Rada Mihalcea and Paul Tarau. 2004. TextRank: Bringing order into text. In *Proceedings of the 2004 Conference on Empirical Methods in Natural Language Processing*, pages 404–411, Barcelona, Spain. Association for Computational Linguistics.

Babak Naderi, Sebastian Möller, Tobias Hossfeld, and Matthias Hirth. 2018. P.808 subjective evaluation of speech quality with a crowdsourcing approach. ITU-T Recommendation P.808, International Telecommunication Union, Geneva.

Ehud Reiter and Anja Belz. 2009. An investigation into the validity of some metrics for automatically evaluating natural language generation systems. *Computational Linguistics*, 35(4):529–558.

Josef Steinberger and Karel Ježek. 2012. Evaluation measures for text summarization. *Computing and Informatics*, 28(2):251–275.

Robert C. Streijl, Stefan Winkler, and David S. Hands. 2016. Mean opinion score (mos) revisited: Methods and applications, limitations and alternatives. *Multimedia Syst.*, 22(2):213–227.

Chris van der Lee, Albert Gatt, Emiel van Miltenburg, and Emiel Krahmer. 2021. Human evaluation of automatically generated text: Current trends and best practice guidelines. *Computer Speech Language*, 67:101151.

Tianyi Zhang*, Varsha Kishore*, Felix Wu*, Kilian Q. Weinberger, and Yoav Artzi. 2020. Bertscore: Evaluating text generation with bert. In *International Conference on Learning Representations*.

Guang Yong Zou. 2007. Toward using confidence intervals to compare correlations. *Psychological methods*, 12(4):399.

On User Interfaces for Large-Scale Document-Level Human Evaluation of Machine Translation Outputs

Roman Grundkiewicz **Marcin Junczys-Dowmunt** **Christian Federmann** **Tom Kocmi**

Microsoft, 1 Microsoft Way, Redmond, WA 98121, USA

{Firstname.Lastname}@microsoft.com

Abstract

Recent studies emphasize the need of document context in human evaluation of machine translations, but little research has been done on the impact of user interfaces on annotator productivity and the reliability of assessments. In this work, we compare human assessment data from the last two WMT evaluation campaigns collected via two different methods for document-level evaluation. Our analysis shows that a document-centric approach to evaluation where the annotator is presented with the entire document context on a screen leads to higher quality segment and document level assessments. It improves the correlation between segment and document scores and increases inter-annotator agreement for document scores but is considerably more time consuming for annotators.

1 Introduction

Recently, several studies have suggested that document context is required for the reliable human evaluation of machine-translated documents (Castilho et al., 2020; Laubli et al., 2020). With the improved performance of neural machine translation systems (NMT) over the past years, this is particularly important when assessing the potential for human parity or super-human performance of MT systems (Läubli et al., 2018; Toral et al., 2018). Following these recommendations, the WMT Conference on Machine Translation[1] has moved towards adopting and presenting document context in their human evaluation campaigns of 2019 and 2020 (Barrault et al., 2019, 2020). The WMT campaigns are the largest academic efforts on human evaluation of machine-translated news articles in the field, running yearly since 2007.

At WMT19, the previous segment-level direct assessment evaluation (Bojar et al., 2017, 2018) — where translated segments were presented to evaluators[2] in random order — was extended by introducing "segment ratings with document context" (Barrault et al., 2019), and assessments of both, individual segments and entire documents, were collected. In this approach, segments from a single document translated by the same MT system were provided sequentially to evaluators in the order as they appear in the document, only one segment shown at a time (Fig. 1a), followed by the entire document comprised of already scored segments (Fig. 1b). WMT 2020 (Barrault et al., 2020) implemented a more document-centric approach, displaying the full translated document on a single screen (Fig. 1c) for most of the out-of-English language pairs.

While the change was primarily about the user interface (UI), we believe it can impact the quality of document-level evaluation to a large extent. Toral (2020) has noticed potential issues arising from the limited inter-sentential context in the WMT19 method, in which the evaluator does not have continuous access to all segments from the document. Unable to revisit previous sentences and never seeing subsequent sentences, the evaluator might forget or lack access to important details necessary to rate the current segment. On the other hand, displaying a long document on a screen can notably increase cognitive load, potentially lowering reliability of assessments over time (Gonzalez et al., 2011), and increase annotation time and costs, especially at the scale of the WMT evaluation campaigns.

In this work, we compare human assessment scores collected during the last two WMT evaluation campaigns and analyze the impacts of the user interface changes between these campaigns. We also attempt to determine whether switching to the

[1] http://www.statmt.org/wmt20/

[2] In this work, we use the terms *evaluator* and *annotator* interchangeably.

Proceedings of the Workshop on Human Evaluation of NLP Systems (HumEval), pages 97–106
Online, April 19, 2021.

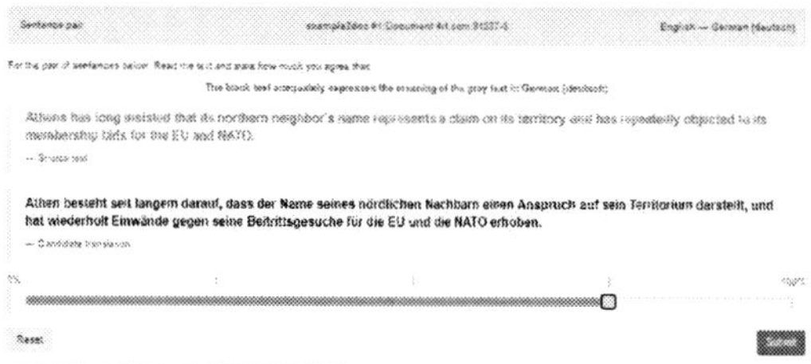

(a) The segment-level portion of the WMT19 interface.

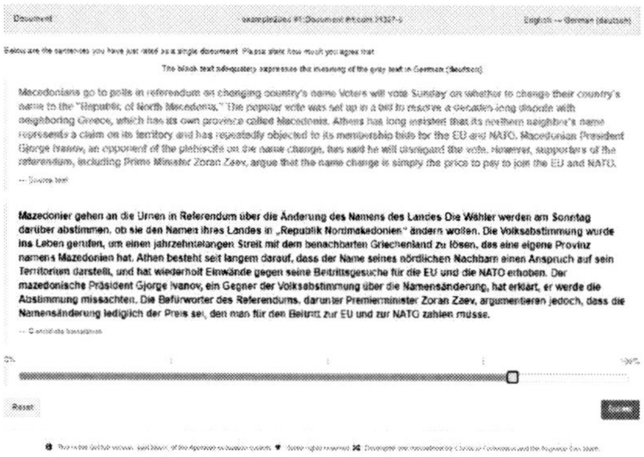

(b) The document-rating portion of the WMT19 interface.

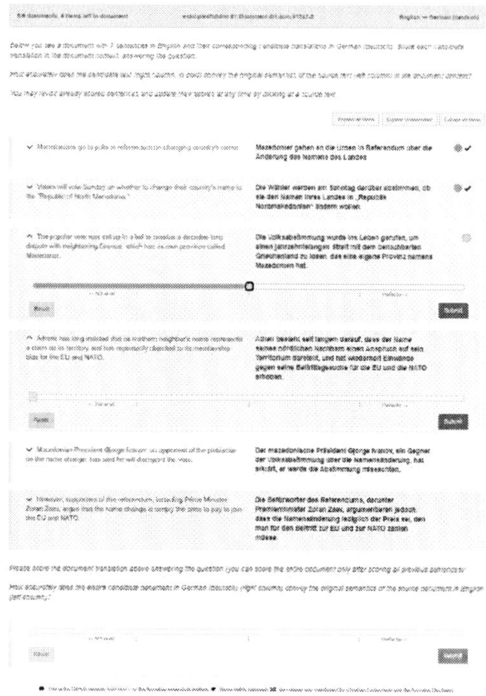

(c) The document-centric WMT20 interface

Figure 1: Screen shots of the Appraise interfaces used for the WMT19 (left) and WMT20 (right) human evaluation campaigns.

document-centric UI was an improvement to the human evaluation procedure and should be adopted in future editions of WMT for all language pairs. We examine if and to what extent human raters make use of the document context, estimate the reliability of document ratings collected through both interfaces, and study potential additional costs resulting from the document-centric evaluation at a large scale.

2 Document context in human evaluation of MT outputs

Recent research emphasized the importance of document context in human evaluation of machine translation, especially in terms of accessing potential human parity or super-human performance (Läubli et al., 2018; Toral et al., 2018; Graham et al., 2020; Toral, 2020).

Several works have compiled sets of recommendations for document-level evaluation. For example, Laubli et al. (2020) recommend evaluation of documents instead of independent sentences as translators tend to judge machine translation more favourably if they cannot identify errors related to textual coherence and cohesion due to lack of context. Castilho et al. (2020) have examined the necessary context span needed for evaluation across different domains, and for relatively short documents like news articles, the authors recommend presenting the whole document during the assessment of individual segments. Using document context has also been recommended by Toral (2020) who reported that this information was needed for evaluators to rank systems in a contrastive evaluation setting. Having the text available during the assessment of fluency or adequacy might be essential for some evaluators who spend more time reading than assessing (Castilho, 2020).

Although the literature is consistent about the need of document context in human evaluation of MT, little research has been done on the impact of experimental design and user interfaces on annotator productivity and the reliability of assessments in this context. The existing research on experimental designs for machine translation evaluation focuses on contrasting direct assessments with pairwise rankings (Novikova et al., 2018; Sakaguchi and Van Durme, 2018) and not on the optimal presentation of the document-level information. However, even the simple UI design decision of aligning document translations on the sentence level impacts efficiency of some evaluators (Popović, 2020). With this work, we want to promote that direction of research.

3 Document-level human evaluation campaigns at WMT

During the WMT evaluation campaigns of 2019 and 2020, segment and document-level assessments of document translations were collected, but using different methods and thus user interfaces. Both were implemented in the Appraise evaluation framework (Federmann, 2018) as a source-based direct assessment task (Graham et al., 2013; Cettolo et al., 2017), i.e. all segments and entire documents were judged on a continuous scale between 0 and 100 by bilingual annotators.

3.1 The WMT19 interface

At WMT19, the evaluation of a translated document consisted of two parts: first, an evaluator would rate all individual segments in a document translated by one MT system, one by one, in the order they appear in the document, followed by assigning a single score to the whole document. Evaluators would be presented with the translation of a single segment (a source sentence and its translation) per screen, or the translation of the entire document. Figures 1a and 1b depict segment-level and document-level portions of the interface, respectively.

This method was a simple document-level extension of the purely segment-level evaluations hosted during the previous editions of the WMT evaluation campaigns and did not require significant changes to the UI. A consequence of this approach was limited inter-sentential context as discussed by Toral (2020), since evaluators could not revisit the previously rated segments nor see subsequent ones. A rating decision could not be corrected in the light of the later-revealed context.

3.2 The WMT20 interface

At WMT20, both segment-level and document-level evaluations were performed on one screen. An evaluator would be presented with a translation of the entire document produced by one MT system. The document and its translation would be placed on a single vertically scrollable screen in two columns with source sentences on the left and their machine-translated counterparts on the right, aligned at segment-level. Figure 1c depicts a screenshot of this interface.

	Statistic	WMT19	WMT20
All	Languages	cs, de, fi, gu kk, lt, ru, zh	cs, de, iu, jp pl, ru, ta, zh
	Annotators	1,271	1,213
	Seg. judgements	207,916	186,813
	Doc. judgements	12,907	13,790
L4	Languages	cs, de, ru, zh	cs, de, ru, zh
	Annotators	779	746
	Seg. judgements	127,178	115,571
	Doc. judgements	7,894	10,019

Table 1: Statistics of data from the WMT19 and WMT20 campaigns, including languages, the total number of annotators and collected segment-level and document-level scores, after excluding documents with quality control items.

In the default scenario, the evaluator would be rating individual segments sequentially and, after rating all segments, on the same screen, the evaluator would rate the translation of the entire document at the bottom of the screen. Evaluators could, however, re-visit and update scores of previously rated segments at any time while still assessing the given document. They could also expand all sliders individually or in full, allowing them to take in all previously assigned scores.

4 Human assessment data

In our experiments, we utilize the human assessment data collected at the WMT19 and WMT20 evaluation campaigns. We limit the data to out-of-English language pairs as the into-English evaluation at WMT20 was done using the WMT19 method of reference-based DA and assessed by crowd workers instead of translators and researchers. Each annotator account provided 200 segment-level scores, and a number of document-level scores depending on the length of documents in the annotator's sample. From our analysis, we exclude all documents that contain one or more quality control segments, which constitute about 12% of all segments.[3]

We use similar amounts of assessments from both campaigns, as seen in Table 1: WMT19 provided 208K segment and 13K document ratings, while 187K and 14K were collected for WMT20, respectively. We either compare data collected for

[3]Please refer to Barrault et al. (2020) for more details on the quality control methods used at WMT.

	WMT19		WMT20		
	Avg.	Std.	Avg.	Std.	Δ (%)
Annotation time for a task (200 seg.)	1:06:08	± 21:47	1:51:09	± 51:12	+68.1
Total time for documents <10 seg.	02:02	± 01:00	02:48	± 01:44	+37.1
Total time for documents >20 seg.	06:54	± 02:48	12:01	± 07:53	+74.0
Time for 1st half of documents	02:06	± 01:09	02:44	± 02:05	+30.5
Time for 2nd half of documents	01:50	± 00:58	01:53	± 01:22	+2.4
Time for first 3 seg. in documents	00:52	± 00:24	01:26	± 01:02	+66.3
Time for last 3 seg. in documents	00:42	± 00:18	00:51	± 00:30	+20.4
Time for single segment score	00:16	± 00:06	00:24	± 00:13	+47.4
Time for single document score	00:12	± 00:09	00:06	± 00:04	-42.7

Table 2: Average annotation times with standard deviations for tasks, documents, parts of documents and segments in the *(hours):minutes:seconds* format.

all eight languages in each campaign or only subsets from four languages that were present in both years, i.e. Czech, German, Russian, and Chinese, minimizing differentiation factors between the data. Note that the WMT19 and WMT20 assessment data concern disjoint sets of segments as *different* test sets and MT systems were evaluated in both campaigns. We are interested in general patterns in the data at a larger scale, so we do not perceive this as an issue, but are aware of the fact in our conclusions. In a more ideal situation, we would have been able to perform A/B testing of different interfaces at the same campaign, but this was not an available option during the actual campaigns.

5 Experiments on WMT data

We aim at comparing the WMT19 and WMT20 interfaces for segment and document-level human assessments of MT outputs by analyzing the data that has been collected using both methods. We analyze annotation times, compare correlations of document and averaged segment ratings, and examine the inter-annotator agreement.

5.1 Annotation times

We analyze annotation times to examine if and to what extent document context is used by annotators if it is available to them during assessment of individual segments.

In both interfaces, two timestamps were collected for each segment or document. In WMT19, timestamps were recorded when a new page opened and when an annotator submitted a score. In the WMT20 document-level interface timestamps were recorded when a segment was (automatically or manually) expanded and when a score was submitted. Note that in the WMT20 campaign, annotators see all segments during the assessment of the document and can read ahead even before the first timestamp is collected. This could make the collected annotation times for WMT20 slightly less reliable.

We report annotation time statistics only for evaluators who completed their task consisting of 200 segments (74% of evaluators at WMT19 and 84% at WMT20). Very quickly annotated items indicate users who potentially gamed the task and assigned random scores. Items that took an excessive amount of time were likely interrupted with unrelated activity or otherwise idle. In order to account for these situations, we remove data points with values smaller than the 10th percentile or larger than the 90th percentile. The results are shown in Table 2.

Our observations are as follows:

- Providing the full document context increases the total annotation time per task by 68% on average. This suggests that annotators do read the context and use it during assessments. Significantly increased annotation time raises the question about cost efficiency of the document-centric evaluations.
- The more context is available, the more time annotators spend on studying it: during WMT20, annotators spent 74% more time on documents with 20 or more segments than on documents of similar length during WMT19, whereas the per-document annotation time for shorter documents with 10 or fewer segments increased by only 37%.
- Comparing the average annotation times for segments from the beginning of the document with those farther into the documents, we can

Aggregation	WMT19	WMT20	Δ
Avg. seg. score	0.907	0.923	0.016
Min. seg. score	0.723	0.736	0.013
Max. seg. score	0.584	0.628	0.044
Avg. of first 5 seg.	0.845	0.861	0.015
Avg. of last 5 seg.	0.883	0.899	0.016
Avg. short doc. 1st half	0.827	0.841	–
Avg. short doc. 2nd half	0.887	0.901	–
Avg. long doc. 1st half	0.868	**0.893**	–
Avg. long doc. 2nd half	0.894	**0.909**	–

(a) All languages

Aggregation	WMT19	WMT20	Δ
Avg. seg. score	0.862	0.919	0.057
Min. seg. score	0.658	0.761	0.103
Max. seg. score	0.520	0.648	0.128
Avg. of first 5 seg.	0.786	0.865	0.078
Avg. of last 5 seg.	0.830	0.903	0.073

(b) 4 common languages (cs, de, ru, zh)

Table 3: Pearson correlations between document-level scores and different aggregations of segment-level scores: average, minimum, maximum, average of first or last 5 segments in the document.

see that with the WMT20 interface annotators significantly increase the pace of annotation throughout the assessment of segments in a document. this is much less prominent for WMT19, which suggests that annotators do read the context ahead before making assessments (Castilho, 2020) and that they can memorize and make better use of the preceding context if it is available to them at all time.

As described in Section 3, the new interface allowed annotators to revise any segment score in a document before submitting the document score. We found that annotators did not use this feature often, and only 1.9% segment-level scores were revised, which resulted in 9.0% documents with one or more revised scores.

These observations suggest that annotators do make use of the available context and spend additional time studying it. Whether using that context results in more reliable quality assessments at segment and document level remains however unanswered.

5.2 Correlation of document and segment-level judgements

We measure the similarity between document-level scores and aggregated segment-level scores using different statistics, for example an average, from the same documents. We use the Pearson coefficient as the correlation measure (Freedman et al., 2007). We hypothesize that an increased correlation may be contributed to an improved capability of the user interface for reliable assessment of document translations by annotators.

Our main results are presented in Table 3 and Figure 2. We excluded all documents that contained one or more segments used for quality control (26% and 22% for WMT19 and WMT20, respectively) before computing the correlation statistics. We did not exclude scores from users who did not pass the quality control as this is not practiced by the WMT organizers when computing human rankings of MT systems for out-of-English languages. These users contributed only a small fraction of the data and excluding their scores does not meaningfully change the results. The scores were not standardized prior to computation.

We observe the following effects of the WMT20 interface compared to the WMT19 interface:

- We can see consistently higher correlations between document-level scores and all tested aggregations of segment-level scores for WMT20. This effect is even more prominent on the four common language pairs used in both campaigns.

- Document-level scores show the highest correlation with the averaged segment-level scores. The very high correlation of 0.92 indicates that the average of segment ratings from a document might be used as a reasonable approximation of the final document ratings in the document-centric evaluation. This might justify dropping the final document score from the assessment.

- The lowest segment score in documents correlates better with the overall document score than the highest segment score (*Min. seg.* vs *Max. seg.*). Intuitively, badly translated segments may impact the overall perception of the document quality more than higher-quality segment translations, or this could be attributed to the fact that shorter sentences are more likely to be translated correctly, but annotators may not see them as contributive to the overall document translation quality as longer sentences.

- Regardless of the user interface, segments

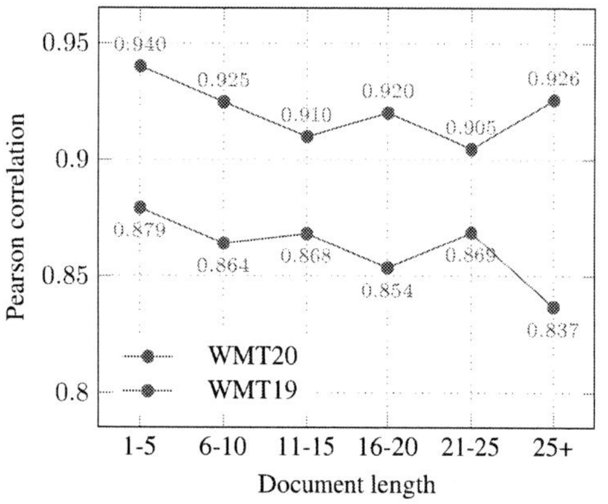

Figure 2: Pearson correlations between document-level and the average of segment-level scores in relation to the number of segments in the document (4 common languages).

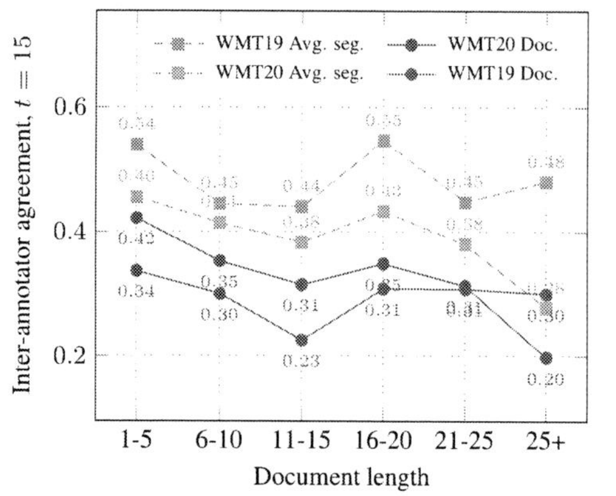

Figure 3: Inter-annotator agreements (Cohen's kappa, $t = 15$) for document-level and averaged segment-level scores in relation to the number of segments in the document (4 common languages).

from the end of a document influence assessment of the entire document more than segments from the beginning of the document (*Avg. of first 5* vs *Avg. of last 5*). From this, we do not observe that showing segments sequentially penalizes the very first segments in the document in contributing to the overall document score. However, the comparison of correlations for short and long documents (up to 10 segments, or more than 20 segments; bottom part of Table 3a) reveals that WMT20 seems to improve the contribution of early segments to the document score for long documents.

- In Figure 2, we computed correlations for averaged segment-level scores in relation to the number of segments in documents. Interestingly, for WMT20, the correlation increases for the longest documents (more than 25 segments).

The same trends are observed if Spearman's or Kendall's rank correlation coefficients are used instead of Pearson's correlation coefficient.

5.3 Inter-annotator agreement

We compute annotator agreement as a measure of reliability between annotators with Cohen's kappa coefficient (Cohen, 1960)

$$\kappa = \frac{P_a - P_e}{1 - P_e},$$

where P_a is the observed proportion of times that two annotators agree, and P_e is the expected mean proportion of agreement due to chance. Values of κ close to 0 are interpreted as no agreement and κ is equal to 1 if there is perfect agreement.

P_a is computed from pairwise comparisons of all documents that have been annotated by two or more annotators by counting the proportion of times that two annotators agree on the score.[4] It is assumed that two annotators agree if their assigned scores s_i and s_j differ no more than a predefined tolerance t, i.e. $|s_i - s_j| \leq t$.

P_e is constant for a given t and computed as the sum of probabilities of randomly assigning a score within the tolerance t (inclusive) over all possible scores from 1 to 100, i.e.:

$$P_e = \sum_{i \in [1,100]} \frac{min(i+t, 100) - max(i-t, 0) + 1}{100^2}.$$

Examples of P_e for different t are presented in Table 5.

We compute inter-annotator agreement (IAA) for $t = 5, 10, 15, 20, 25, 30$, and compare agreement for document-level and averaged segment-level scores, presenting the results in Table 4. Since there are very few annotators who have annotated the same documents more than once, we do not compute document-level intra-annotator agreement.

Here, our main observations are as follows:

- Obviously, the larger the tolerance t, the higher the agreement. Because the average dif-

[4]If a document is annotated by more than two annotators, pairwise comparisons between all annotators are counted.

	Doc. scores			Avg. seg. scores		
t	WMT19	WMT20	Δ	WMT19	WMT20	Δ
5	0.110	0.118	0.007	0.148	0.132	-0.016
10	0.195	0.215	0.020	0.290	0.254	-0.036
15	0.280	0.333	0.053	0.433	0.390	-0.044
20	0.378	0.443	0.065	0.560	0.514	-0.046
25	0.481	0.554	0.073	0.669	0.634	-0.035
30	0.559	0.639	0.080	0.760	0.737	-0.023
			Documents	12,907	13,790	
			Distinct documents	10,132	7,020	
			With multiple judgements	26.2%	66.1%	

(a) All languages

	Doc. scores			Avg. seg. scores		
t	WMT19	WMT20	Δ	WMT19	WMT20	Δ
5	0.115	0.124	0.009	0.182	0.144	-0.039
10	0.202	0.226	0.024	0.329	0.272	-0.057
15	0.302	0.343	0.040	0.481	0.406	-0.075
20	0.403	0.456	0.053	0.637	0.536	-0.101
25	0.509	0.569	0.059	0.756	0.657	-0.100
30	0.580	0.648	0.068	0.851	0.753	-0.098
			Documents	7,894	10,019	
			Distinct documents	6,376	4,798	
			With multiple judgements	23.0%	74.3%	

(b) 4 common languages (cs, de, ru, zh)

Table 4: Inter-annotator agreement (Cohen's kappa) on document-level scores and averaged segment-level scores for different tolerances t, i.e. two scores are assumed equal if they differ no more than t.

t	5	10	15	20	25	30
P_e	0.107	0.199	0.286	0.368	0.445	0.517

Table 5: Examples of P_e for different tolerances t.

ference of document-level and segment-level scores for documents assessed multiple times is between 15.0 and 19.6 (not shown in the table), we can assume that a t value of 15 or 20 is the most reasonable. In this case, the inter-annotator agreement is fair or sometimes moderate according to the recommended interpretation scale proposed by Landis and Koch (1977).

- For both methods, agreement for document-level scores is lower than for segment-level scores. This confirms the finding of Castilho (2020) that document-level evaluation efforts where annotators assign one score per document leads to lower levels of inter-annotator agreement for adequacy when compared to segment-level evaluation. In contrary to that work, our analysis is done at a much larger scale and for multiple language pairs.

- Inter-annotator agreement of document-level scores is higher for WMT20 than for WMT19 (4th column). Interestingly, the opposite is true for averaged segment-level scores (7th column), and it is even more prominent for the subset of four common languages. We will discuss this some more in Section 6.

- As shown in Figure 3, inter-annotator agreement decreases with increasing document length for WMT20, but it flattens for the longest documents in the case of WMT19.

In Appendix A we provide inter-annotator agreement results computed with the Krippendorff's alpha coefficient (Hayes and Krippendorff, 2007) for reference.

6 Discussion

In the presented experiments, we have observed interesting differences in correlation and inter-annotator agreement for long documents. In WMT19, for long documents, the correlation between segment-level scores and document-level scores significantly decreases, while IAA flattens out and eventually ends up being higher than for WMT20. We think this might be an effect of cognitive overload when annotators are presented with long document translation text pairs without visual help in the form of sentence alignment and similar hints.[5] A large wall of text might discourage annotators and they might fall back to assigning default or less diverse "safe" scores. Analyzing annotation times in relation to the document length, presented in Figure 4 supports this explanation. The average time of document ratings flattens for documents longer than 20 segments for WMT19, while it increases for WMT20.

Another non-intuitive observation we have made is that the inter-annotator agreement for averaged segment scores is higher in WMT19 than in WMT20. The agreement for document scores is, as expected, consistently higher for WMT20. If this is not solely attributed to the different data sets used in both campaigns, we would explain it by a tendency of annotators to assign higher scores if they cannot identify errors due to insufficient context

[5]See the example on Figure 1b consisting only of 6 segments. A thoughtful evaluation of an article with 20 or more segments would appear even more challenging.

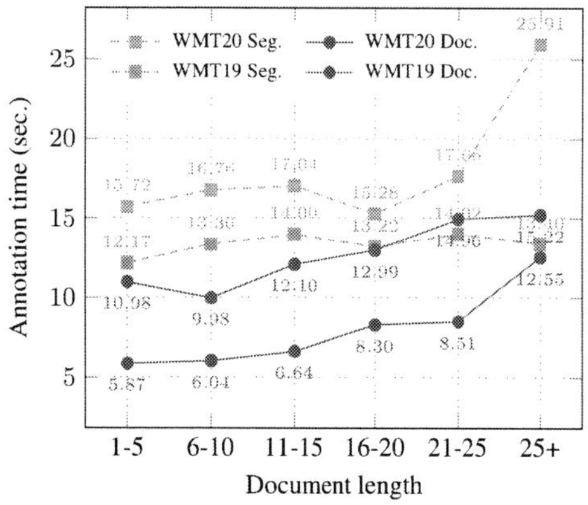

Figure 4: Annotation times (sec.) for single segment or document score in relation to the number of segments in the document (all languages).

(Laubli et al., 2020), which may occur for WMT19 because of its limited inter-sentential context. Another explanation would be that the WMT20 interface presenting all sentences from the document at once, encourages annotators to assign more diversified scores across segments; this may then lower the agreement at segment level. However, we were not able to confirm this based on an analysis of histograms of segment scores and their standard deviations.

Our study is conducted post-hoc, i.e. we cannot test for scenarios that were not anticipated during the actual evaluation campaigns. A more conclusive interpretation would require A/B testing with the same sets of documents, translations and annotators used for both evaluation methods. Nevertheless, we think that the presented comparison of two WMT evaluation campaigns supports the assumption that the document-centric evaluation conducted during WMT20 produced more reliable document ratings. We believe this to be an important finding because higher quality of collected document assessments should help to avoid statistical issues arising from low statistical power as observed by Graham et al. (2020).

7 Summary

In this work, we have compared two methods for document-level human evaluation of MT outputs through an analysis of the large-scale human assessment data from WMT evaluation campaigns, consisting of 8 different out-of-English language pairs. Our main findings are:

- Showing the entire document can extend the annotation time of individual segments by as much as 68% — presumably because annotators make use of the available context during evaluation.
- Annotators rarely change their segment-level ratings even if this option is available to them. Nevertheless, in some instances they do.
- Annotators tend to rate documents more consistently with their segment ratings if the entire document context is available at all time.
- In the document-centric evaluation, document ratings can be approximated reasonably well by averaged segment level scores.
- Inter-annotator agreement for document ratings increases if segment level evaluation is made in the global context.

Our analysis suggests that not only the entire document context is needed for reliable human evaluation of news translations, as recent studies have shown, but that the method in which the context is presented to evaluators is also important for collecting good-quality segment and document-level assessments. We conclude that the WMT20 method produces more reliable ratings, and thus can be adopted for future editions of the WMT document-level human evaluation campaigns for all languages.

In future work, we plan to strengthen our findings by comparing the WMT19 and WMT20 methods in A/B testing with common sets of documents, translations and annotators for both settings.

References

Loïc Barrault, Magdalena Biesialska, Ondřej Bojar, Marta R. Costa-jussà, Christian Federmann, Yvette Graham, Roman Grundkiewicz, Barry Haddow, Matthias Huck, Eric Joanis, Tom Kocmi, Philipp Koehn, Chi-kiu Lo, Nikola Ljubešić, Christof Monz, Makoto Morishita, Masaaki Nagata, Toshiaki Nakazawa, Santanu Pal, Matt Post, and Marcos Zampieri. 2020. Findings of the 2020 conference on machine translation (WMT20). In *Proceedings of the Fifth Conference on Machine Translation*, pages 1–55, Online. Association for Computational Linguistics.

Loïc Barrault, Ondřej Bojar, Marta R. Costa-jussà, Christian Federmann, Mark Fishel, Yvette Graham, Barry Haddow, Matthias Huck, Philipp Koehn, Shervin Malmasi, Christof Monz, Mathias Müller, Santanu Pal, Matt Post, and Marcos Zampieri. 2019.

Findings of the 2019 conference on machine translation (WMT19). In *Proceedings of the Fourth Conference on Machine Translation (Volume 2: Shared Task Papers, Day 1)*, pages 1–61, Florence, Italy. Association for Computational Linguistics.

Ondřej Bojar, Rajen Chatterjee, Christian Federmann, Yvette Graham, Barry Haddow, Shujian Huang, Matthias Huck, Philipp Koehn, Qun Liu, Varvara Logacheva, Christof Monz, Matteo Negri, Matt Post, Raphael Rubino, Lucia Specia, and Marco Turchi. 2017. Findings of the 2017 conference on machine translation (WMT17). In *Proceedings of the Second Conference on Machine Translation*, pages 169–214, Copenhagen, Denmark. Association for Computational Linguistics.

Ondřej Bojar, Christian Federmann, Mark Fishel, Yvette Graham, Barry Haddow, Philipp Koehn, and Christof Monz. 2018. Findings of the 2018 conference on machine translation (WMT18). In *Proceedings of the Third Conference on Machine Translation: Shared Task Papers*, pages 272–303, Belgium, Brussels. Association for Computational Linguistics.

Sheila Castilho. 2020. On the same page? Comparing inter-annotator agreement in sentence and document level human machine translation evaluation. In *Proceedings of the Fifth Conference on Machine Translation*, pages 1150–1159, Online. Association for Computational Linguistics.

Sheila Castilho, Maja Popović, and Andy Way. 2020. On context span needed for machine translation evaluation. In *Proceedings of the 12th Language Resources and Evaluation Conference*, pages 3735–3742, Marseille, France. European Language Resources Association.

Mauro Cettolo, Marcello Federico, Luisa Bentivogli, Niehues Jan, Stüker Sebastian, Sudoh Katsuitho, Yoshino Koichiro, and Federmann Christian. 2017. Overview of the IWSLT 2017 evaluation campaign. In *International Workshop on Spoken Language Translation*, pages 2–14.

J. Cohen. 1960. A coefficient of agreement for nominal scales. *Educational and Psychological Measurement*, 20(1):37.

Christian Federmann. 2018. Appraise evaluation framework for machine translation. In *Proceedings of the 27th International Conference on Computational Linguistics: System Demonstrations*, pages 86–88, Santa Fe, New Mexico. Association for Computational Linguistics.

David Freedman, Robert Pisani, and Roger Purves. 2007. Statistics (international student edition). *Pisani, R. Purves, 4th edn. WW Norton & Company, New York.*

Cleotilde Gonzalez, Brad Best, Alice F Healy, James A Kole, and Lyle E Bourne Jr. 2011. A cognitive modeling account of simultaneous learning and fatigue effects. *Cognitive Systems Research*, 12(1):19–32.

Yvette Graham, Timothy Baldwin, Alistair Moffat, and Justin Zobel. 2013. Continuous measurement scales in human evaluation of machine translation. In *Proceedings of the 7th Linguistic Annotation Workshop and Interoperability with Discourse*, pages 33–41, Sofia, Bulgaria. Association for Computational Linguistics.

Yvette Graham, Barry Haddow, and Philipp Koehn. 2020. Statistical power and translationese in machine translation evaluation. In *Proceedings of the 2020 Conference on Empirical Methods in Natural Language Processing (EMNLP)*, pages 72–81, Online. Association for Computational Linguistics.

Andrew F. Hayes and Klaus Krippendorff. 2007. Answering the call for a standard reliability measure for coding data. *Communication Methods and Measures*, 1(1):77–89.

J. Richard Landis and Gary G. Koch. 1977. The measurement of observer agreement for categorical data. *Biometrics*, 33(1).

Samuel Laubli, Sheila Castilho, Graham Neubig, Rico Sennrich, Qinlan Shen, and Antonio Toral. 2020. A set of recommendations for assessing human–machine parity in language translation. *Journal of Artificial Intelligence Research (JAIR)*, 67.

Samuel Läubli, Rico Sennrich, and Martin Volk. 2018. Has machine translation achieved human parity? a case for document-level evaluation. In *Proceedings of the 2018 Conference on Empirical Methods in Natural Language Processing*, pages 4791–4796, Brussels, Belgium. Association for Computational Linguistics.

Jekaterina Novikova, Ondřej Dušek, and Verena Rieser. 2018. RankME: Reliable human ratings for natural language generation. In *Proceedings of the 2018 Conference of the North American Chapter of the Association for Computational Linguistics: Human Language Technologies, Volume 2 (Short Papers)*, pages 72–78, New Orleans, Louisiana. Association for Computational Linguistics.

Maja Popović. 2020. Informative manual evaluation of machine translation output. In *Proceedings of the 28th International Conference on Computational Linguistics*, pages 5059–5069, Barcelona, Spain (Online). International Committee on Computational Linguistics.

Keisuke Sakaguchi and Benjamin Van Durme. 2018. Efficient online scalar annotation with bounded support. In *Proceedings of the 56th Annual Meeting of the Association for Computational Linguistics (Volume 1: Long Papers)*, pages 208–218, Melbourne, Australia. Association for Computational Linguistics.

Antonio Toral. 2020. Reassessing claims of human parity and super-human performance in machine translation at WMT 2019. In *Proceedings of the 22nd*

Annual Conference of the European Association for Machine Translation, pages 185–194, Lisboa, Portugal. European Association for Machine Translation.

Antonio Toral, Sheila Castilho, Ke Hu, and Andy Way. 2018. Attaining the unattainable? reassessing claims of human parity in neural machine translation. In *Proceedings of the Third Conference on Machine Translation: Research Papers*, pages 113–123, Belgium, Brussels. Association for Computational Linguistics.

A Appendix

Table 6 and Figure 5 provide inter-annotator agreement for document-level and averaged segment-level scores in the form of Krippendorff's alpha coefficient (Hayes and Krippendorff, 2007) for 4 common languages from WMT19 and WMT20. We present coefficients computed with interval and ratio metrics, and for a direct comparison with the results presented in Section 5.3, with the nominal metric with different tolerances t, i.e. two scores are assumed equal if they differ no more than t.

Krippendorff's alpha coefficients computed using the interval or ratio metrics do not show the higher agreement on document ratings for WMT20 compared to WMT19 that has been observed with Cohen's Kappa, but the difference is again smaller than for averaged segment ratings. Coefficients computed using the nominal metric with tolerance thresholds align with the inter-annotator agreement results obtained with the other statistic measure.

	Doc. scores			Avg. seg. scores		
t	WMT19	WMT20	Δ	WMT19	WMT20	Δ
Inter.	0.340	0.282	-0.058	0.465	0.297	-0.168
Ratio	0.294	0.246	-0.048	0.461	0.277	-0.184
5	0.030	0.046	0.016	0.060	0.053	-0.007
10	0.061	0.077	0.016	0.103	0.085	-0.018
15	0.100	0.130	0.030	0.194	0.138	-0.056
20	0.153	0.188	0.035	0.329	0.202	-0.127
25	0.237	0.258	0.021	0.462	0.290	-0.172
30	0.286	0.311	0.025	0.612	0.370	-0.242

Table 6: Inter-annotator agreement (Krippendorff's alpha) on document-level and averaged segment-level scores for different metrics (4 common languages).

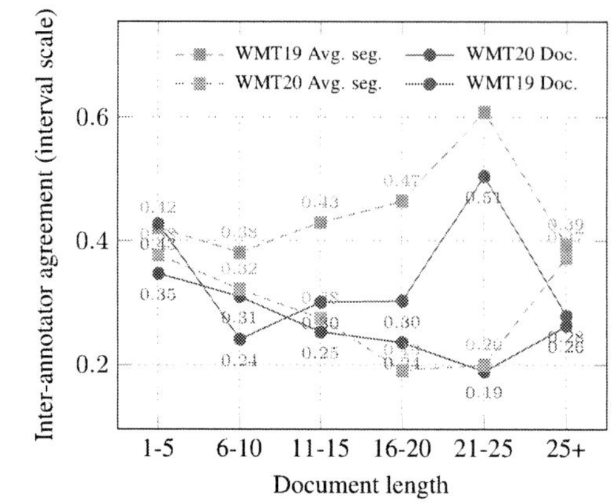

Figure 5: Inter-annotator agreements (Krippendorff's alpha, interval metric) for document-level and averaged segment-level scores in relation to the number of segments in the document (4 common languages).

Eliciting explicit knowledge from domain experts in direct intrinsic evaluation of word embeddings for specialized domains

Goya van Boven
Utrecht University
j.g.vanboven@students.uu.nl

Jelke Bloem
University of Amsterdam
j.bloem@uva.nl

Abstract

We evaluate the use of direct intrinsic word embedding evaluation tasks for specialized language. Our case study is philosophical text: human expert judgements on the relatedness of philosophical terms are elicited using a synonym detection task and a coherence task. Uniquely for our task, experts must rely on explicit knowledge and cannot use their linguistic intuition, which may differ from that of the philosopher. We find that inter-rater agreement rates are similar to those of more conventional semantic annotation tasks, suggesting that these tasks can be used to evaluate word embeddings of text types for which implicit knowledge may not suffice.

1 Introduction

Philosophical research often relies on the close reading of texts, which is a slow and precise process, allowing for the analysis of a few texts only. Supporting philosophical research with distributional semantic (DS) models (Bengio et al., 2003; Turney and Pantel, 2010; Erk, 2012; Mikolov et al., 2013) has been proposed as a way to speed up the process (van Wierst et al., 2016; Ginammi et al., in press; Herbelot et al., 2012), and could increase the number of analysed texts, decreasing reliance on a canon of popular texts (cf. addressing the great unread, Cohen, 1999). However, we cannot evaluate semantic models of philosophical text using a general English gold standard, as philosophical concepts often have a very specific meaning. For example, the term *abduction*, usually meaning a kidnapping, denotes a specific type of inference in philosophy (Douven, 2017). Therefore, models must be evaluated in a domain-specific way.

The critical difference between the general case and the philosophy case is the following. It is easy to find native speakers of e.g. British English who have a good intuition of the meaning of its terms in general use, and the relations between them. This yields e.g. the SimLex-999 word similarity dataset (Hill et al., 2015), covering frequent words and their typical senses. More difficult is finding 'native speakers' who have an intuition of the meaning of the terms used by a particular philosopher. The only candidate would be that philosopher themselves, and even then, the meaning of some of the terms used is the result of explicit analysis and definition rather than implicit language knowledge of the philosopher. Uncommon terms with highly specific meanings are explicitly defined and debated, leading them to differ between philosophers or even within the works of a single philosopher. Any accurate evaluation or annotation would require expert knowledge, and methods that can incorporate explicit knowledge, rather than judgements based on implicit knowledge of a standard language or jargon by one of its speakers.

We test two direct evaluation methods for DS models described by Schnabel et al. (2015) on our case study, the works of Willard V. O. Quine, a 20th century American philosopher. Instead of native English speaking crowdworkers, we selected expert participants who have studied this philosopher extensively. We aim to test whether these methods produce reliable results when participants need to use explicit rather than implicit knowledge, and consider the methods to be successful if inter-rater agreement matches that of other semantic evaluations. More broadly, our methodological findings apply to evaluation of DS models for specialized domains, language for specific purposes (LSP), historical language varieties or other language (varieties) for which no native annotators are available.

2 Related work

Most intrinsic evaluations compare word embedding similarities (e.g. in terms of cosine distance)

Proceedings of the Workshop on Human Evaluation of NLP Systems (HumEval), pages 107–113
Online, April 19, 2021.

to premade datasets of human similarity or relatedness judgements. Sets of words are created and evaluated on semantic relations by participants, and the similarity between the assessments and an embedding space is used as a measure of performance. In specific domains, examples of such datasets of term ratings can be found for identifier names in source code (Wainakh et al., 2019), in the medical domain (Pakhomov et al., 2010, 2011; Pedersen et al., 2007) and in geosciences both for English (Padarian and Fuentes, 2019) and Portuguese (Gomes et al., 2021). The last two studies compare domain-specific embeddings to general domain embeddings and both find that the former perform better. A problem of these indirect datasets is that only naturally occurring, often high-frequency terms without any spelling variations, are evaluated, while DS models include many more variations (Batchkarov et al., 2016).

Direct intrinsic evaluation methods, where participants respond directly to the output of models, can be categorized as *absolute* and *comparative* intrinsic evaluation (Schnabel et al., 2015). The former method evaluates embeddings individually and compares their final scores, while in the latter participants directly express their preferences between models. To our best knowledge, the only example of a domain-specific direct human evaluation is Dynomant et al. (2019) who evaluate French embeddings of health care terms by a human evaluation in which two medical doctors rate the relevance of the first five nearest neighbours of target terms from models trained on in-domain text.

In the philosophical domain some evaluations have been conducted with other methods, sometimes incorporating expert explicit knowledge, but none are direct. In each of these studies the work of Quine is utilized as data. Firstly, Bloem et al. (2019) propose a method of evaluating word embedding quality by measuring model consistency, not making use of expert knowledge. Secondly, Oortwijn et al. (2021a) construct a conceptual network which serves as a *ground truth* of expert knowledge. They compare the similarity of embeddings for target philosophical terms to their position in the manually created network. Here, the conceptual relatedness between terms is restricted to the property of sharing hypernyms, and only terms that were predefined in the ground truth can be considered for evaluation. Betti et al. (2020) introduce a more elaborate ground truth that is concept-focused, including more types of conceptual relations and including irrelevant as well as relevant terms for better evaluation of model precision. Still, evaluation remains restricted to terms in the ground truth. Only using direct evaluation methods we can attempt to evaluate all model output.

3 Task description

We perform a synonym detection task and a coherence task. In these tasks, participants are asked to judge model-generated candidate terms that semantic models deem closest to a target term. In the synonym detection task, participants select the most similar word to target term t out of a set of options: the k-nearest neighbours of the target term in each model that is being compared. In the coherence task, the participant selects a semantical outlier in a set of words, where one of the words is not close to t in the model. We refer to Schnabel et al. (2015) for details and a comparison to other tasks for general semantic evaluation. Our participant instructions are based on Schnabel et al., who use the instructions of the WordSim-353 dataset (Finkelstein et al., 2001). But as this study focuses on explicit knowledge, several adjustments are needed.

Although explicit knowledge is easier to verbalize than implicit knowledge, it involves controlled rather than automatic processing (Bowles, 2011; Ellis, 2004, 2005), so our version of the task might take longer. Yet in order to retain the required focus, the test should not take too long. We therefore conduct a pilot study in which response times are measured to estimate task durations, and we adapt the size of the main study accordingly.

The original task instructions do not define similarity, while other studies define it as co-hyponymy (Turney and Pantel, 2010) or synonymy (Hill et al., 2015). According to Batchkarov et al. (2016) defining similarity is difficult as it depends on the context and downstream application in which the terms are used. We keep a consistent context, both training and evaluating in the domain of a particular philosopher, although the concern of capturing the multidimensional concept of *similarity* in a single number is valid also in this context. Gladkova and Drozd (2016) claim participants are likely to prefer synonyms when asked to select the most similar word. In this study we are looking to find any relationship present, rather than a specific one, and expect the experts to explicitly consider this, so we ask for *relatedness*. Gladkova and Drozd further argue that when asked for relatedness participants must choose between various relations present, a choice that can be subjective or random, and might reflect other factors such as "frequency, speed of association, and possibly the order of presentation of words". The first two factors are alleviated in this study as the participants must take Quine's definitions of words into account rather than their own. This forces participants to think their answers through, which should reduce the association effects typical of fast-paced online studies. To account for effects of order of presentation, we randomize the order of the options. In our instructions, we define relatedness as synonymy, meronymy, hyponymy, and co-hyponymy, and provide examples. Participants are also allowed to base their judgements on other types of relations.

After the experiment we present a post-test survey, querying the types of relation participants based their judgements on, and task difficulty. Furthermore, we change the option *I don't know the meaning of one (or several) of the words* in the synonym detection task to be *None of these words is even remotely related*, and also include a similar option in the coherence task, namely *No coherent group can be formed from these words*. This is done to avoid any random selection of words when there are no meaningful relations, making the responses more accurate. As we aim to gather explicit knowledge, participants are allowed to look up relevant information on presented words. For reproducibility, our instructions (and results) are included in the supplementary materials. [1]

As the tasks require participants to be experts on the work of Quine, the number of possible participants is limited. Although participants are philosophers trained to work precisely and make consistent judgements, subjectivity can be a risk as participant must choose the relation they deem most important, while lacking context. We use inter-rater agreement to evaluate this. We report joint probability of agreement (percentage of agreement) as we have added the *none* options to avoid chance agreement. As joint probabilities cannot be compared across studies, we also report Cohen's κ.

All experiments[2] are conducted on the survey platform *Qualtrics*[3]. Participants are asked to execute the experiments in a silent environment.

4 Case study for philosophy

We make use of the QUINE corpus (v0.5, Betti et al., 2020), which includes 228 philosophical books, articles and bundles Quine authored, consisting of 2.15 million tokens in total. As target terms for evaluation, we use Bloem et al.'s (2019) test set for the the book *Word & Object* (Quine, 1960), one of Quine's most influential works. It consists of 55 terms that were selected from the book's index. We used 10 of these terms in the pilot study, 25 in the synonym detection task, 14 in the coherence task and 6 in both experiments.[4]

One Quine expert participated in the pilot study. The pilot study consists of short versions of the two tasks, both testing five target terms. In the synonym detection task, each target term has six candidate related terms from the models, that the participant should choose between. Each term is tested three times with candidates of differing similarity from the model (nearest neighbour ranks $k \in \{1, 5, 50\}$). The pilot coherence (outlier) task has ten questions. The average response time for the synonym detection task was 109.5s and 42.1s for the coherence task. Because for the first task this was higher than anticipated, we reduced the number of ranks to two and divided the task across two separate surveys.

4.1 Experiment 1: Synonym detection task

Three experts on the work of Quine, including the participant of the pilot study, participated in this experiment. They all hold a Master's degree in philosophy and have studied the philosopher extensively.

This task includes 31 target words, which are all tested on two ranks k, with $k \in \{1, 10\}$, resulting in 62 questions. Of the 45 test set terms not used in the pilot study, we took the fifteen highest frequency terms ($n > 275$) and the sixteen lowest ($n < 84$). The experiment was conducted through two surveys, each consisting of 31 questions, lasting around 50 minutes, with a break halfway. [5]

The data from one of the participants was excluded, as the participant indicated that the test was too difficult and that their expertise on the work of Quine did not suffice. Moreover the response times of this participant were a lot lower than for the other participants. For this experiment, the overall

[1] To be found at https://github.com/gvanboven/direct-intrinsic-evaluation

[2] Experiments were approved by The Ethics Committee of the Faculty of Humanities of the University of Amsterdam.

[3] www.qualtrics.com

[4] Listed in the supplemental materials, with frequencies

[5] Example surveys and raw results for each participant are included in the supplementary materials.

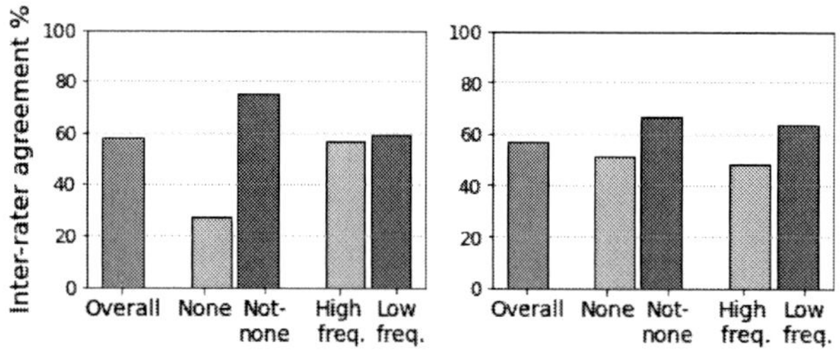

(a) (b)

Figure 1: Inter-rater agreement in different conditions of (a) the synonym detection task and (b) the coherence task

	Response time	
	Exp. 1	**Exp. 2**
Overall	45.5 s	25.8 s
None	53.4 s	28.2 s
Not-none	43.4 s	23.4 s
High frequency	35.7 s	26.9 s
Low frequency	54.9 s	24.9 s

Table 1: Response times in different conditions of 1. synonym and 2. coherence tasks

inter-rater agreement was 58.1%, with $\kappa = 0.492$.

4.2 Experiment 2: Coherence task

Two of the participants from the previous experiments also participated in this study. 20 target words are used: the 14 test set terms not used in the pilot or Exp. 1, and the 3 highest and lowest frequency terms from Exp. 1. We divide these into eleven low frequency words ($n < 142$) and nine high frequency words ($n > 187$). Using 3 DS models this results in 60 questions, the test takes approximately 40 minutes with a break. The inter-rater agreement was 56.7%, with $\kappa = 0.345$.

5 Analysis

To assess whether the method was successful we discuss some reliability metrics and examine disagreement examples. First of all, the fact that the data from one participant had to be excluded confirms the high standard of expertise required for participating in our version of the tasks. The results might have differed had there been more or different participants. However, other studies on expert explicit knowledge also execute tasks with two (Dynomant et al., 2019) or three (Padarian and Fuentes, 2019; Gomes et al., 2021) participants.

Inter-rater agreement scores for the two tasks were 58.1% ($\kappa = 0.492$) and 56.7% ($\kappa = 0.345$), indicating moderate or fair agreement. Batchkarov et al. (2016) found the average inter-rater agreement of two raters of the WordSim-353 (Finkelstein et al., 2001) and MEN (Bruni et al., 2014) dataset to lie between $\kappa = 0.21$ and $\kappa = 0.62$. Thus, agreement scores in this study are not lower than that of commonly used similarity datasets, despite participants having to agree on another person's semantics and including a *None* option.

Both experiments yield lower inter-rater agreement for the *None* option than for the other choices, shown in Figure 1(a) and (b). Response times were also higher for the *None* option in both tasks (Table 1), suggesting this choice is more difficult. Most disagreement thus concerned the presence of a semantic relationship, but if the annotators agreed there was one, they mostly preferred the same relation. This suggests a *None* option increases annotation quality in general. In the coherence task, there was more agreement on low than high frequency words, which may be due to their lesser ambiguity.

According to the post-test survey, participants mostly based their judgements on sharing the same super term. Relationships that were used without being listed in the instructions were antonymy, forming a technical bigram term together, having the same stem and being used in the same context by Quine. We see this reflected when examining some examples of disagreement. In Table 2, we see disagreement on the related term for *adjectives* because both chosen terms have a relation to this target term, but these are two different relations. We see agreement for *information*, as *collateral information* is a meaningful bigram in Quine's thought experiment on radical translation. In Table 3 we see disagreement on the *ambiguity* outlier. While *believe* has a tenuous relation to *ambiguity*, participant 2 may have considered this relation too tenuous and went for *none*. One expert stated that unclear boundaries of the *none* option were the reason for many *none* disagreements. The *sense datum* disagreement was guessed to be over a rare non-mathematics sense of *divisibility* that one participant remembered but the other might not have.

6 Discussion

In the post-test survey, participants commented that it was sometimes difficult to select the most related

adjectives	*information*	*application*
translation	learning	**numbers**$_1$
embodying	reduction	ambiguity
modifiers$_2$	**collateral**$_{12}$	multiplicity
specious_present	application	subtraction
	ordered_pair	belong
verbs$_1$	*None*	abbreviative
None		***None***$_2$

Table 2: Example of disagreement and agreement in the synonym detection task. To be read vertically, with target terms in italics. Bolded/marked model terms were chosen by participants to be related to the target term.

ambiguity	*objects*	*sense_datum*
parts	object	**prediction**$_1$
phoneme	physical	construction
believe$_1$	**them**$_{12}$	**divisibility**$_2$
None$_2$	*None*	*None*

Table 3: Example of disagreement and agreement in the coherence task. Bolded/marked terms were chosen by participants to be outliers, underlined terms were model outliers with lower word embedding similarity.

word, as different relations were present and selecting the most important one is partly a matter of preference. Such ambiguity is prevalent in any semantic annotation task in which context is unspecified, and in other language annotation tasks in which no explicit choice is made in the guidelines among possible competing valid interpretations (Plank et al., 2014). As noted by Sommerauer et al. (2020), justified disagreement is possible, though detecting it requires meta-annotation and this is in itself a difficult task. However, it might yield additional insights, i.e. that certain DS models might prioritize certain relation types in their nearest neighbours, and that these are equally valid because the experts disagreed on them. Disagreement can also be caused by poorly specified tasks and insufficient conceptual alignment among annotators, especially when the goal is creating a ground truth (Oortwijn et al., 2021b) or otherwise annotating for a specific theory or interpretation.

In future experiments, more specific instructions on when to consider a relation to be relevant, or guidelines on prioritizing certain relations over others, can reduce the difficulty of the task. Our expert participants used many semantic relation types in their interpretation with no clear hierarchy among them. However, applying this to DS model evaluation may require more insight into what exactly the geometric relationships between embeddings in a DS model capture. It may also be interesting for philosophers to make use of models trained to represent particular relations, such as antonymy (Dou et al., 2018). With more specific instructions explicitly directing participants to prioritize or ignore specific relations, our evaluation approach can be adapted to evaluate such models and we expect higher agreement in this type of task. In other cases different interpretations can be desirable, e.g. where there is no hierarchy of relations and a model should capture *relatedness* in a broad sense. For this purpose, we should consider allowing multiple answers — while a forced choice helps to elicit implicit knowledge, explicit knowledge may not always support a categorical decision, though this adds the complication of deciding when an option is relevant enough, similar to the *none* option.

Our results show that absolute and comparative intrinsic evaluation tasks can be used to agree on semantic relatedness between word embeddings even when the target language variety is highly specific. By instructing domain experts to perform the evaluation task using explicit expert knowledge rather than implicit knowledge, inter-rater agreement rates similar to other semantic annotation tasks can be reached. Due to the inherent lack of context in evaluating type-based non-contextual word embeddings, participants struggled with the generality of the task. Based on our analysis and post-test survey, we expect more specific guidelines on word relatedness to increase the reliability of the annotators' judgements, while limiting their generalizability. The addition of a *None* option seemed particularly beneficial for obtaining more reliable annotations based on explicit knowledge. We expect these findings to apply in the context of other domains for which no 'native' annotators are available — for example, language for specific purposes (LSP), historical language varieties or idiolects. In future work, the absolute and comparative intrinsic evaluation tasks we have described can be used to compare the quality of the representations of different word embedding models on these specialized language varieties.

Acknowledgements

We are grateful to Yvette Oortwijn, Thijs Ossenkoppele and Arianna Betti for their input as Quine domain experts. This research was supported by VICI grant *e-Ideas* (277-20-007), financed by the Dutch Research Council (NWO).

References

Miroslav Batchkarov, Thomas Kober, Jeremy Reffin, Julie Weeds, and David Weir. 2016. A critique of word similarity as a method for evaluating distributional semantic models. In *Proceedings of the 1st Workshop on Evaluating Vector-Space Representations for NLP*, pages 7–12.

Yoshua Bengio, Réjean Ducharme, Pascal Vincent, and Christian Jauvin. 2003. A neural probabilistic language model. *Journal of machine learning research*, 3(Feb):1137–1155.

Arianna Betti, Martin Reynaert, Thijs Ossenkoppele, Yvette Oortwijn, Andrew Salway, and Jelke Bloem. 2020. Expert concept-modeling ground truth construction for word embeddings evaluation in concept-focused domains. In *Proceedings of the 28th International Conference on Computational Linguistics*, pages 6690–6702.

Jelke Bloem, Antske Fokkens, and Aurélie Herbelot. 2019. Evaluating the consistency of word embeddings from small data. In *Proceedings of the International Conference on Recent Advances in Natural Language Processing (RANLP 2019)*, pages 132–141.

Melissa A Bowles. 2011. Measuring implicit and explicit linguistic knowledge: What can heritage language learners contribute? *Studies in second language acquisition*, pages 247–271.

Elia Bruni, Nam-Khanh Tran, and Marco Baroni. 2014. Multimodal distributional semantics. *Journal of Artificial Intelligence Research*, 49:1–47.

Margaret Cohen. 1999. *The sentimental education of the novel*. Princeton University Press.

Zehao Dou, Wei Wei, and Xiaojun Wan. 2018. Improving word embeddings for antonym detection using thesauri and SentiWordNet. In *CCF International Conference on Natural Language Processing and Chinese Computing*, pages 67–79. Springer.

Igor Douven. 2017. Abduction. In Edward N. Zalta, editor, *The Stanford Encyclopedia of Philosophy*, summer 2017 edition. Metaphysics Research Lab, Stanford University.

Emeric Dynomant, Romain Lelong, Badisse Dahamna, Clément Massonnaud, Gaétan Kerdelhué, Julien Grosjean, Stéphane Canu, and Stefan J Darmoni. 2019. Word embedding for the French natural language in health care: comparative study. *JMIR medical informatics*, 7(3):e12310.

Rod Ellis. 2004. The definition and measurement of L2 explicit knowledge. *Language learning*, 54(2):227–275.

Rod Ellis. 2005. Measuring implicit and explicit knowledge of a second language: A psychometric study. *Studies in second language acquisition*, 27(2):141–172.

Katrin Erk. 2012. Vector space models of word meaning and phrase meaning: A survey. *Language and Linguistics Compass*, 6(10):635–653.

Lev Finkelstein, Evgeniy Gabrilovich, Yossi Matias, Ehud Rivlin, Zach Solan, Gadi Wolfman, and Eytan Ruppin. 2001. Placing search in context: The concept revisited. In *Proceedings of the 10th international conference on World Wide Web*, pages 406–414.

Annapaola Ginammi, Rob Koopman, Shenghui Wang, Jelke Bloem, and Arianna Betti. in press. Bolzano, Kant, and the traditional theory of concepts: A computational investigation. In *The Dynamics of Science: Computational Frontiers in History and Philosophy of Science*. Pittsburgh University Press.

Anna Gladkova and Aleksandr Drozd. 2016. Intrinsic evaluations of word embeddings: What can we do better? In *Proceedings of the 1st Workshop on Evaluating Vector-Space Representations for NLP*, pages 36–42.

Diogo da Silva Magalhães Gomes, Fábio Corrêa Cordeiro, Bernardo Scapini Consoli, Nikolas Lacerda Santos, Viviane Pereira Moreira, Renata Vieira, Silvia Moraes, and Alexandre Gonçalves Evsukoff. 2021. Portuguese word embeddings for the oil and gas industry: Development and evaluation. *Computers in Industry*, 124:103347.

Aurélie Herbelot, Eva Von Redecker, and Johanna Müller. 2012. Distributional techniques for philosophical enquiry. In *Proceedings of the 6th Workshop on Language Technology for Cultural Heritage, Social Sciences, and Humanities*, pages 45–54. Association for Computational Linguistics.

Felix Hill, Roi Reichart, and Anna Korhonen. 2015. Simlex-999: Evaluating semantic models with (genuine) similarity estimation. *Computational Linguistics*, 41(4):665–695.

Tomas Mikolov, Kai Chen, Greg Corrado, and Jeffrey Dean. 2013. Efficient estimation of word representations in vector space. *CoRR*, abs/1301.3781.

Yvette Oortwijn, Jelke Bloem, Pia Sommerauer, Francois Meyer, Wei Zhou, and Antske Fokkens. 2021a. Challenging distributional models with a conceptual network of philosophical terms. In *Proceedings of the 2021 Conference of the North American Chapter of the Association for Computational Linguistics: Human Language Technologies (NAACL-HLT)*. In press.

Yvette Oortwijn, Thijs Ossenkoppele, and Arianna Betti. 2021b. Interrater disagreement resolution: A systematic procedure to reach consensus in annotation tasks. In *Proceedings of the First Workshop on Human Evaluation of NLP Systems (HumEval)*.

José Padarian and Ignacio Fuentes. 2019. Word embeddings for application in geosciences: development, evaluation, and examples of soil-related concepts. *Soil*, 5(2):177–187.

Serguei Pakhomov, Bridget McInnes, Terrence Adam, Ying Liu, Ted Pedersen, and Genevieve B Melton. 2010. Semantic similarity and relatedness between clinical terms: an experimental study. In *AMIA annual symposium proceedings*, page 572. American Medical Informatics Association.

Serguei VS Pakhomov, Ted Pedersen, Bridget McInnes, Genevieve B Melton, Alexander Ruggieri, and Christopher G Chute. 2011. Towards a framework for developing semantic relatedness reference standards. *Journal of biomedical informatics*, 44(2):251–265.

Ted Pedersen, Serguei VS Pakhomov, Siddharth Patwardhan, and Christopher G Chute. 2007. Measures of semantic similarity and relatedness in the biomedical domain. *Journal of biomedical informatics*, 40(3):288–299.

Barbara Plank, Dirk Hovy, and Anders Søgaard. 2014. Linguistically debatable or just plain wrong? In *Proceedings of the 52nd Annual Meeting of the Association for Computational Linguistics (Volume 2: Short Papers)*, pages 507–511.

Willard Van Orman Quine. 1960. Word and object. *MIT Press*.

Tobias Schnabel, Igor Labutov, David Mimno, and Thorsten Joachims. 2015. Evaluation methods for unsupervised word embeddings. In *Proceedings of the 2015 conference on Empirical Methods in Natural Language Processing*, pages 298–307.

Pia Sommerauer, Antske Fokkens, and Piek Vossen. 2020. Would you describe a leopard as yellow? Evaluating crowd-annotations with justified and informative disagreement. In *Proceedings of the 28th International Conference on Computational Linguistics*, pages 4798–4809.

Peter D Turney and Patrick Pantel. 2010. From frequency to meaning: Vector space models of semantics. *Journal of artificial intelligence research*, 37:141–188.

Yaza Wainakh, Moiz Rauf, and Michael Pradel. 2019. Evaluating semantic representations of source code. *CoRR*, abs/1910.05177.

Pauline van Wierst, Sanne Vrijenhoek, Stefan Schlobach, and Arianna Betti. 2016. Phil@Scale: Computational Methods within Philosophy. In *Proceedings of the Third Conference on Digital Humanities in Luxembourg with a Special Focus on Reading Historical Sources in the Digital Age. CEUR Workshop Proceedings, CEUR-WS.org*, volume 1681, Aachen.

Detecting Post-edited References and Their Effect on Human Evaluation

Věra Kloudová, Ondřej Bojar, Martin Popel
Charles University,
Faculty of Mathematics and Physics,
Institute of Formal and Applied Linguistics,
Malostranské náměstí 25, 118 00
Prague, Czech Republic
{bojar,kloudova,popel}@ufal.mff.cuni.cz

Abstract

This paper provides a quick overview of possible methods how to detect that reference translations were actually created by post-editing an MT system. Two methods based on automatic metrics are presented: BLEU difference between the suspected MT and some other good MT and BLEU difference using additional references. These two methods revealed a suspicion that the WMT 2020 Czech reference is based on MT. The suspicion was confirmed in a manual analysis by finding concrete proofs of the post-editing procedure in particular sentences. Finally, a typology of post-editing changes is presented where typical errors or changes made by the post-editor or errors adopted from the MT are classified.

1 Introduction

Over ten years of WMT (Conference on Machine Translation, Barrault et al., 2020)[1] saw a number of manual evaluation methods and established the best strategies for obtaining reference translations for automatic evaluation, see Appendix B in WMT 2020 Findings (Barrault et al., 2020).

One of the instructions for preparing the reference translations explicitly prohibits using any machine translation. Yet, in 2020, one of the agencies has not followed this instruction. Not only was it easy to recognize, but we learned several novel insights into manual evaluation of translation, by examining post-edited and independent reference translations and providing a small contrastive style of manual evaluation.

2 Dataset

We used the English-Czech part of WMT2020 (Barrault et al., 2020) news test set, which consists of 130 documents (1418 segments) originally written in English – news stories downloaded from web. The test set comes with an official reference translation into Czech (REF1) provided by the WMT organizers and done by a professional translation agency. There are also 8 machine translations submitted by the participants of the WMT news translation shared task and 4 translations by online systems anonymized as ONLINE-A, ONLINE-B, ONLINE-G and ONLINE-Z.

We focused on three translations: the official reference, REF1; the best-performing MT system (according to the official WMT manual evaluation), CUNI-DOCTRANSFORMER (Popel, 2020); and the best-performing online system, ONLINE-B.

We hired two professional translators (native Czech speakers) to translate the whole WMT20 test set, thus creating additional references REF2 and REF3. We also hired 18 annotators to judge the translation quality of REF1, CUNI-DOCTRANSFORMER and ONLINE-B.[2] The annotators assessed 90 of the 130 documents, using the RankME evaluation (Novikova et al., 2018) following the methodology of Popel et al. (2020). In this RankME evaluation, fluency, adequacy and overall quality are evaluated in a source-based sentence-level document-aware fashion, on a 0–10 scale, where all the evaluated translations are shown on the same screen, allowing thus better reliability in comparisons; see Section 5 for details.

3 Automatic analysis of references

Table 1 shows the translation quality of the three references and two selected MT systems according to two manual evaluations, DA (Direct Assessment, Graham et al., 2013) and RankME, and four types of BLEU scores. The first three types use

[1] http://www.statmt.org/wmt06 till wmt20

[2] The additional references REF2 and REF3 were not available before our RankME evaluation started. We plan to evaluate them in future.

Proceedings of the Workshop on Human Evaluation of NLP Systems (HumEval), pages 114–119
Online, April 19, 2021.

system	manual		BLEU			
	DA	RankME	REF1	REF2	REF3	REF2+3
REF1	**85.6**	**8.17**	–	28.91	24.18	37.22
REF2	–	–	28.90	–	26.43	–
REF3	–	–	24.20	26.45	–	–
CUNI-DOCTRANSFORMER	82.8	7.39	35.88	**36.50**	**30.17**	**47.59**
ONLINE-B	70.5	5.62	**41.11**	31.08	26.39	41.00

Table 1: Manual and automatic evaluation scores of the systems in our study. DA is the source-based Direct Assessment average score (un-normalized). RankME is the average Overall quality score over all 90 documents (not sentences) evaluated in our study. BLEU is computed with SacreBLEU (Post, 2018) with signature BLEU+case.mixed+numrefs.1+smooth.exp+tok.13a+version.1.4.13. The best score in each column is in bold.

REF1, REF2 and REF3, respectively, as the reference translation in BLEU. The fourth type uses BLEU with two reference translations: REF2+3.

While both manual evaluations, DA and RankME, agree that REF1 is better than both CUNI-DOCTRANSFORMER and ONLINE-B, the automatic metric BLEU evaluates one of the two MT systems as better than REF1.[3] For brevity, we report only BLEU, but we confirmed this with several other automatic metrics, e.g. chrF (Popović, 2015).

The reason for this surprising observation is that most sentences in REF1 are actually post-edited versions of ONLINE-B, as we show in Sections 3.1 and 4 and as was acknowledged by the agency after our investigation. Thus, REF1 and ONLINE-B are more similar than if REF1 had been translated from scratch.[4]

It is well-known that BLEU (and other automatic metrics based on similarity with reference translations) is biased when evaluating a system which was used as a basis for post-editing the reference translation.

It is important to note that the official (manual) evaluation carried out by WMT for the affected English-to-Czech translation direction was *source-based* DA. The annotators of the DA thus were not affected by the quality of references; instead, they blindly rated REF1 as if it was another competing translation system. The resulting scores of DA document that source-level DA is sufficiently reliable, robust to invalid references. At the same time, it was a little surprising to us that "mere post-editing" can increase translation quality so substantially that REF1 significantly outperformed all other systems. Despite the remaining translation errors in REF1, see below, the translator/post-editor did the job well.

For a finer analysis, we process the news test set at the level of individual documents in the following.

3.1 Automatic detection of post-editing

Our first suspicion that REF1 is actually post-edited ONLINE-B stems from the fact that ONLINE-B achieved the highest $\text{BLEU}_{\text{REF1}}$ score (i.e. BLEU with REF1 as the reference) out of all the MT systems, including the best one according to the manual evaluation, CUNI-DOCTRANSFORMER, as shown in Table 1. In order to confirm this suspicion, we wanted to automatically find documents where the probability of being post-edited is the highest.

Below, we suggest two methods for such document-level automatic detection of post-editing. The first method needs just an output of another MT system. The second method needs one or more additional human references.

3.1.1 Detection using another MT system

We selected CUNI-DOCTRANSFORMER as the other MT system for two reasons. First, it is the best MT system in English-Czech WMT20 according to the official manual evaluation. Second, as far

[3] Actually, both MT systems are better than all three references according to all BLEU scores, with a single exception of $\text{BLEU}_{\text{REF3}}(\text{ONLINE-B}) = 26.39 < 26.43 = \text{BLEU}_{\text{REF3}}(\text{REF2})$, which is not statistically significant (bootstrap resampling, $p < 0.05$). Obviously, we cannot use e.g. $\text{BLEU}_{\text{REF1}}$ to judge the quality of REF1 (it would be 100, by definition).

[4] One of the instructions for the translation agency preparing references for WMT 2020 was: *All translations should be "from scratch", without post-editing from MT. Using post-editing would bias the evaluation, so we need to avoid it. We can detect post-editing so will reject translations that are post-edited.* (Barrault et al., 2020). Unfortunately, the WMT organizers did not detect the post-editing in this case (as we do in this paper) and did not reject the translation.

as we know, CUNI-DOCTRANSFORMER was not available online at the time of creating the WMT20 references, so it could not be used as the basis for post-editing REF1.

For each document d, we computed

$$Detection1 = \text{BLEU}_{\text{REF1}}(\text{ONLINE-B}, d) - \text{BLEU}_{\text{REF1}}(\text{CUNI-DOCTRANSFORMER}, d). \quad (1)$$

This score was positive for 104 out of the 130 documents. In other words, for 80% of documents, the reference is more similar to ONLINE-B than to the best-performing CUNI-DOCTRANSFORMER, a likely indicator that most of the documents were post-edited.

We inspected manually three documents with the most negative $Detection1$ score and did not find any clues of post-editing, but we noticed the quality of ONLINE-B was low for these documents, so perhaps the translator throw away the MT output and translated these documents from scratch (or post-edited so heavily that the original MT output cannot be detected).

We inspected manually three documents with the most positive $Detection1$ score and observed these well translated with a reasonably high quality by ONLINE-B, and required just few minor post-edits, as was done in REF1.

Finally, we inspected sentences from other documents and found further signals of post-editing (even when the $Detection1$ score was not high enough to be a convincing proof alone). These examples are discussed in Section 4.

3.1.2 Detection using additional references

A similar detection can be used with an additional human reference instead of an MT system. We had available two such references, REF2 and REF3. We thus opted for a slightly different detection formula which allows to use two-reference BLEU:

For each document d, we computed

$$Detection2 = \text{BLEU}_{\text{ONLINE-B}}(\text{REF1}, d) - \text{BLEU}_{\text{REF2+3}}(\text{REF1}, d). \quad (2)$$

This resulted in a similar ordering of documents as the $Detection1$ method.

3.2 Human translation is more similar to MT than other humans

For each document d, we computed

$$Score3 = \text{BLEU}_{\text{REF2+3}}(\text{REF1}, d) - \text{BLEU}_{\text{REF2+3}}(\text{ONLINE-B}, d). \quad (3)$$

This $Score3$ score was negative for 96 out of the 130 documents. This means that the similarity of ONLINE-B to the additional references REF2 and REF3 is higher than the similarity of REF1 to REF2 and REF3. When focusing just on REF2, we can see that $\text{BLEU}_{\text{REF2}}(\text{ONLB}) = 31.08 > 28.91 = \text{BLEU}_{\text{REF2}}(\text{REF1})$. This is very surprising given our hypothesis that REF2 is actually translated from scratch without any post-editing.

We have two possible explanations for this. First, the REF1 translator tried to "hide" the fact that the translation is post-edited, by doing edits which do not affect the translation quality. Second, the REF1 translator actually improved the ONLINE-B translation quality by post-edits which result in less literal translations, while the REF2 translator opted more frequently translations which were likely to be independently produced also by the MT system.

Given the fact that both DA and RankME manual evaluations show REF1 is significantly better than ONLINE-B, we hypothesize most of the post-edits were actually improvements. We noticed just a few opposite cases (see below, category 3).

4 Post-editing changes typology

In this part of our study, we would like to present a classification of post-editing changes observed in texts which we claim to be post-edited machine translations. These changes signal that the reference translation REF1 has been actually created by post-editing a MT system. For this purpose, we used MT-ComparEval (Klejch et al., 2015) to select 27 sentences which show the highest n-gram overlap with the suspected MT system. We analyzed the edits made by a post-editor in a MT output and compared the source text (English), the MT output (Czech) and the output of the manual post-editing process (Czech).

Based on the particular changes found after comparing these three versions of our sentences, we defined the following categories (with examples where SRC is the source sentence, ONLB is the MT ONLINE-B and REF1 is the human post-editing). In each category, we would like to present particularly noticeable changes which we assume to be clear evidence of the post-editing procedure. We classify these changes into three categories:

- Category 1: minor changes, particularly focused on grammar categories, in long adopted structures from the MT (preserving or improving the overall quality of the output),

- Category 2: unnecessary shifts (without a significant impact on the quality of the output),
- Category 3: negative shifts (errors made by the post-editor, preserving or even worsening the quality of the MT output).

Furthermore, we also found these errors or conspicuous structures in the post-edited output:

- Category 4: errors adopted from the MT which the post-editor has not discovered; therefore, they have been preserved in the final text of REF1.

For all these four categories, we can state they prove the final output is a result of a post-editing process.

4.1 Typology 1: Changes by the post-editor

4.1.1 Changes in spelling

Category 3: Errors in writing:

SRC their 17-month-old daughter
ONLB jejich **17měsíční** dcerou
REF1 jejich **17timěsíční** dcerou

The standard Czech grammar allows only forms *17měsíční* or *sedmnáctiměsíční* (17-month). The form *17timěsíční* (where "*ti*" reflects the pronunciation) is considered an error.

4.1.2 Grammatical changes

Category 1: Changes in verb tenses:

SRC Wang's death follows after those of other activists [...]
ONLB Wangova smrt **následuje** po těch dalších aktivistech [...]
REF1 Wangova smrt **následovala** po úmrtí dalších aktivistů [...]

The present tense (*následuje = follows*) used in ONLB was changed into past tense (*následovala = followed*). Changes between past and present tense (while keeping the same verb) occurred relatively often (8 cases) in the investigated 27 sentences.

Category 3: Case and noun number changes:

SRC Nobel laureate winner Liu Xiaobo [...]
ONLB Nositel Nobelovy ceny **za laureát** Liu Xiaobo [...]
REF1 Nositel Nobelovy ceny **laureátů** Liu Xiaobo [...]

Despite the changes made, the semantic defectiveness of ONLB has been preserved. In Czech, the Nobel prize is *Nobelova cena* and the word *laureátů* (genitive sg.) is wrong. In this case, *Laureát Nobelovy ceny* would be acceptable.

Category 3: Changes in adjective comparison:

SRC The market was more receptive to lesser-known names [...]
ONLB Trh byl **vnímavější** k méně známým jménům [...]
REF1 Trh byl **více vnímavý** k méně známým firmám [...]

The correct comparative of *vnímavý = receptive* is *vnímavější*. The phrase *více vnímavý* is considered non-standard and rather rare.[5]

4.1.3 Changes in accuracy of information

Category 3: Changes incompatible with the meaning of the source text:

SRC from some 3 billion cu ft at the start of 2019
ONLB z **přibližně** 3 miliard cu ft na začátku roku 2019
REF1 ze **současných** 3 miliard kubických stop na začátku roku 2019

ONLB uses *přibližně = approximately*, but REF1 changed it to *současných = current*, which is wrong because the article was written in September 2019, when the amount was already much higher than 3 billion cu ft, according to the source text.

4.2 Typology 2: Errors adopted from ONLB

4.2.1 Errors in spelling

Category 4: English spelling in foreign names:

SRC [...], Uighur scholar
ONLB [...], **Uighurský** učenec
REF1 [...], **Uighurský** učenec

The correct Czech spelling would be *ujgurský* (with lowercase *u*, in this sentence).

Category 4: MT spelling errors:

SRC Endeavor Group Holdings
ONLB Společnost **Endeavour** Group Holdings
REF1 Společnost **Endeavour** Group Holdings

ONLB introduced a spelling error – *Endeavour*, which remained unnoticed by REF1.

[5]Such analytic comparatives can be seen as a proof of translationese (Toury, 1995), i.e. in this case, influenced by the English analytic comparative *more receptive*.

4.2.2 Lexical and stylistic errors

Category 4: Errors in lexical meaning:

SRC [...] then evidence showed the officers had reason to believe their lives were in danger [...]

ONLB [...] důkazy ukazují, že **důstojníci** měli důvod se domnívat, že jejich životy jsou v nebezpečí [...]

REF1 [...] podle svědectví důkazů měli **důstojníci** důvod domnívat se, že jejich životy byly v ohrožení [...]

Given the context of the source article, *officers* should be translated as *policisté = police officers*. It is questionable whether the translation *důstojníci = commissioned officers* is acceptable.

Category 4: Errors in meaning of a syntactic structure:

SRC an invite from Khloe to a 'Taco Tuesday' dinner at her mansion

ONLB pozvání od Khloe **na večeři "Taco Tuesday" u jejího sídla**

REF1 pozván od Khloé **na večeři v "Taco Tuesday" u jejího sídla**

In the highlighted example, REF1 added only the preposition *v = in*, which bears out the superficial reading of the machine translation output *a dinner in a "Taco Tuesday" restaurant near her mansion*. However, the original meaning is quite different: "Taco Tuesday" is a custom of going out to eat tacos, not a name of a restaurant.

Category 4: Improper collocations:

SRC The California attorney general's office in March declined to issue state criminal charges after a nearly yearlong investigation.

ONLB Kancelář generálního prokurátora v Kalifornii v březnu po téměř celoročním vyšetřování odmítla **vydat státní trestní obvinění**.

REF1 Kancelář generálního prokurátora v Kalifornii v březnu po téměř celoročním vyšetřování odmítla **podat trestní obvinění**.

In this example, solely the verb prefix changed (*vydat* → *podat*), but not the noun (*obvinění = accusation, charge*). The correct translation would be *podat trestní oznámení*.

5 Human evaluation – RankME

In our blind RankME evaluation by 18 human judges (6 professional translators, 6 students from MA Study Program Translation: Czech and English at the Institute of Translation Studies, Charles University's Faculty of Arts,[6] and 6 non-professionals with excellent knowledge of the English language), 90 documents (887 segments, typically sentences) were evaluated on a sentence level in terms of adequacy, fluency and overall quality (as defined by Popel et al. (2020)). Every document was scored by two evaluators, and every evaluator scored ten different documents. Then we could compare the ratings of the post-edited REF1 and of the suspected ONLB. According to the ratings, the translation quality is, in all cases, better in REF1 compared to ONLB. The post-editor improved the quality of the ONLB in all three categories: in adequacy (increased by 2.23 on average), fluency (2.70) and overall quality (2.55), on a 0–10 scale. As could be expected, the most significant improvement occurred in fluency. Apparently, the post-editor was more sensitive to errors in fluency rather than adequacy, as shown also in our analysis of post-editing changes.

6 Conclusion

We suspected that WMT20 reference translations were actually post-edits of one of the participating systems, ONLINE-B, and not created independently. We proposed two methods to detect this situation, both confirming our suspicion.

In a subsequent manual analysis, we provided numerous examples of translation choices in the reference translation which are extremely unlikely to happen when translating from scratch.[7]

The result of this analysis is a draft typology of post-editing strategies. We see this typology as an interesting basis for further inspection of translations in a world where post-editing becomes the industry standard.

By contrasting Direct Assessment scores with our manual evaluation (RankME), we observed the post-editor improved primarily *fluency* of the translation and less so its adequacy. It would be useful to confirm this observation on a larger sample.

[6] `https://utrl.ff.cuni.cz/`

[7] Such choices are also likely to be changed in paraphrasing, which opens a new view on the results of Freitag et al. (2020), who show that using paraphrases as references in BLEU may lead to higher correlation with human evaluation.

Acknowledgments

The work was supported by the grants 19-26934X (NEUREM3) and GX20-16819X (LUSyD) by the Czech Science Foundation. The work has been using language resources developed and distributed by the LINDAT/CLARIAHCZ project of the Ministry of Education, Youth and Sports of the Czech Republic (project LM2018101).

References

Loïc Barrault, Magdalena Biesialska, Ondřej Bojar, Marta R. Costa-jussà, Christian Federmann, Yvette Graham, Roman Grundkiewicz, Barry Haddow, Matthias Huck, Eric Joanis, Tom Kocmi, Philipp Koehn, Chi-kiu Lo, Nikola Ljubešić, Christof Monz, Makoto Morishita, Masaaki Nagata, Toshiaki Nakazawa, Santanu Pal, Matt Post, and Marcos Zampieri. 2020. Findings of the 2020 conference on machine translation (WMT20). In *Proceedings of the Fifth Conference on Machine Translation*, pages 1–55, Online. Association for Computational Linguistics.

Markus Freitag, David Grangier, and Isaac Caswell. 2020. BLEU might be guilty but references are not innocent. In *Proceedings of the 2020 Conference on Empirical Methods in Natural Language Processing (EMNLP)*, pages 61–71, Online. Association for Computational Linguistics.

Yvette Graham, Timothy Baldwin, Alistair Moffat, and Justin Zobel. 2013. Continuous measurement scales in human evaluation of machine translation. In *Proceedings of the 7th Linguistic Annotation Workshop and Interoperability with Discourse*, pages 33–41, Sofia, Bulgaria. Association for Computational Linguistics.

Ondřej Klejch, Eleftherios Avramidis, Aljoscha Burchardt, and Martin Popel. 2015. MT-ComparEval: Graphical evaluation interface for Machine Translation development. *The Prague Bulletin of Mathematical Linguistics*, 104:63–74.

Jekaterina Novikova, Ondřej Dušek, and Verena Rieser. 2018. RankME: Reliable human ratings for natural language generation. In *Proceedings of the 2018 Conference of the North American Chapter of the Association for Computational Linguistics: Human Language Technologies, Volume 2 (Short Papers)*, pages 72–78, New Orleans, Louisiana. Association for Computational Linguistics.

Martin Popel. 2020. CUNI English-Czech and English-Polish Systems in WMT20: Robust Document-Level Training. In *Proceedings of the Fifth Conference on Machine Translation*, pages 269–273, Online. Association for Computational Linguistics.

Martin Popel, Marketa Tomkova, Jakub Tomek, Łukasz Kaiser, Jakob Uszkoreit, Ondřej Bojar, and Zdeněk Žabokrtský. 2020. Transforming machine translation: a deep learning system reaches news translation quality comparable to human professionals. *Nature Communications*, 11(4381):1–15.

Maja Popović. 2015. chrF: character n-gram F-score for automatic MT evaluation. In *Proceedings of the Tenth Workshop on Statistical Machine Translation*, pages 392–395, Lisbon, Portugal. ACL.

Matt Post. 2018. A call for clarity in reporting BLEU scores. In *Proceedings of the Third Conference on Machine Translation: Research Papers*, pages 186–191, Belgium, Brussels. Association for Computational Linguistics.

Gideon Toury. 1995. *Descriptive translation studies and beyond*. John Benjamins Publishing.

A Case Study of Efficacy and Challenges in Practical Human-in-Loop Evaluation of NLP Systems using Checklist

Shaily Bhatt[1] **Rahul Jain**[2] **Sandipan Dandapat**[2] **Sunayana Sitaram**[1]
[1] Microsoft Research, Bangalore, India
[2] Microsoft R&D, Hyderabad, India
{t-shbhatt, jain.rahul, sadandap, sunayana.sitaram}@microsoft.com

Abstract

Despite state-of-the-art performance, NLP systems can be fragile in real-world situations. This is often due to insufficient understanding of the capabilities and limitations of models and the heavy reliance on standard evaluation benchmarks. Research into non-standard evaluation to mitigate this brittleness is gaining increasing attention. Notably, the behavioral testing principle 'Checklist', which decouples testing from implementation revealed significant failures in state-of-the-art models for multiple tasks. In this paper, we present a case study of using Checklist in a practical scenario. We conduct experiments for evaluating an offensive content detection system and use a data augmentation technique for improving the model using insights from Checklist. We lay out the challenges and open questions based on our observations of using Checklist for human-in-loop evaluation and improvement of NLP systems. *Disclaimer: The paper contains examples of content with offensive language. The examples do not represent the views of the authors or their employers towards any person(s), group(s), practice(s), or entity/entities.*

1 Introduction

NLP systems have been known to learn spurious patterns from data to achieve high accuracy on test sets (Goyal et al., 2017; Gururangan et al., 2018; Glockner et al., 2018; Tsuchiya, 2018; Geva et al., 2019). Evaluating models on static benchmarks and on test sets that have a similar distribution to the training data has resulted in an overestimation of model performance (Belinkov and Bisk, 2018; Recht et al., 2019) and models becoming increasingly fragile or less useful in real-world settings. This can be due to various factors such as language complexity and variability, the difference between training, testing, and real-world data, and insufficient understanding of the capabilities and limitations of the model itself. When deployed in the wild, such systems tend to break down, resulting in grossly incorrect predictions. This leads to mistrust in the system at two levels – first, on individual predictions and second, on the system's soundness in uncontrolled environments such as usage after deployment (Ribeiro et al., 2016).

Further, evaluation benchmarks are also becoming increasingly obsolete due to the exponential rise in data and compute-heavy systems that exceed performance expectations, bringing the benchmark's 'toughness' and hence, its reliability into question (Nie et al., 2020). In order to mitigate this limitation of static evaluation, several approaches are used to evaluate other model aspects including, but not limited to, robustness (Rychalska et al., 2019), fairness (Prabhakaran et al., 2019), consistency (Ribeiro et al., 2019), explanations (Ribeiro et al., 2016), and adversarial performance (Ribeiro et al., 2018b; Iyyer et al., 2018; Nie et al., 2020).

Human-in-Loop processes can be used to complement the capabilities of automation with human expertise (Ribeiro et al., 2020; Potts et al., 2020; Nie et al., 2020; Ribeiro et al., 2018b). Previous studies have shown that using humans to close the loop of the process of evaluation, explanation, or improvement can lead to a much better understanding of the system through higher explainability (Ribeiro et al., 2018a, 2016), better detection of model failures (Ribeiro et al., 2020; Iyyer et al., 2018), and easier bug-fixing (Ribeiro et al., 2020, 2018b), resulting in robustness of the model in practical scenarios and increased trust in its predictions.

Ribeiro et al. (2020) introduced a behavioral testing strategy that decouples testing from model implementation. Using human-generated test sets, they showed that state-of-the-art NLP models for multiple tasks fail to perform well for basic capabilities. We describe the framework in detail in section 2.

In this paper, we describe a case study of using the Checklist paradigm of evaluation in a practi-

Proceedings of the Workshop on Human Evaluation of NLP Systems (HumEval), pages 120–130
Online, April 19, 2021. ©2021 Association for Computational Linguistics

cal scenario. Specifically, we used Checklist to evaluate and debug an offensive content detection system. We found that Checklist can lead to effective pinpointing of specific capabilities for which the model, despite impressive performance on a standard benchmark test set, failed. Further, these insights can be used to improve the model using targeted data augmentation to debug specific model failures. However, we found that using Checklist for evaluation and improvement is not always foolproof. We discuss the challenges and open questions observed during these experiments.

The rest of the paper is organized as follows: First, we give a brief overview of the Checklist framework. In Section 3, we describe our case study, including the capabilities we test, results on the base model, the method applied to use these insights for improvement, and the results thereafter. Finally, we present a detailed analysis of some of the most imminent challenges with using Checklist for our experiments.

2 Overview of Checklist

The Checklist framework (Ribeiro et al., 2020) introduces a human-in-loop behavioral testing technique for evaluating NLP systems. The authors argue that even though models perform well on static benchmarks, they fail to perform in real-world scenarios for basic capabilities. They release an open-source package [1] with functionality to create template sets and run software engineering-like decoupled testing on black-box models.

The individual phenomena tested using Checklist are known as capabilities. These capabilities are based on model expectations and the language usage that it needs to handle. For example, Negation is a capability of a Sentiment Analysis model - the model should be able to distinguish 'happy' and 'not happy' as two opposite sentiments despite the overlapping word 'happy'.

The Checklist framework provides three different test types. The Minimum Functionality Tests (MFTs) are simple tests, similar to unit tests in software testing, that can test predictions on specific model capabilities. Most of the capabilities tested in our case study are MFTs. Invariance tests (INVs) are a test type where small semantic-preserving perturbations are applied to the test cases, and it is expected that the model output should not change. For example - in our case, while testing for the Robustness of the model, small typos are introduced. Directional Expectation tests (DIRs) are similar to INV, except that the model output is expected to change in a certain way.

In order for humans to generate test cases, Checklist uses Templates and Lexicons. For example: 'I {POSITIVE_VERB} {ACTIVITY}.' is a template. 'POSITIVE_VERB' and 'ACTIVITY' in this template are two different keywords in the lexicon, each taking a specific set of values. For example, POSITIVE_VERB = ['like', 'love', 'enjoy'] and ACTIVITY = ['dancing', 'hiking' 'cooking', 'coding']. The template generates 12 examples - the Cartesian product of the values of the two lexicon keywords in the template.

In the original Checklist work, the authors test state-of-the-art and commercial systems across three tasks revealing unprecedented failure rates even for the most basic capabilities. For more detailed information on these results, we refer the reader to the original paper.

3 A Case Study of Using Checklist

We used Checklist to evaluate and improve an in-house offensive content detection system. While we studies a particular system as a use case, the process can be applied to any NLP model.

The first step was to create a documentation of expectations. This documentation was important to lay out guidelines for what constitutes positive or negative examples in specific settings. In accordance with standard text classification annotation, for this task, offensive content is the positive class, and non-offensive content is the negative class. The documentation or guidelines contained concrete definitions of various offensive content categories that the model is expected to detect. These are henceforth known as the model capabilities and are described in section 3.1. This is important for Checklist evaluation because it relies on building templates that target specific model capabilities. We gave this documentation to the annotators who were expected to use these guidelines to come up with templates of specific capabilities that could be used to find bugs.

Since offensive classification is a task that inherently has a class imbalance with fewer examples in the positive class in most publicly available datasets (de Gibert et al., 2018; Davidson et al., 2017), including ours, we asked the annotators to develop templates that would result in offensive data. An-

[1] https://github.com/marcotcr/checklist

other reason for this design decision was that while offensive content is more likely to follow a certain pattern - a combination of entities and offensive language, non-offensive content would not follow any discernible patterns making it difficult to convert it into templates. Further, from an application perspective in real-world settings, where such a model is employed to flag or filter offensive content, a higher recall is preferable, as false negatives (examples that are offensive but predicted as non-offensive) need to be avoided even at the cost of a few false positives.

3.1 Capabilities

Based on the documentation the capabilities tested for detection of offensive content were:

1. **Characterization**: Derogatory content/Defamation targeted towards individuals or groups (people who share certain attributes like sex, race, religion, nationality, occupation, age, etc.) including stereotypes. Also includes positive and negative characterizations of individuals or groups including comments on sexual orientation, ethics, morality, habits, physical appearance, or other characteristics.
   (a) **Simple Characterization of Individuals**: Characterizing individuals. *Example*: *Trump is an idiot, is Joe Biden racist?, Kevin Spacey gay, Fat Meghan Markle, Bin Laden was amazing*, etc.
   (b) **Simple Characterization of Groups**: Characterizing groups *Example*: *Mexicans are lazy, Are all whites racist, Jews are greedy, females belong in the kitchen, all men are pigs, people from middle east stink*, etc.
2. **Negation**: Negation of characteristics targeted towards individuals or groups. Also includes negation of positive and negative characterizations of individuals or groups including comments on sexual orientation, ethics, morality, habits, physical appearance, or other characteristics.
   (a) **Negation of Positive characterization of Individuals**: Negating a positive characterization of any individual. Also includes content that seeks or suggest negation of rights or equality to specific entities. *Example*: *Trump is not smart, Justin Beiber is not an ethical person, Gandhi was not honest*, etc.
   (b) **Negation of Positive Characterization of Groups**: Negating positive characterization of groups. Also includes content that seeks or suggest negation of rights or equality to specific groups. *Example*: *Females are not smart, Muslims are not honest, Policemen cannot be good, Women should not be allowed to go to college*, etc.
   (c) **Negation of Negative Characterization of Individuals**: Negating negative characterization of individuals. *Example*: *Bin Laden was not bad, Hitler was not brutal*, etc.
   (d) **Negation of Negative Characterizations of Groups**: Negating negative characterization of groups. *Example*: *Jihadists are not bad, Racist people are not awful*, etc
3. **Violence** Explicitly seeking or suggesting violence against Groups or Individuals. Also includes content that in general talks about violent actions in an offensive fashion but is not directed towards any specific entity. *Example: ISIS beheadings, Trump should be assassinated, Should men hit women, North korea should be nuked*, etc.
4. **Unsafe**: Seeking or suggesting unsafe content related to topics including, but not limited to, suicide, self-harm, illegal drugs, addictive or harmful medication, etc. *Example: Easy ways to kill oneself, Where to buy levothyroxine without prescription, How to make meth at home*, etc.
5. **Racy**: Sexually suggestive content which may or may not be targeted to individuals or groups. *Example*: *Pictures of hot women swimmers, Japanese men in bedroom*, etc
6. **Robustness**: To test if the system is robust to minor perturbations like typos or punctuation that are consistent with intentional or unintentional usage in writing offensive content.
   (a) **One Typo**: Introducing one random typo in the example by flipping adjacent characters. *Example*: *fcuk.*
   (b) **Two Typo**: Introducing one random typo in the example by flipping adjacent characters. *Example*: *All mne ar epigs.*
   (c) **Punctuation Insertion**: Random inser-

tion of punctuation marks in the example. *Example*: *f*ck*.

3.2 Using Checklist to Evaluate the Base Model

We used one template set and documented the failure rates of an in-house XLMR-based offensive content detection model, henceforth referred to as the base model. This base model had a good performance on the standard static benchmark test sets of 10k instances,[2] similar to other state-of-the-art systems for offensive content detection. The static test set had a similar distribution to the training data and has roughly 2.5k positive and 7.5k negative examples. The metrics on the static test set are available in the base model row of Table 1. The model was a 24-layer transformer-based XLM-R model fine-tuned with 481k examples of offensive and hate speech data, out of which 198k were positive examples. The model was trained with a learning rate of 5e-6 for 10 epochs with a batch size of 128.

Targeting specific capabilities using Checklist showed huge failure rates, indicating that the model still failed to meet the expectations even with good performance metrics. This is consistent with the original findings of Ribeiro et al. (2020), where multiple state-of-the-art models were found to have huge failure rates for the many basic capabilities.

Particularly in derogatory content, offensive content against a specific person seemed to be tougher to detect as compared to offensive content against a group. This may be because the names used to generate the test cases for offensive content against a person may not necessarily be names of famous people seen in training data, and the model was unable to generalize offensive language detection to unseen named entities. It is also possible that offensive content against specific groups is a more sensitive issue and is thus represented more in the base model's training data. Further, the model was unable to handle negation very well. This is consistent with the findings of Ribeiro et al. (2020) who also found that state-of-the-art sentiment analysis models failed much more when dealing with negation.

In capabilities of unsafe and violent content, the failure rates were comparatively lower. This can be attributed to the fact that such content is more likely to contain specific keywords or patterns that the model has learned to classify as offensive during training, resulting in lower failure rates even when tested using templates. In Racy content, however, this might have been tougher. This is because racy content is often observed to be multi-intentioned. The same content can be an innocent statement or a racy statement. For example, words like 'cock' or 'chicks' that are often used in an explicit or racy sense and can also refer to their actual (non-racy) meaning.

[2]Created by three human judges with majority voting

Model	Precision	Recall	F1 Score
Base	79.75	80.13	79.94
Aug-1	80.20	79.30	79.75
Aug-2	79.27	80.13	79.70
Aug-3	79.50	80.13	79.81
Aug-4	80.56	80.25	80.40
Aug-5	80.14	80.13	80.14

Table 1: Metrics on static benchmark test set

Finally, Checklist evaluation revealed that the model was NOT robust to minor perturbations. This is an important finding because it is expected that the model would come across content that the user intentionally or unintentionally mistypes. However, such perturbations may not have been reflected in the training and standardized testing data.

As seen in the Base Model row of Table 2, the failure rates for examples generated by templates of specific capabilities is high.

3.3 Improving the Model

So far, consistent with previous results, Checklist evaluation revealed important gaps in the base model. The interesting follow-up question is how to use these insights to improve the model to overcome current limitations. Typically, in deep learning models, model improvements result from improved model architectures, better training or fine-tuning strategies, or more data. However, these strategies do not directly address the limitation of models in specific capabilities in the way that Checklist reveals. Thus, we explored the use of insights from the human-in-loop evaluation that can help improve the model in these specific settings while also testing the improved model against standard benchmarks used to evaluate the model.

3.3.1 Data Augmentation Methodology

We used an iterative process of data augmentation to improve the model using the insights of model failures from Checklist evaluation and data generated by templates. We chose this iterative data augmentation method due to its demonstrated

	1.a	1.b	2.a	2.b	2.c	2.d	3	4	5	6.a	6.b	6.c
Base	47.37	22.84	32.13	36.73	37.77	46.16	18.70	6	44.70	46.62	59.11	42.61
Aug-1	22.21	0.05	0.03	0	1.07	0.02	0	0	0	3.54	4.23	1.08
Total Examples	10k	5.5k	3k	6k	7.5k	5.5k	4.3k	1k	2.7k	12.3k	12.3k	12.7k

Table 2: Failure Rates (%) of Base and Improved models for Test holdout set for different capabilities 3.1

Model	Training Data	TS-1	TS-2	TS-3	TS-4	TS-5
Base	Base training data (BTD)	38.0 (0)	20.05 (0)	28.24 (0)	26.35 (0)	34.14 (0)
Aug-1	BTD + data from TS-1	4.0* (-34)	12.67 (-7.38)	5.66 (-22.58)	18.83 (-7.52)	13.67 (-20.47)
Aug-2	BTD + data from TS-2	31.73 (-6.27)	0.01* (-20.04)	19.34 (-8.9)	13.28 (-13.28)	26.97 (-7.17)
Aug-3	BTD + data from TS-3	30.21 (-7.79)	15.53 (-4.52)	0.01* (-28.23)	26.11 (-0.24)	23.57 (-10.57)
Aug-4	BTD + data from TS-4	34.29 (-3.71)	9.61 (-10.44)	24.98 (-3.26)	0* (-26.35)	30.29 (-3.85)
Aug-5	BTD + data from TS-5	32.18 (-5.82)	15.74 (-4.31)	19.34 (-8.9)	19.35 (-7.0)	0.01* (-34.13)

Table 3: Average (weighted across different capabilities by number of examples in each) failure rates (%) of different models on independently created template sets. Figures in bracket show change in failure rate from the failure rate of base model tested on the particular template set (* refers to tested on the test holdout set such that the testing examples are disjoint from training data of the augmented model but come from the same template set)

success in improving NLI models by Nie et al. (2020), who proposed iterative Human-And-Model-in-the-Loop-Enabled-Training (HAMLET) to create dynamic and harder adversarial test sets for that 'fools'[3] the model. These harder examples are then used to re-train the model, and the process is repeated. Potts et al. (2020) also successfully use a similar human-in-loop feedback process with data augmentation to create iterations of datasets and better models for sentiment analysis.

Our process in spirit is similar, except instead of adversarial examples, we focused on specific capabilities from the Checklist evaluation using templates. A set of examples generated from the same Checklist templates, which is disjoint from the test examples themselves, were appended to the model's original training set, and the model was re-trained. This yielded a new model, henceforth called the augmented model. The augmented model was then tested on the set of examples that was earlier used to test the base model.

Specifically, TS-1 was the set of templates used to test the base model. This template set was generated by a human annotator, known to have sufficient expertise of English. The data generated from the TS-1 was divided into a training subset (TrS) and test subset (TeS) with a ratio of 60:40. First, the base model's failure rates on TeS were recorded as shown in Table 2. Now the TrS was combined with the base model's training data, and the model was re-trained. This re-trained model is called the augmented model. The data from TeS was now used to test this augmented model for the capabilities captured in TS-1.

3.3.2 Performance After Data Augmentation

We found that the failure rates of the augmented model dropped significantly. Interestingly, the performance on the static evaluation test sets neither improved nor degraded substantially, which can be seen in Table 1. Here, Aug-1 was the model obtained by retraining the base model with the original data plus data from TrS of TS-1. The rest of the four augmented models, Aug 2-5, will be described subsequently. This shows that while data augmentation helps specific capabilities, it does not degrade performance on the static benchmark leading to the conclusion that the retrained model is not over-fitted to the examples generated using Checklist.

The fact that the performance on the benchmark test set did not improve showed that static benchmark evaluation sets failed to evaluate the model rigorously enough for important capabilities. Adding data points that make the model more robust to such examples improves the model overall. However, this improvement was not captured in the static evaluation as the test set might not have contained such specific examples for these capabilities in the first place. This is why the failure of model in these scenarios went unnoticed till it was evaluated specifically for those capabilities using Checklist. This observation bolsters the case of using Checklist evaluation for better understanding and explainability of the limitations of the model.

[3]flips the output of the model

3.3.3 Testing on Multiple Template Sets

The fact that TrS and TeS have very similar (but not the same) examples as they were generated from the same set of templates can be one reason for the augmented model's extremely low failure rate. However, to analyze whether the model learned generalizable capabilities from the TS-1 and ascertain that these gains in performance corresponding to lower failure rates are not specific to a template set, we asked a new independent annotator to use the documentation guidelines to create templates from scratch. The data generated from this independently generated template set is used to evaluate the base and augmented model (Aug-1, which was trained on data from TS-1). This process was carried out with four different annotators, resulting in 4 new augmented models (Aug 2-5).

Specifically, we created a larger study and asked four more annotators to create template sets independently using the documentation guidelines. These template sets are called TS-2, TS-3, TS-4, and TS-5. Data from each template set was also split into training and testing sets with a ratio of 60:40. The same base model was first used, and failure rates were recorded on each template set. Next, four more augmented models were created (Aug-2, Aug-3, Aug-4, and Aug-5). For creating Aug-i ($2 \leq i \leq 5$), the training data from TS-i was combined with the base model's training data, and the model was re-trained on this entire dataset. Now the failure rates of Aug-i were recorded on the held out test set (data points coming from the same templates but disjoint from the training augmented data) of TS-i and the entire data from the rest of the template sets.

All template sets were generated by annotators with expertise of English language and were cross-checked for correctness. The number of templates in each template sets ranged from 18-25 distributed among the different capabilities. The number of examples generated from template sets that were added to retraining of the model (including perturbed examples for robustness test) were close to 50k for each of the augmented models. There were no templates that were exactly the same in any pairs of template sets, though, there were some templates that were similar. The overlap in terms of examples generated was less than 0.02% between any of the sets. The lexicon keywords had some common vocabulary. However, this can be expected due to the specificity of the task and the words that are commonly used in such offensive statements.

3.3.4 Performance on Multiple Template Sets

We report the average failure rates in Table 3. The reported average is the weighted average of failure rates across different capabilities, weighted according to the number of examples the template set has for that capability. The results across template sets vary, and we discuss the challenge of ascertaining template quality in detail in section 4.3.

We found that for all our augmented models, the failure rates between the base and augmented model significantly differed for the test holdout of its own template set. Further, the augmented models showed better performance than the base model across all examples from all other template sets that were generated independently by different annotators. In fact, we saw improvements up to 15-20% in multiple cases (e.g. Aug-1 on Ts-3 and Ts-5) . This indicates that the model did learn some generalizable capabilities irrespective of the template set used for augmentation.

Grouping the results by capability, we found a general trend of lower failure rates in augmented models. There were no clear trends of a particular capability consistently benefitting more or less. The failure rates of Template Sets 2-5 on the Augmented models 2-5 and base model grouped by capabilities are in the Appendix.

4 Challenges and Open Questions

Our case study was an experiment of using Checklist to debug NLP systems. It presents optimistic findings for using human-in-loop for improving model performance. However, using this technique for evaluation and improvement is not straightforward or foolproof. In this section, we discuss some nuances and challenges that we observed while conducting these experiments.

4.1 Resource Requirement

The process, while effective, is intensive in both human and computational resources.

Generating templates from scratch required a significant amount of annotator hours. In our experiments, it took 1 hour to create 5-7 templates spanning 1-2 capabilities. This time can vary from person to person. A single annotator required a minimum of half of a workday[4] and a maximum of 2 workdays to come up with template sets. The

[4] a workday is taken as 8 hours

time may also vary based on the task for which templates are being generated.

Once the template sets are created, generating Checklist reports for evaluation is computationally cheap, the cost of model inference notwithstanding. However, using the insights of this evaluation to carry out the targeted data augmentation procedure can be compute-heavy. Retraining the model can cost significant time, money, and energy. Fine-tuning, though computationally cheaper *can* lead to over-fitting on template sets, which is why we chose not to take the approach. Further, going through the iterative and parallel versions of the process would require further investment of human and computational resources to generate more template sets, employ more annotators, and repeated retraining of the model.

4.2 Methods to Improve the Model

In the current version of the process, we used a simple but effective iterative data augmentation procedure. While this is effective in our case it *can* lead to over-fitting or catastrophic forgetting in deep learning models. Furthermore, as stated earlier, the process itself is compute-expensive.

Data augmentation may not be the only (or the most optimal) solution. Some other methods that can be utilized are continual training or fine-tuning. Furthermore, there can be more than one way to combine the initial training and template generated datasets to yield better performance. Thus, the effective use of the insights from Checklist evaluation still remains an open question for future studies.

4.3 Template and Template Set Quality

An important question for any evaluation technique, whether static benchmark or human-generated templates, is its quality. In both cases, it is difficult to quantify quality.

The main reason why it is important to estimate the quality of template sets is evident from the results of Table 3. None of the augmented models are better for all the template sets across the board, and performance on the same template set can vary significantly for different augmented models created by augmenting different data points. Thus, the templates that humans come up with and the examples that those templates generate can significantly impact how much the model improves.

Quality can be viewed in two ways, absolute quality, and relative quality. Absolute quality of a template refers to easily quantifiable measures such as the number of examples it generates and the capabilities it covers. On the other hand, two templates are compared for their quality in the case of relative quality. In this case, the higher quality template would intuitively be one that can find more bugs or result in higher failure rates in the model. It is important to note that higher absolute quality may not always result in higher relative quality. A template can generate more examples and cover more capabilities and give low failure rates, leading to finding fewer bugs than another template that generates fewer examples or spans fewer capabilities.

Relative template quality is a more effective way for quality analysis of templates because it is driven by failure rates of the model on the template compared to other templates, and this is the basis of finding bugs using Checklist. However, whether a template is 'tougher' (hence, of higher quality with respect to relative quality evaluation) or 'easier' is subjective to the model and its training data. In other words, a template that results in higher failure rates for a particular model as compared to another template of the same capability can show lower failure rates when used with another model and vice versa. Furthermore, human analysis of template quality may not always sync with the model performance. That is, a template that a human may deem to be 'tougher' for a model may not be so.

Following the definition of template quality for individual templates may not always extrapolate to a template set's quality. That is, while comparing the quality of two template sets, it can be possible (and in fact, often observed in our study) that a template set may contain some templates that are of a higher relative quality and some templates that are of lower relative quality as compared to the templates of another template set. This makes it even more difficult to quantify even the relative quality of template sets that span multiple templates and capabilities.

Further, template generation by humans is an endless process; one can keep on generating more and more templates given time. In fact, in the extreme situation, it is possible that the an iteration of Checklist evaluation may not reveal any actionable bugs, in such a scenario, it would be unclear as to how many iterations would be needed in order to claim that the model does not have any bugs.

Moreover, within template sets, multiple capabilities are covered by putting together different templates by annotators. Our results show that this does not lead to consistent improvements across capabilities. Thus, obtaining the best combination of different templates is not straight-forward. A detailed study into what constitutes better quality templates can help ascertain a more effective selection process from a large set.

Finally, multiple templates can be combined to form template sets, and how to put together template sets that uniformly benefit all capabilities is unclear. Thus, techniques to find the optimal and representative template sets generated with little human effort and can be relied upon for holistic evaluation are an imminent challenge and makes quality estimation of templates and template set an important open question.

4.4 Experience of Annotators

Since annotators are an indispensable part of this study, it was important to understand their perspective. We thus interviewed the annotators in order to gain insight into their experience.

For our study, the annotators can be considered as 'experts' [5]. The common feedback we received was that it was difficult to come up with the template sets from scratch. On further probing, this difficulty could be broken down into multiple steps.

First, generating offensive content templates needs specific vocabulary, also known as lexicons in Checklist. Creating these lexicons from scratch can be subject to creativity and offensive language usage. Further, using these lexicons to generate templates is again subject to creativity, which varies from person to person, and can be difficult to replicate from a scientific perspective. This difficulty can be ported to almost any task for which templates are to be generated as it would need the creation of specific lexicon vocabulary and their combinations.

Secondly, it is not easy to ascertain what set of templates is best. As discussed in the template quality section, while the quality of individual templates can be judged by failure rates, for an annotator developing templates in a limited time-frame, the template set generated may not always be optimal, or the best possible set that finds the maximum bugs. Thus, without instant model feedback, deciding which templates are good and which are not is difficult, and finding the most optimal template set may not be feasible.

Finally, from the perspective of this particular task of the case-study, offensive content itself is a topic open to interpretation from perspectives of communities coming from varied socio-cultural backgrounds and individual sentiments, philosophy, and beliefs. What one person may find offensive, another person may not, and vice versa. As a result, despite well-documented qualitative guidelines of expectations from the models, individual examples can have debatable annotation. This ambiguity is also carried into the template generation process, where an annotator's individuality may reflect in the offensive templates that they generate.

Typically, it is easier for humans to verify annotations or explanations rather than generating them from scratch. This can be extended to judging whether a template is correct and useful. Thus developing techniques that can be utilized for automated template creation from small seed data followed by verification and labeling by humans can be an important future research direction.

4.5 Multilinguality

Given the rapid adoption of massive multilingual systems in NLP, there is an increasing need for evaluation in other languages. Thus it is intuitive to feel the need to use Checklist for multilingual models. However, template generation would typically need a native or fluent speaker of the language. It can often be difficult for researchers building massive multilingual systems to find experts fluent in multiple or specific languages. While the open-source Checklist framework provides limited capability of generating multilingual templates, it is not powerful enough to automate the process for different languages without sufficient human supervision. Thus, developing ways to create multilingual Checklists using Checklists in one language easily has immense scope.

5 Conclusion

State-of-the-art systems have been known to break down when deployed in the wild because of heavy reliance on static evaluation benchmarks that fail to holistically test the system. Several non-standard forms of evaluation into specific aspects of the models can lead to insights that might otherwise go unnoticed. Human-in-loop processes have been known to aid better explainability, trust, debugging,

[5] educated in English and having understanding equivalent to graduate-level courses in natural language processing and machine learning

and improvement of NLP models by combining automation with human-expertise of language use. The Checklist framework introduced a behavioral testing approach for finding bugs in NLP models, which showed that state-of-the-art systems fail on the simplest of capabilities.

We presented a case study of using Checklist to debug an English offensive content detection system. The process we utilized was two-staged: First, we employed a human annotator to generate templates for evaluating specific model capabilities. These results were leveraged to find bugs, or capabilities in which the model is not performing as per expectation. The second step was to augment the data generated from these templates and re-train the model. This led to targeted bug-fixing and better performance not just on the test sets created from the same templates, but more generally, on independently created template sets.

Using this technique led to not only improved models but also a better understanding of the limitations and capabilities of the model in context of specific requirements. Our findings add to the growing optimism of using human expertise and non-standard evaluation to improve performance, better explainability, and increase trust in NLP systems deployed in real-world uncontrolled usage environments.

We also discuss various challenges of employing such a human-in-loop strategy. These include resource requirements, different methods to improve the model, determining the quality of templates and template sets, finding the optimal and representative template set, the difficulty for human subjects to create templates from scratch, and extension of the paradigm to languages other than English. This leads to the conclusion that the process, even though beneficial, leaves many open questions that need to be addressed.

We hope that our work further increases attention to the Checklist paradigm and motivates researchers to evaluate and improve black box NLP models using non-standard and explainable human-in-loop evaluation and investigate its challenges.

Acknowledgments

We would like to thank our colleagues Monojit Choudhary, Kalika Bali, Somak Aditya, Anirudh Srinivasan, and Karthikeyan K for their invaluable inputs during the course of this work. We extend gracious thanks to our five amazing annotators who put a lot of time and effort in understanding the problem, creating templates, and giving us their feedback.

References

Yonatan Belinkov and Yonatan Bisk. 2018. Synthetic and natural noise both break neural machine translation. In *6th International Conference on Learning Representations, ICLR 2018, Vancouver, BC, Canada, April 30 - May 3, 2018, Conference Track Proceedings*. OpenReview.net.

Thomas Davidson, Dana Warmsley, Michael Macy, and Ingmar Weber. 2017. Automated hate speech detection and the problem of offensive language. In *Proceedings of the 11th International AAAI Conference on Web and Social Media*, ICWSM '17, pages 512–515.

Mor Geva, Yoav Goldberg, and Jonathan Berant. 2019. Are we modeling the task or the annotator? an investigation of annotator bias in natural language understanding datasets. In *Proceedings of the 2019 Conference on Empirical Methods in Natural Language Processing and the 9th International Joint Conference on Natural Language Processing (EMNLP-IJCNLP)*, pages 1161–1166, Hong Kong, China. Association for Computational Linguistics.

Ona de Gibert, Naiara Perez, Aitor García-Pablos, and Montse Cuadros. 2018. Hate speech dataset from a white supremacy forum. In *Proceedings of the 2nd Workshop on Abusive Language Online (ALW2)*, pages 11–20, Brussels, Belgium. Association for Computational Linguistics.

Max Glockner, Vered Shwartz, and Yoav Goldberg. 2018. Breaking NLI systems with sentences that require simple lexical inferences. In *Proceedings of the 56th Annual Meeting of the Association for Computational Linguistics (Volume 2: Short Papers)*, pages 650–655, Melbourne, Australia. Association for Computational Linguistics.

Yash Goyal, Tejas Khot, Douglas Summers-Stay, Dhruv Batra, and Devi Parikh. 2017. Making the V in VQA matter: Elevating the role of image understanding in visual question answering. In *2017 IEEE Conference on Computer Vision and Pattern Recognition, CVPR 2017, Honolulu, HI, USA, July 21-26, 2017*, pages 6325–6334. IEEE Computer Society.

Suchin Gururangan, Swabha Swayamdipta, Omer Levy, Roy Schwartz, Samuel Bowman, and Noah A. Smith. 2018. Annotation artifacts in natural language inference data. In *Proceedings of the 2018 Conference of the North American Chapter of the Association for Computational Linguistics: Human Language Technologies, Volume 2 (Short Papers)*, pages 107–112, New Orleans, Louisiana. Association for Computational Linguistics.

Mohit Iyyer, John Wieting, Kevin Gimpel, and Luke Zettlemoyer. 2018. Adversarial example generation with syntactically controlled paraphrase networks. In *Proceedings of the 2018 Conference of the North American Chapter of the Association for Computational Linguistics: Human Language Technologies, Volume 1 (Long Papers)*, pages 1875–1885, New Orleans, Louisiana. Association for Computational Linguistics.

Yixin Nie, Adina Williams, Emily Dinan, Mohit Bansal, Jason Weston, and Douwe Kiela. 2020. Adversarial NLI: A new benchmark for natural language understanding. In *Proceedings of the 58th Annual Meeting of the Association for Computational Linguistics*, pages 4885–4901, Online. Association for Computational Linguistics.

Christopher Potts, Zhengxuan Wu, Atticus Geiger, and Douwe Kiela. 2020. Dynasent: A dynamic benchmark for sentiment analysis. *arXiv preprint arXiv:2012.15349*.

Vinodkumar Prabhakaran, Ben Hutchinson, and Margaret Mitchell. 2019. Perturbation sensitivity analysis to detect unintended model biases. In *Proceedings of the 2019 Conference on Empirical Methods in Natural Language Processing and the 9th International Joint Conference on Natural Language Processing (EMNLP-IJCNLP)*, pages 5740–5745, Hong Kong, China. Association for Computational Linguistics.

Benjamin Recht, Rebecca Roelofs, Ludwig Schmidt, and Vaishaal Shankar. 2019. Do imagenet classifiers generalize to imagenet? In *Proceedings of the 36th International Conference on Machine Learning, ICML 2019, 9-15 June 2019, Long Beach, California, USA*, volume 97 of *Proceedings of Machine Learning Research*, pages 5389–5400. PMLR.

Marco Tulio Ribeiro, Carlos Guestrin, and Sameer Singh. 2019. Are red roses red? evaluating consistency of question-answering models. In *Proceedings of the 57th Annual Meeting of the Association for Computational Linguistics*, pages 6174–6184, Florence, Italy. Association for Computational Linguistics.

Marco Túlio Ribeiro, Sameer Singh, and Carlos Guestrin. 2016. "why should I trust you?": Explaining the predictions of any classifier. In *Proceedings of the 22nd ACM SIGKDD International Conference on Knowledge Discovery and Data Mining, San Francisco, CA, USA, August 13-17, 2016*, pages 1135–1144. ACM.

Marco Túlio Ribeiro, Sameer Singh, and Carlos Guestrin. 2018a. Anchors: High-precision model-agnostic explanations. In *Proceedings of the Thirty-Second AAAI Conference on Artificial Intelligence, (AAAI-18), the 30th innovative Applications of Artificial Intelligence (IAAI-18), and the 8th AAAI Symposium on Educational Advances in Artificial Intelligence (EAAI-18), New Orleans, Louisiana, USA, February 2-7, 2018*, pages 1527–1535. AAAI Press.

Marco Tulio Ribeiro, Sameer Singh, and Carlos Guestrin. 2018b. Semantically equivalent adversarial rules for debugging NLP models. In *Proceedings of the 56th Annual Meeting of the Association for Computational Linguistics (Volume 1: Long Papers)*, pages 856–865, Melbourne, Australia. Association for Computational Linguistics.

Marco Tulio Ribeiro, Tongshuang Wu, Carlos Guestrin, and Sameer Singh. 2020. Beyond accuracy: Behavioral testing of NLP models with CheckList. In *Proceedings of the 58th Annual Meeting of the Association for Computational Linguistics*, pages 4902–4912, Online. Association for Computational Linguistics.

Barbara Rychalska, Dominika Basaj, Alicja Gosiewska, and Przemysław Biecek. 2019. Models in the wild: On corruption robustness of neural nlp systems. In *International Conference on Neural Information Processing*, pages 235–247. Springer.

Masatoshi Tsuchiya. 2018. Performance impact caused by hidden bias of training data for recognizing textual entailment. In *Proceedings of the Eleventh International Conference on Language Resources and Evaluation (LREC 2018)*, Miyazaki, Japan. European Language Resources Association (ELRA).

Appendix

Model	Characterization	Negation	Violence	Unsafe	Robustness
Base	21.23	2.59	0.2	28.3	24.17
Aug-2	0.01*	0*	0*	0.06*	0.00*
Aug-3	19.93	1.35	0.2	28.25	17.24
Aug-4	11.85	2.19	0.3	6.27	11.49
Aug-5	19.22	1.82	0.2	29.02	17.84

Table 4: Failure Rates (%) of grouped capabilities on Template Set - 2. (* refers to tested on the test holdout set such that the testing examples are disjoint from training data of the augmented model but come from the same template set)

Model	Characterization	Negation	Violence	Unsafe	Robustness
Base	21.21	18.27	20.98		35.26
Aug-2	16.88	3.90	12.43		24.22
Aug-3	0*	0*	0*	Annotator did not create Template	0.01*
Aug-4	23.56	9.15	15.69		32.04
Aug-5	15.03	7.24	17.35		22.88

Table 5: Failure Rates (%) of grouped capabilities on Template Set - 3. (* refers to tested on the test holdout set such that the testing examples are disjoint from training data of the augmented model but come from the same template set)

Model	Characterization	Negation	Violence	Unsafe	Robustness
Base	12.99	21.01	32.98	56.03	32.63
Aug-2	8.50	12.56	9.65	33.12	13.68
Aug-3	13.46	17.64	12.73	50.35	30.38
Aug-4	0*	0.01*	0*	0*	0*
Aug-5	9.43	11.89	15.28	43.5	21.99

Table 6: Failure Rates (%) of grouped capabilities on Template Set - 4. (* refers to tested on the test holdout set such that the testing examples are disjoint from training data of the augmented model but come from the same template set)

Model	Characterization	Negation	Violence	Unsafe	Robustness
Base	14.41	24.21	98.48		37.29
Aug-2	6.57	9.58	97.79		29.07
Aug-3	3.85	3.70	96.98	Annotator did not create Template	25.07
Aug-4	8.32	16.01	72.22		33.35
Aug-5	0*	0*	0*		0.01*

Table 7: Failure Rates (%) of grouped capabilities on Template Set - 5. (* refers to tested on the test holdout set such that the testing examples are disjoint from training data of the augmented model but come from the same template set)

Interrater Disagreement Resolution
A Systematic Procedure to Reach Consensus in Annotation Tasks

Yvette Oortwijn[*†] and **Thijs Ossenkoppele**[*] and **Arianna Betti**[*]
[*]University of Amsterdam, Institute for Logic, Language and Computation
[†]Eindhoven University of Technology, Algorithms, Geometry & Applications
{y.oortwijn, t.ossenkoppele, a.betti}@uva.nl

Abstract

We present a systematic procedure for interrater disagreement resolution. The procedure is general, but of particular use in multiple-annotator tasks geared towards ground truth construction. We motivate our proposal by arguing that, barring cases in which the researchers' goal is to elicit different viewpoints, interrater disagreement is a sign of poor quality in the design or the description of a task. Consensus among annotators, we maintain, should be striven for, through a systematic procedure for disagreement resolution such as the one we describe.

1 Introduction

A growing body of literature signals a thorny issue with assessing general progress in the field of natural language processing (NLP) as part of artificial intelligence. Benchmarks that are considered 'general', and are widely used as standards to assess NLP systems' performance, turn out to be rather specific, and hence of more limited significance than commonly acknowledged (Raji et al. 2020; Schlangen 2020). Good performance on specific benchmarks does not guarantee good performance across the board (Faruqui et al. 2016; Bakarov 2018; Ethayarajh and Jurafsky 2020): it only helps with gaining understanding of how certain systems work for those specific benchmarks. In order to claim progress across the board, one would need to evaluate system performance on a certain reasoned series of such specific benchmarks, that is, results on a host of "more focused and explicitly defined problems" (Raji et al., 2020, 1). To enact this, one would need a ground truth for the evaluation of each specific task-*cum*-dataset, including ground truths in expert domains.

Ground truth construction is challenging. In this paper we focus on the process of constructing ground truths via semantic annotations tasks. Recent studies stress the intrinsic difficulty of semantic annotation due to vagueness and ambiguity (Aroyo and Welty 2015; Kairam and Heer 2016; Pavlick and Kwiatkowski 2019). Importantly, some argue that interpretative disagreements due to different conceptualizations or perspectives cannot be seen as just 'mistakes' (Sommerauer et al. 2020; Herbelot and Vecchi 2016). It is our tenet that in ground truth construction differences in conceptualizations or perspectives can and must be explicitly specified as an integral part of annotation tasks; moreover, interrater disagreement is not necessarily due to inherent ambiguities in the data, but at least in part to the annotation task being underspecified, in particular as to the right context to consider.

Take annotation tasks involving relatedness or similarity judgments, which are key types of judgment for NLP evaluation. Similarity is not a property of two things by themselves in isolation: it is always judged by a specific standard, and by weighing properties of the things compared in different ways, according to a context (Goodman 1972; Batchkarov et al. 2016). When people judge by different standards[1], disagreement arises as a matter of course - and is especially likely when annotating texts of high conceptual density, as this requires a lot of prior knowledge and interpretation. In order to get comparable and meaningful annotations, judgment standards need to be aligned and made extremely transparent.

In this paper we propose a six-step systematic procedure for interrater disagreement resolution in which conceptual alignment figures as one of the steps. The procedure is designed to facilitate the resolution of interrater disagreement that fre-

[1]As Gladkova and Drozd (2016) point out, similarity is defined by Turney and Pantel (2010) as co-hyponymy (e.g. car and bicycle), whereas Hill et al. (2015) define it as "exemplified by pairs of synonyms; words with identical referents" (e.g. mug and cup).

Proceedings of the Workshop on Human Evaluation of NLP Systems (HumEval), pages 131–141
Online, April 19, 2021.

quently arises in annotation tasks in which multiple annotators participate. The emergence of disagreement in annotation tasks is valuable information, albeit of a negative type: barring cases in which the researchers' goal is none other than eliciting disagreement, interrater disagreement, we maintain, is a sign of poor quality in the design or the description of a task. In ground truth construction, consensus among annotators should be striven for. The procedure applies to a wide range of annotation tasks, namely every task involving the application of one or more concepts to a unit of annotation (a fragment of text, such as a paragraph or a sentence, or a more artificial unit, such as a string with a length of n characters). We hold that the benefit of a systematic procedure of resolving interrater disagreement is twofold: first, such a procedure leads to the construction of reliable and well-grounded datasets, and second, it ensures that the resolution proceeds in a non-arbitrary fashion allowing for proper documentation and replicability of the data.

2 Related work

Computational research: interrater agreement, dataset creation and ground truths Standard methods for measuring interrater agreement and reliability (Artstein and Poesio, 2008) such as (Cohen's) kappa (Cohen 1960; Landis and Koch 1977) and Krippendorff's alpha (Krippendorff, 2013) output a single score to represent the agreement between different raters. Methods such as the CrowdTruth framework (Aroyo and Welty 2014; Aroyo and Welty 2015) give a more detailed disagreement analysis, though only in post-annotation phase. Similarly, Kairam and Heer (2016) mention that disagreement cannot simply be treated as noise and propose a post-annotation method for identifying different valid interpretations annotators may use to come to different conclusions. By contrast, we take disagreement analysis and resolution as internal to the annotation procedure.

Sommerauer et al. (2020) stress difficulties with annotation due to ambiguity or vagueness in language while studying cases in which disagreement between different annotators is expected and multiple answers are legitimate. Our focus is datasets that are meant to be used as ground truths. In ground truth construction, we argue, it is necessary to resolve cases of disagreement (disagreement resolution phase, see *step 5* below), and, more importantly, dispel the ambiguities that cause disagreement (if ambiguity is the cause of the disagreement) by task specification, either by redesigning the task or by making the annotation guidelines more precise (conceptual alignment phase, see *step 2* below). We do recognize that genuine disagreement might exist due to e.g. ambiguity in language in existing datasets (see also, Palomaki et al. (2018)), but we see legitimate disagreement as having a specific meaning: it is either a signal that further resolution is needed (through annotation task redesign or guideline redefinition), or it is the possible result of a task specifically designed to chart or elicit instances of disagreement, as in Sommerauer et al. (2020) or Herbelot and Vecchi (2016).

We offer a procedure by which annotators can avoid disagreement due to unclarity of the task, accurately discern the reason for disagreement whenever it arises, and make a deliberate decision on how these cases should be annotated. Any differences between 'people's beliefs about the world' (or the data), we say, should be explicitly integrated in task design such that annotators are required to judge according to a certain perspective or set of beliefs, and not from an absolute point of view. We agree with Pavlick and Kwiatkowski (2019) that disagreement between annotators cannot simply be seen as noise in the data supposedly due to low-quality annotations. However, while they divide the annotations into consistent units to get sets of consistent gold labels, we argue that in ground truth construction the variety of human judgments can and should be narrowed down to exactly one type by specification of the task. In our case, the process of identifying reasons for disagreement is part of the annotation process, which allows for resolution of disagreement and thereby a dataset suitable for use as a ground truth for the task at hand.

In Betti et al. (2020), a general method for constructing expert-controlled ground truths for concept-focused domains is proposed, and the construction for an actual ground truth for a philosophical corpus is described. Disagreement resolution is mentioned, and one example of resolution is reported, but no explicit general methodology for disagreement resolution is offered.

It has been emphasized that the conditions under which a dataset has been created need to be properly documented to allow for reproducibility and replicability (Bender and Friedman 2018; Paullada et al. 2020; Hutchinson et al. 2021). Language models are known to pick up and reinforce existing biases in data (see, e.g., Bolukbasi et al. 2016; Zhao et al. 2017). Bender and Friedman (2018) offer instructions on how to document data using data statements to help reproducibility and replicability, bring existing biases to the surface and improve representation in future dataset creation. The procedure we propose asks for explicit decisions from raters after deliberation. This requirement makes the conditions of dataset creation clear, thus allowing proper documentation.

Philosophy Peer disagreement is a topic of investigation in philosophy, in particular in the subfield of social epistemology. A large amount of literature exists on issues concerning both peer disagreement (e.g. Goldman and Whitcomb 2011; Christensen and Lackey 2013) and group decision making in the face of such disagreement (e.g. List 2005), but resolution procedures that aid in moving from peer disagreement to unanimously agreed upon results are not proposed, and are in general '[...] at best rare in scientific contexts.' (de Ridder, 2014). One of the scarce examples is Gius and Jacke's (2017) procedure for resolving interrater disagreement in literary corpus annotation. Although similar in approach, our work improves on the latter in terms of applicability: we intend our procedure to be fit for all annotation tasks that involve the application of one or more concepts to units of annotation, while Gius & Jacke focus on tasks within literary analysis exclusively. Note that annotation tasks in which concepts are applied to units of annotation are frequent: any task involving the identifying of instances of any concept qualifies. For example, in our validation example in section 5.2 the annotation task requires annotators to identify wide-scope claims in the text of journal articles (that is, instances of the concept of *wide-scope claim*).

3 Ground truths and interrater agreement

In Pivovarov and Elhadad (2012) a Cohen's kappa of 0.68 is "accepted as representing a substantial amount of agreement between annotators". By contrast, in Betti et al. (2020) the initial interrater agreement of 0.65 was taken as a starting point to reach further consensus. When the aim of the annotation is e.g. to get an overview of the variety of ways in which people interpret statements, then interrater agreement need only be high on statements for which there is only one obvious interpretation and so agreement is expected. However, when the annotations are supposed to establish a ground truth, interrater agreement, we argue, should be 1.

One strategy used for getting the interrater agreement on the ground truth to 1, is to discard disputed annotation(s) (see, e.g., Kenyon-Dean et al. (2018)). But clearly this is loss of valuable information: for the purpose of training and evaluating a computational system we want to be as specific as possible as to what its output needs to be; by tossing out disputed annotation we underspecify what the right output on the matter is. Consider one of the examples in Herbelot and Vecchi (2016): "MISSILES EXPLODE received the labels SOME, MOST and ALL. It is likely that the SOME interpretation quantifies over missiles which actually explode, while the MOST/ALL interpretation considers the potential of a missile to explode". For ground truth construction, it is necessary to specify whether an annotator should e.g. take an actual or potential interpretation, to prevent annotators from making arbitrary choices or introducing unknown biases.

So, if an annotation data set is to be used as a ground truth, agreement should be the aim. When disagreement arises, it is important to identify why it arises, and make well-grounded decisions on how to deal with it. In the next section, we will outline a procedure for annotation through which different reasons for disagreement can be identified and which specifies directions for resolution of each of these types of disagreements. The procedure results in a reproducible dataset by forcing annotators to make well-grounded, and thereby traceable decisions on their annotations. Note that traceability makes the procedure relevant to all annotations, not just ground truth construction.

The annotation procedure supposes what we call an 'annotation toolbox' consisting of (i) the annotation task or question, (ii) the guidelines specifying the instructions for annotation and (iii) some kind of definition or characterisation of the key concepts involved (see *step 2*). Fixing the definitions and characterisations of these concepts is essential to the conceptual alignment of annotators and for subsequent use of the resulting annotations. The use of the annotation toolbox also facilitates disagreement resolution insofar as annotators can refer to elements of the toolbox to give a justification for their scoring. This also means that if disagreement cannot be resolved by referring to elements of the toolbox, the toolbox is incomplete, or in any case insufficient as a basis for annotation. In this case, further expert research might be necessary to supplement the annotation toolbox. Based on the newly supplemented annotation toolbox, previous annotations might have to be redone, for there is no guarantee that these would end up receiving the same scoring. If such a resolution or supplementation is deemed impossible, the annotation cannot be completed and cannot lead to a dataset that is suitable as a ground truth.

4 The annotation procedure

What follows is a description of the steps of the annotation procedure (see flowchart in figure 1). Throughout this description we will talk of 'scoring' as the act of annotating a single unit. This is intended to also refer to types of annotation that are more adequately called 'categorizing', 'labelling' or otherwise. Note that with the exception of cases in which *step 0-2* is performed by the same group of researchers as *step 3-5* (see, e.g., section 5.1 in which the annotation procedure of Betti et al. (2020) is described), the annotators should be under close supervision of the researchers formulating the research question, and those setting the annotation task and guidelines, throughout all steps of the procedure.

4.1 The procedure

Step 0: Research setup and hypothesis forming In this initial phase, the prior research is done which indicates the need for an annotation task, research question(s) and hypotheses to be tested are formulated, and an annotation task is distilled to test these hypotheses. If at any point it is noticed that the research question or hypotheses are ill-defined or the annotation task does not match the research question, one should return to this step and start the process anew.

Step 1: Setting up annotation task and guidelines In this phase, the annotators are either presented with or set up themselves both 1) the annotation task, and 2) a set of annotation guidelines that guide 1). Ideally the annotators are already involved in the task and guideline set up since this improves the understanding of the task. 1) is immutable; if for some reason during the annotation procedure the task changes, the annotation procedure is reset and new guidelines must be set up that correspond to the new task. 2), however, is mutable; it can happen that new insights emerge during the annotation procedure that call for additional annotation guidelines or for an improvement of the existing ones. In case setting up the annotation task and guidelines requires additional research, one should return to *step 0*.

In developing the guidelines, researchers should consider how to score units that are ambiguous and therefore might endorse more than one interpretation. We recommend that instead of using, e.g., a simple binary scoring system, an "ambiguous" score is added to prevent forcing a decision. Forcing decisions could lead to arbitrariness, while ambiguity is still a real part of natural language that should be reflected in annotation. It should be ensured that this category won't mask unclarity in the task or the guidelines, by asking annotators to specify the source of unclarity (e.g. lexical ambiguity).

Step 2: Interrater conceptual alignment In this phase, the researchers identify the key concepts[2], and make sure that all annotators agree on the meaning or function of those concepts in the context of the task by specifying the definitions and characterisations for these concepts. In case researchers and annotators are two different sets of people, the annotators should be trained by the researchers in the concepts relevant to the task. The annotation procedure cannot move beyond this step if no interrater conceptual consensus is reached; this type of mismatch will almost certainly result in irresolvable conflicting annotations. Complex concepts, viz. concepts that involve many subconcepts when unpacked (e.g. philosophical concepts) require unpacking in the form of an interpretive model in the sense of Betti and van den Berg (2014). In these interpretive models, relations between subconcepts in the definition or characterisation of the concept modelled are made explicit. This facilitates the identification of instances of complex, rich concepts such as *epistemology* (see section 5.1). Such elaborate specification might not be required for simpler, or already well-defined concepts used consensually in different domains; in such cases, we expect less elaborate methods to suffice.

After consensus is reached on all key concepts that the annotators are aware of at this stage, the annotators can be expected to have an equal understanding of these concepts, which they can apply in

[2]By 'key concepts' we mean concepts mentioned in both task and guidelines. Note that settling on a definition for a concept at this step might require adding further new concepts to the guidelines in *step 1*, which should in turn be settled in *step 2*.

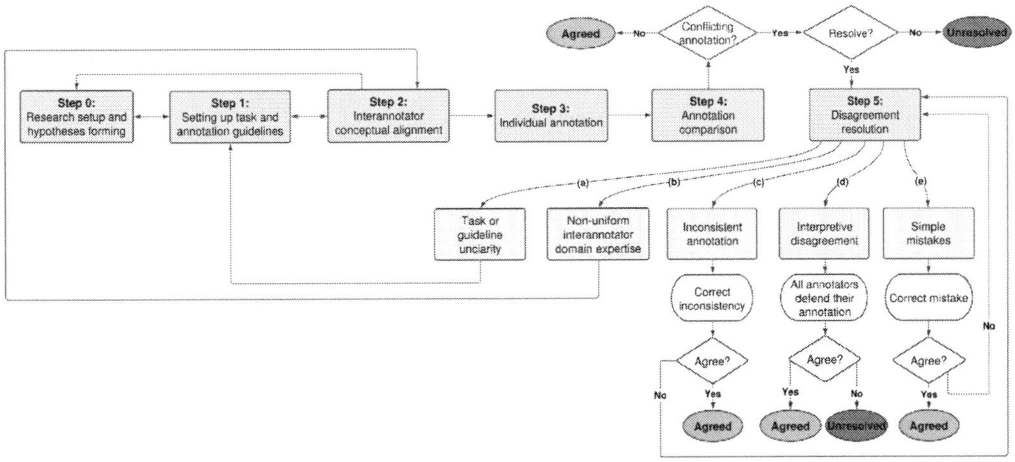

Figure 1: This flowchart serves as a summary of the annotation procedure detailed in section 4. The oval boxes contain the resulting annotations, green for agreed and pink for unresolved annotations. See `https://github.com/YOortwijn/HumEvalDisRes` to view the image separately.

annotating the units. As we observe in our second test case (section 5.2), questions for which there are issues with conceptual alignment receive lower interrater agreement than questions without such issues. The annotations for these questions should be redone after returning to this step for proper conceptual alignment.

Similar to *step 1*, it is possible that for the definition of concepts it is necessary to do further research, in which case one should return to *step 0*, or to further specify the task or guidelines, in which case one should return to *step 1*.

Step 3: Individual annotation Next, the annotations are performed according to the annotation guidelines specified in *step 1*. The manner in which the individual annotation proceeds depends on the guidelines, but as a general rule all annotators should score independently from each other to prevent being influenced by each other's scores.

Step 4: Annotation comparison After the individual annotation process, the annotations are compared. The comparison ideally yields a large set of agreed-upon annotations, but will likely also yield a set of conflicting annotations. For the latter, the disagreement resolution procedure should be put into operation. As mentioned in section 3, if conflicting annotations are simply discarded, we obtain an incomplete dataset which is not fit for use as a ground truth. Moreover, in such cases, hidden unclarities are likely to persist in the task or guidelines (see *step 5, a* below); as a consequence, we cannot trust previously agreed-upon annotations to reflect genuine agreement. We recommend in any case that it be specified whether the annotation procedure for the dataset under consideration has proceeded beyond this step; for, if not, then no attempt has been made to even check for inconsistent scoring by the same annotator (see *step 5, c*).

Step 5: Disagreement resolution We identify five main sources of interrater disagreement:

(a) *Task or guideline unclarity*. Among the possible reasons for interrater disagreement are 1) at least one annotator made a judgment based on a deviant interpretation of the nature of the task, and 2) the guidelines harbor residual unclarity as to the individual annotation procedure due to e.g. missing or vague instructions.

In case 1), the annotators should achieve a uniform understanding of the task through discussion. Different construal of the task can be due to poor or missing definition of the concepts involved in it. In this case the annotators should return to *step 2*. For other task unclarities the annotators should return to *step 1*. Recall that the task is immutable, so if it becomes apparent that the annotators cannot agree on what the task to be performed is, the whole annotation procedure should be abandoned; there is no justification for continuing an annotation task that is not equally clear for all annotators. The annotators will have to restart the procedure and redefine the task in such a way that all annotators understand what is expected of them.

In case of 2), the annotators should return to *step 1* to reconsider the guidelines and, depending on the source of confusion, amend or supplement them. This should not be a controversial practice: it is not the task itself that is amended, but only the lines along which it is carried out most successfully. Note that in cases of drastic changes to the guidelines[3], the whole individual annotation process likely needs to be redone. This option should be duly considered since this situation casts doubts also on the cases of agreement in the dataset .

(b) *Non-uniform interrater domain expertise.* Despite having gone through *step 2*, there still may be differences in the amount of background knowledge that the annotators bring to the individual annotations. A difference in background knowledge used in annotating can cause diverging annotations. An example of divergence of this kind is when annotators align on the wrong width of some concept, i.e. a too narrow or too broad definition or characterisation of the concept, in which too many or too few aspects of that concept are considered. Mismatch in concept width among annotators is bound to lead to diverging annotations. In such a case, the annotators have to return to *step 2*.

(c) *Inconsistent annotation.* An annotator can have annotated inconsistently by scoring two units differently that should be given the same score (e.g. because the two units are functionally synonymous). In this case, the inconsistent annotator must decide whether they agree with the other annotators. If so, the scoring of the inconsistent units can simply be corrected and the disagreement is resolved. Reconsideration might however lead to rescoring such that the inconsistency is resolved, but the disagreement is not. In such cases, disagreement resolution won't be of type (c), though, and must be discussed under (a), (b), (d), or (e).

(d) *Interpretive disagreement.* Interpretive disagreement arises when, despite the fact that the annotators have reached conceptual alignment, there is disagreement about the purported meaning of certain terms in some unit. Annotators might hold a different interpretation of a certain unit even when they have an equal understanding of the concepts used in that unit, for example due to the use of an ambiguous term. The way these disagreements will have to be resolved is case-dependent. All annotators should defend their choice by stating the reasons for annotating the way they did. They should try to convince the other annotators by (rational) argumentation that their reading is the correct one. The annotators should then together weigh each others' reasons and see whether agreement can be reached. Whether the disagreement can be resolved or not depends on whether the annotators can settle for one interpretation that they all agree on. In some complex cases, deliberation might need to be postponed until research on the phenomenon encountered has sufficiently progressed.

(e) *Simple mistakes.* If it is suspected that an annotator has made a simple mistake somewhere (a typo, or disagreement about a unit that should not be controversial), this has to be pointed out to the annotator concerned. If they agree that they have made a mistake, the annotation can be corrected.

4.2 Unresolved Annotations

By identifying the source of disagreement and, if necessary, clarifying the task or guidelines for annotation, updating and repeating the (relevant parts of the) annotation procedure should result in a complete set of agreed-upon annotations. If there are structural unclarities in the task or annotation guidelines, it might be necessary to redo the individual annotations at *step 3*, and subsequent steps, after the task and guidelines have been clarified (*step 1-2*). Further research might also be needed to solve some disagreement (*step 0*) in which case the annotation process should be halted.

In case the resolution procedure has still failed to resolve all disagreements but the annotation process has to be finished, it is possible to settle for a deprecated dataset. Two strategies to complete the annotation process commonly used in current annotation dataset creation are: 1) the conflicting annotations remain disagreed upon, with the resulting data loss and problems with usage of the dataset as a ground truth mentioned in section 3 as its consequence, or 2) a pre-appointed 'dictator' has the last say and resolves the disagreements by force. The dictator does so by either forcing particular decisions of their own choosing (in which case this part of the dataset is a single-annotator portion), or by applying some judgment aggregation method, such as majority rule. The benefit of choosing 1) is having a fully peer consensus-based

[3]What "drastic changes" are depends on the nature of the task, and on whether the changes have any bearing on the scoring of other, previously completed annotations.

annotation dataset, but this option imposes limits on the applicability of the resulting dataset as a ground truth. If 2) is chosen, there will be no unresolved disagreements, but the epistemic status of the annotation procedure is significantly compromised, not to mention the risk of having a dictator that makes wrong or capricious decisions. These options are up to those responsible for the resulting dataset. We argue against keeping any disagreements essentially unresolved (see section 3); at the same time, we also advise strongly against appointing dictators, as persistent peer disagreements reflect poorly specified tasks or unclear guidelines, and the forced resolution of these disagreements obfuscate such defects. Instead, a higher degree of conceptual alignment or a better specification of the annotation task or guidelines should be aimed for. If this is not possible, both the dataset and the cases of interpretive disagreement should be flagged as such, and a report should be made.

5 Test cases

By way of illustration and validation, in this section we outline two different user applications of the procedure we have observed, by two non-overlapping teams of domain expert annotators. The first application concerns a study of a complex, rich philosophical concept in the complete corpus of the works of a specific author. In this case, the annotators worked through the entire procedure. The second application concerns a study of the methodological justification given to wide-scope claims in academic literature. Although the corpus used in the second case is also from the field of philosophy, the annotation task is generic, and could have been performed on any type of scholarly article. The second team set up the research (*step 0*), annotation task and guidelines (*step 1*), but they did not settle on the meaning of all key concepts (*step 2*) before annotation. For the first case we will give examples for each of the reasons for disagreement, while for the second case we will focus on an issue due to the lack of conceptual alignment.

5.1 Epistemology in Quine

In this task, the annotators scored paragraphs in the work of the philosopher W. V. O. Quine for relevance on his views on epistemology.[4]

[4]For more information about the dataset, see Betti et al. (2020) and https://github.com/YOortwijn/HumEvalDisRes

The annotators started by creating an initial interpretive model at *step 0*. The annotation task and guidelines, formulated as part of *step 1*, were as follows: The annotators have to score paragraphs based on the degree of evidence they contain with respect to a research question (RQ) concerning the nature of Quine's naturalistic epistemology.

Guidelines: The annotators have three scoring options:

1: the paragraph contains strong evidence for some answer to the RQ.

0: the paragraph contains mild evidence for some answer to the RQ, or the annotator is not sure whether the paragraph contains sufficient evidence to answer the RQ.

-1: the paragraph does not contain enough evidence to answer the RQ.

As part of *step 2* the annotators expanded the initial interpretive model to make sure they had a clearly defined, shared conception of all key concepts. Without this, the annotators might have started the individual annotation phase with diverging understandings of the concept of e.g. epistemology and would presumably fail to score the same way, leading to many disagreements.

After *step 3* (individual annotations), the annotators had an interrater agreement of about $\kappa \approx 0.65$. After *step 4* and *step 5*, the identification and resolution of all the cases of disagreement, an interrater agreement of 1 was reached. The following are examples of each of the possible reasons for disagreement and how they were resolved:

(a) *Task or guideline unclarity*: In some of the annotated paragraphs, Quine merely talks about the views of different philosophers on epistemology, instead of expressing his own. After discussion it was decided to add to the guidelines the rule that these paragraphs do not provide evidence for the research question and hence should be scored -1.

(b) *Non-uniform interrater domain expertise*: There was disagreement about a passage in which the term "first philosophy" occurred without an explanation of that term in the same passage. Not all annotators agreed on the degree of evidence the passage provided without an explication of "first philosophy". After further conceptual alignment, the annotators agreed that "first philosophy" expressed a concept of central importance, and that an equal understanding of the matter among annotators was thus essential to the task. A characterisation for the term was fixed, and the units containing "first philosophy" were re-annotated in unanimous agreement.

(c) *Inconsistent annotation*: Two paragraphs that had to be annotated indicated Quine's blurring of the boundary between ontological statements and (natural) scientific statements, only in different wording. One annotator scored the two passages differently, and corrected this after notice from and discussion with another annotator.

(d) *Interpretive disagreement*: One annotator scored 1, the other two 0. Upon discussion, the first annotator explained to have read the unit as if Quine defended a view mentioned as the "straightforward view". After discussion, the annotator became convinced that this cannot be clearly said from the fragment, and thus consensus was reached on scoring 0, resolving the disagreement.

(e) *Simple mistake*: An annotator noticed disagreement about a paragraph that should not be controversial. In that paragraph, Quine quite straightforwardly states that mathematical logic is an example of a hard science. The unit was rescored and the disagreement was resolved.

5.2 Literature Reviews in the History of Philosophy

In this annotation task, annotators scored articles from the *British Journal of History of Philosophy* between 2017 and 2019 by checking their abstracts, introduction and methodological information for clear statements of inclusion/exclusion criteria for the sources the authors take into account, the completeness of the sources consulted, and the scope of the claims authors made on this basis.[5]

The annotation task was as follows: for each article, the annotators answer the following questions:

Exclusion/Inclusion

1. Does the article use a reproducible methodology with explicit inclusion and exclusion criteria to identify and find primary literature?
2. Does the article use a reproducible methodology with explicit inclusion and exclusion criteria to identify and find secondary literature?

Completeness

3. Does the article explicitly attempt to identify all available primary literature relative to the research question?
4. Does the article explicitly attempt to identify all available secondary literature relative to the research question?

Wide-scope claims

5a. Does the article argue for wide-scope historical claims, i.e., claims spanning multiple decades or periods or intellectual movements?

5b. If 5a is answered positively, does the article qualify the wide-scope claims?

Guidelines: The annotators will annotate the article by scoring '1' for yes, otherwise, by scoring '0'. In case of a discrepancy between the abstract and body of the article, the body (represented by the introduction and methodology section) will be leading. The annotators will also check section and subsection headings in order to identify other relevant sections related to the finding and use of primary and secondary literature.

The annotators did not construct interpretive models for the key concepts in the task/guidelines. This is understandable, given the low complexity of concepts involved. The problem, though, is that the team did not fix definitions or characterisations of all relevant terms from the outset either, as will be clear below, and by contrast with the annotations in section 5.1. Missing this essential part of the annotation toolbox is a shortcoming that resulted in an interrater agreement unnecessarily lower than it should have been. We will highlight one case of task or guideline unclarity (*step 5, a*).

During discussion on specific disagreements on the basis of our flowchart, the annotators noticed that they used different construals of what constitutes a *wide-scope claim*. While the annotators were able to resolve these disagreements on a case-by-case basis, it cannot be guaranteed that the agreed annotations would still receive the same scoring by the new considerations on what constitutes a *wide-scope claim*. Therefore, when in *step 5* of the procedure it is discovered that the interpretation of key terms should be refined, it is necessary to revisit all annotations. By following the first three steps of the procedure before starting the individual annotations, annotators are forced to settle on an interpretation of terms such as *wide-scope claim* before annotating. This way disagreement on many passages and the need to redo all annotations can be avoided.

The interrater agreement on this task was $\kappa \approx 0.71$ before disagreement resolution. The annota-

[5]For more information about the dataset, see `https://github.com/YOortwijn/HumEvalDisRes`

tors resolved all cases of disagreement using *step 5* of the procedure. 62% of the disagreements were determined to be inconsistent annotations (*5, c*), 21% were due to guideline or task unclarity (*5, a*), 10% were due to non-uniform interrater expertise (*5, b*) and 7% were simple mistakes (*5, e*).

Note that the two questions about *wide-scope claims* have a much lower interrater agreement of $\kappa \approx 0.45$. This can be explained by the problems concerning the different construals of what constitutes a *wide-scope claim* discussed above and emphasized the need for conceptual alignment. Note also that no cases of interpretive disagreement were identified. This is likely because, after the interpretation of concepts has been settled in *step 2*, there is not much need for extensive interpretation of the units of annotation in this annotation task.

6 Further applications

We have shown how the procedure applies to the two test cases discussed in section 5. However, our procedure is not limited to cases of that type. Concepts are involved in any type of annotation task, and any concept necessitates both interpretation and conceptual alignment.

Consider the case of Herbelot and Vecchi (2016) again: "MISSILES EXPLODE received the labels SOME, MOST and ALL.". Suppose we want to construct a ground truth of property-object pairs. The example shows that the guidelines should specify whether to use an actual or potential interpretation of property possession. Note, though, that settling for an interpretation often won't be enough: while annotating under a potential interpretation, the issue may arise whether objects should have the potential to have a property *actually* (most do, but some are faulty) or *teleologically* (all). By our procedure, these ambiguities become apparent, and disagreement can be resolved.

The two test cases of section 5 both have academics as annotators, but this is no intrinsic requirement of our procedure. For some linguistic tasks, being a native speaker of the relevant language is enough expertise to be able to grasp and apply the concepts involved in the task. Another matter is the common practice of resorting to crowdsourcing platforms[6] to construct large, non-academic annotation datasets. The practice is useful, but ill-suited to accommodate the type of disagreement resolution we envisage. Our take is that even though it might not always be possible to adopt the entire procedure for ground truth construction, we see no fundamental, theoretical problems with its application in a wide variety of cases.

7 Conclusion and further work

In this paper we proposed a six-step systematic procedure for annotation focused on disagreement resolution. We argued that disagreement is the result of poorly specified tasks or guidelines, or of insufficient conceptual alignment among annotators. To avoid incomplete datasets unfit for use as ground truths, we set up the procedure in such a way that the identification and non-arbitrary resolution of different types of disagreement is facilitated. Disagreement resolution by a clearly defined procedure results in more reliable and well-grounded datasets. By identifying the cause of disagreement and giving appropriate instructions for resolution for each type of disagreement, our procedure ensures that the resolution proceeds in a non-arbitrary fashion allowing for proper documentation and increasing replicability of the data.

We have validated the effectiveness and the importance of our annotation procedure by two test cases. The first case shows that conceptual alignment by itself does not guarantee that annotators make no mistakes or only come across clarified concepts, indicating the need for disagreement resolution after annotation. The second case emphasizes the importance of task clarification and conceptual alignment prior to annotation. Without this, the likeliness increases of having to redo annotations due to different construals of terms influencing both conflicting and agreed-upon annotations.

In further work we aim to collect more use cases to test the applicability of the procedure to more varied types of annotations. Moreover, we want to consider in more depth the interplay of *step 0-2* and further elaborate on the idea of *key concept* at *step 2*.

Acknowledgements

We thank the anonymous reviewers for their time and helpful comments. We thank the UvA e-Ideas team for their valuable discussion of a draft of this paper. This research was supported by grants *e-Ideas* (VICI, 277-20-007) and *CatVis* (314-99-117), funded by the Dutch Research Council (NWO), and by the Human(e)AI grant *Small data, big challenges* funded by the University of Amsterdam.

[6] See e.g. `https://www.mturk.com/`

References

Lora Aroyo and Chris Welty. 2014. The three sides of CrowdTruth. *Human Computation*, 1(1).

Lora Aroyo and Chris Welty. 2015. Truth is a lie: Crowd truth and the seven myths of human annotation. *AI Magazine*, 36(1):15–24.

Ron Artstein and Massimo Poesio. 2008. Survey article: Inter-coder agreement for computational linguistics. *Computational Linguistics*, 34(4):555–596.

Amir Bakarov. 2018. A survey of word embeddings evaluation methods. arXiv:1801.09536.

Miroslav Batchkarov, Thomas Kober, Jeremy Reffin, Julie Weeds, and David Weir. 2016. A critique of word similarity as a method for evaluating distributional semantic models. In *Proceedings of the 1st Workshop on Evaluating Vector-Space Representations for NLP*, pages 7–12, Berlin, Germany. Association for Computational Linguistics.

Emily M. Bender and Batya Friedman. 2018. Data statements for natural language processing: Toward mitigating system bias and enabling better science. *Transactions of the Association for Computational Linguistics*, 6:587–604.

Arianna Betti, Martin Reynaert, Thijs Ossenkoppele, Yvette Oortwijn, Andrew Salway, and Jelke Bloem. 2020. Expert Concept-Modeling Ground Truth Construction for Word Embeddings Evaluation in Concept-Focused Domains. In *Proceedings of the 28th International Conference on Computational Linguistics*, pages 6690–6702, Barcelona, Spain (Online). International Committee on Computational Linguistics.

Arianna Betti and Hein van den Berg. 2014. Modelling the History of Ideas. *British Journal for the History of Philosophy*, 22(4):812–835.

Tolga Bolukbasi, Kai-Wei Chang, James Zou, Venkatesh Saligrama, and Adam Kalai. 2016. Man is to computer programmer as woman is to homemaker? Debiasing word embeddings. In *Proceedings of the 30th International Conference on Neural Information Processing Systems*, NIPS'16, pages 4356–4364, Red Hook, NY, USA. Curran Associates Inc.

David Christensen and Jennifer Lackey, editors. 2013. *The Epistemology of Disagreement: New Essays*. Oxford University Press, Oxford, UK.

Jacob Cohen. 1960. A coefficient of agreement for nominal scales. *Educational and Psychological Measurement*, 20(1):37–46.

Jeroen de Ridder. 2014. Epistemic dependence and collective scientific knowledge. *Synthese*, 191(1):37–53.

Kawin Ethayarajh and Dan Jurafsky. 2020. Utility is in the eye of the user: A critique of NLP leaderboards. arXiv:2009.13888.

Manaal Faruqui, Yulia Tsvetkov, Pushpendre Rastogi, and Chris Dyer. 2016. Problems with evaluation of word embeddings using word similarity tasks. In *Proceedings of the 1st Workshop on Evaluating Vector-Space Representations for NLP*, pages 30–35, Berlin, Germany. Association for Computational Linguistics.

Evelyn Gius and Janina Jacke. 2017. The Hermeneutic Profit of Annotation: On Preventing and Fostering Disagreement in Literary Analysis. *International Journal of Humanities and Arts Computing*, 11(2):233–254.

Anna Gladkova and Aleksandr Drozd. 2016. Intrinsic evaluations of word embeddings: What can we do better? In *Proceedings of the 1st Workshop on Evaluating Vector-Space Representations for NLP*, pages 36–42, Berlin, Germany. Association for Computational Linguistics.

Alvin I. Goldman and Dennis Whitcomb, editors. 2011. *Social Epistemology: Essential Readings*. Oxford University Press, Oxford, NY.

N. Goodman. 1972. Seven strictures on similarity. In *Problems and Projects*, pages 437–450. Bobbs Merrill, Indianapolis, IN.

Aurélie Herbelot and Eva Maria Vecchi. 2016. Many speakers, many worlds: Interannotator variations in the quantification of feature norms. In *Linguistic Issues in Language Technology, Volume 13, 2016*. CSLI Publications.

Felix Hill, Roi Reichart, and Anna Korhonen. 2015. SimLex-999: Evaluating semantic models with (genuine) similarity estimation. *Computational Linguistics*, 41(4):665–695.

Ben Hutchinson, Andrew Smart, Alex Hanna, Emily Denton, Christina Greer, Oddur Kjartansson, Parker Barnes, and Margaret Mitchell. 2021. Towards accountability for machine learning datasets: Practices from software engineering and infrastructure. In *Proceedings of the 2021 ACM Conference on Fairness, Accountability, and Transparency*, FAccT '21, page 560–575, New York, NY, USA. Association for Computing Machinery.

Sanjay Kairam and Jeffrey Heer. 2016. Parting crowds: Characterizing divergent interpretations in crowdsourced annotation tasks. In *Proceedings of the 19th ACM Conference on Computer-Supported Cooperative Work & Social Computing*, CSCW '16, pages 1637–1648, New York, NY, USA. Association for Computing Machinery.

Kian Kenyon-Dean, Eisha Ahmed, Scott Fujimoto, Jeremy Georges-Filteau, Christopher Glasz, Barleen Kaur, Auguste Lalande, Shruti Bhanderi, Robert

Belfer, Nirmal Kanagasabai, Roman Sarrazingendron, Rohit Verma, and Derek Ruths. 2018. Sentiment analysis: It's complicated! In *Proceedings of the 2018 Conference of the North American Chapter of the Association for Computational Linguistics: Human Language Technologies, Volume 1 (Long Papers)*, pages 1886–1895, New Orleans, Louisiana. Association for Computational Linguistics.

Klaus H. Krippendorff. 2013. *Content Analysis - 3rd Edition : An Introduction to Its Methodology*. SAGE Publications, Inc., Thousand Oaks, CA.

J. Richard Landis and Gary G. Koch. 1977. The Measurement of Observer Agreement for Categorical Data. *Biometrics*, 33(1):159–174.

Christian List. 2005. Group Knowledge and Group Rationality: A Judgment Aggregation Perspective. *Episteme*, 2(1):25–38.

Jennimaria Palomaki, Olivia Rhinehart, and Michael Tseng. 2018. A case for a range of acceptable annotations. In *Proceedings of the 1st Workshop on Subjectivity, Ambiguity and Disagreement in Crowdsourcing, and Short Paper Proceedings of the 1st Workshop on Disentangling the Relation Between Crowdsourcing and Bias Management (SAD 2018 and CrowdBias 2018), Zürich, Switzerland*, volume 2276 of *CEUR Workshop Proceedings*, pages 19–31. CEUR-WS.org.

Amandalynne Paullada, Inioluwa Deborah Raji, Emily M. Bender, Emily Denton, and Alex Hanna. 2020. Data and its (dis)contents: A survey of dataset development and use in machine learning research.

Ellie Pavlick and Tom Kwiatkowski. 2019. Inherent disagreements in human textual inferences. *Transactions of the Association for Computational Linguistics*, 7:677–694.

Rimma Pivovarov and Noémie Elhadad. 2012. A hybrid knowledge-based and data-driven approach to identifying semantically similar concepts. *Journal of Biomedical Informatics*, 45(3):471–481.

Inioluwa Deborah Raji, Emily M. Bender, Emily Denton, Alex Hanna, and Amandalynne Paullada. 2020. AI and the Everything in the Whole Wide World Benchmark. In *Proceedings of the NeurIPS 2020 Workshop: ML Retrospectives, Surveys & Meta-Analyses (ML-RSA)*, Online.

David Schlangen. 2020. Targeting the benchmark: On methodology in current natural language processing research. arXiv:2007.04792.

Pia Sommerauer, Antske Fokkens, and Piek Vossen. 2020. Would you describe a leopard as yellow? Evaluating crowd-annotations with justified and informative disagreement. In *Proceedings of the 28th International Conference on Computational Linguistics*, pages 4798–4809, Barcelona, Spain (Online). International Committee on Computational Linguistics.

Peter D. Turney and Patrick Pantel. 2010. From frequency to meaning: Vector space models of semantics. *Journal of Artificial Intelligence Research*, 37(1):141–188.

Jieyu Zhao, Tianlu Wang, Mark Yatskar, Vicente Ordonez, and Kai-Wei Chang. 2017. Men also like shopping: Reducing gender bias amplification using corpus-level constraints. In *Proceedings of the 2017 Conference on Empirical Methods in Natural Language Processing*, pages 2979–2989, Copenhagen, Denmark. Association for Computational Linguistics.

Author Index

Association for Computational Linguistics
209 N. Eighth Street
Stroudsburg, Pennsylvania 18360

ISBN 978-1-7138-2911-9

CURRAN ASSOCIATES INC.
proceedings.com